A HISTORY OF
THE WESTERN BOUNDARY
OF THE
LOUISIANA PURCHASE, 1819-1841

A Da Capo Press Reprint Series

THE AMERICAN SCENE
Comments and Commentators

GENERAL EDITOR: WALLACE D. FARNHAM
University of Illinois

A HISTORY OF
THE WESTERN BOUNDARY
OF THE
LOUISIANA PURCHASE, 1819-1841

By Thomas M. Marshall

DA CAPO PRESS · NEW YORK · 1970

A Da Capo Press Reprint Edition

This Da Capo Press edition of *A History of the Western Boundary of the Louisiana Purchase, 1819-1841,* is an unabridged republication of the first edition published in Berkeley, California, in 1914.

Library of Congress Catalog Card Number 73-87411

SBN 306-71554-6

Published by Da Capo Press
A Division of Plenum Publishing Corporation
227 West 17th Street, New York, N.Y. 10011

UNIVERSITY OF CALIFORNIA

PUBLICATIONS IN HISTORY

VOLUME II

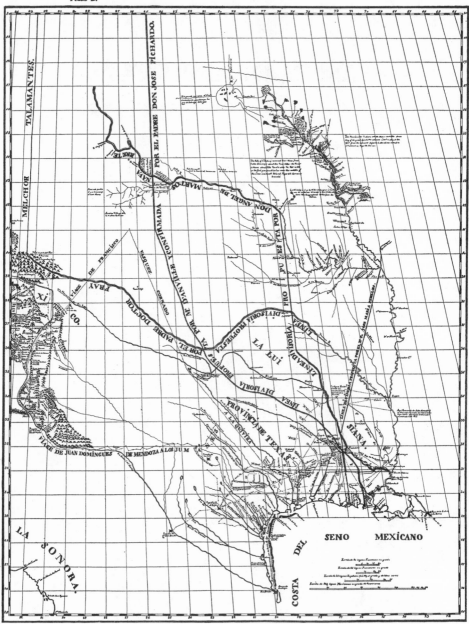

Map 1. Eastern half of the Pichardo Boundary Commission Map. (Now for the first time printed)

A HISTORY OF THE WESTERN BOUNDARY OF THE LOUISIANA PURCHASE, 1819-1841

BY

THOMAS MAITLAND MARSHALL, Ph. D.

UNIVERSITY OF CALIFORNIA PRESS

BERKELEY

1914

TO MY WIFE

VESTA WOODBURY MARSHALL

PREFACE

Ever since the appearance of Justin Winsor's *Narrative and Critical History* and the monumental works of Hubert Howe Bancroft, scholars have been attracted by the richness of the Southwest as a field for historical investigation. The immense collection of manuscripts and rare books, known as the Bancroft Library, now owned by the University of California, the archives of the United States, Mexico, Spain, England, and France, and the published documents of the United States government, contain a vast store of materials relating to this field, much of which has not yet been appraised. Any work, therefore, for many years to come, must be temporary in its nature, a fact which none recognizes more fully than the author of this monograph.

Its appearance seems justifiable, however, when it is considered that no one has attempted to view in its entirety the history of the western boundary of the Louisiana Purchase. Various historians, realizing the importance of the subject, have touched it at occasional points, but usually as incidental to some other theme; such a treatment must necessarily lead to error of fact and to faulty placing of emphasis. Even here the present work is open to criticism, for it is confined to those questions which primarily involve the United States, without attempting to explore the original documents which pertain to the history of the boundary during the Spanish-French régime. This, however, has already been done with considerable care by Cox, Ficklen, Garrison, Clark, Bolton, and Heinrich,[1] and upon their findings the writer has depended for the background of his subject.

[1] See the general bibliography for full reference to the work of all historians mentioned in the preface.

Preface

The first three chapters of this work should be regarded as an introduction to the main thesis, which covers the boundary question from the treaty of 1819 until the final survey of the Sabine line in 1841, a phase of the subject which has received but slight treatment by historians. Especially have the events from 1836 to 1841 been inadequately reviewed.

It seems necessary to call attention to the most important works dealing with the diplomacy of the southwestern frontier which have appeared in recent years. Although differing with some of them at certain points, nevertheless the writer acknowledges that he has gained much from the writings of each. Of first importance is the history by Henry Adams, which contains the most complete account of the diplomacy of Jefferson and Madison; Herbert B. Fuller's *Purchase of Florida* gives the most scholarly treatment of the diplomatic relations with Spain which led to the treaty of 1819. The late George P. Garrison made accessible the major part of the diplomatic correspondence of the Republic of Texas. To Walter F. McCaleb we owe the best account of the Neutral Ground Treaty. The various writings of I. J. Cox have added materially to our knowledge of the details of transactions on the border. A considerable body of material for the history of Louisiana from 1785 to 1807 has been placed in usable form by James A. Robertson. F. E. Chadwick has produced the only work which attempts to give in its entirety a history of the relations of the United States and Spain. The recent study of the diplomatic relations of the United States and Mexico, 1821-1848, by Rives is unique in its field and necessarily supplements the more slender though scholarly work of Reeves. Eugene C. Barker has developed the field of the diplomacy of Jackson and the history of the Texan revolution in numerous magazine articles of recognized merit. Justin Smith's detailed study of the annexation of Texas is the only adequate treatment of the subject, a work which must be supplemented, however, by

Preface

Ephraim Adams' account of the British interests in Texas, 1838-1846. The latter has also recently edited the British correspondence covering the same field. Recent articles by Professor Manning have added much to our knowledge of the diplomatic relations of the United States and Mexico. Several of the writings above cited have appeared since this work was undertaken, thus demonstrating the interest in the subject here treated.

The appearance of Herbert E. Bolton's *Guide to the Archives of Mexico* makes known a vast storehouse of unworked historical documents which a generation of scholars cannot exhaust. The writer has profited greatly from the use of the notes from which the guide was compiled, and from manuscripts in Professor Bolton's private collection. The list would be incomplete if attention were not also called to the invaluable and ever increasing mass of material which has appeared in *The Quarterly* of the Texas State Historical Association (continued as *The Southwestern Historical Quarterly*), the excellence of which is largely due to its discerning editors, George P. Garrison, Eugene C. Barker, and Herbert E. Bolton. The above list is by no means complete, but space requirement prevents further mention.

The writer wishes to indicate some of the more important phases of the subject in which he has differed with accepted theory or in which he believes that he has added somewhat to the history of the subject. He finds that Napoleon decided to sell Louisiana several months earlier than the date set by Henry Adams. The conception of the size of Louisiana gradually developed in the mind of Jefferson; the conclusion which he reached became the basis of American diplomacy for half a century; the evolution of this idea and its importance have not been fully appreciated. The sale of Louisiana by France having been consummated, Spain carried out an effective plan for restricting the limits of the purchase; this has never received adequate treatment. The reason for Wilkinson's betrayal of Burr and for entering into the Neutral Ground Treaty has been the subject of much discussion and various theories have been advanced; the truth of the matter seems to lie in the fact that Wilkinson sold his services to the Spanish government while he was stationed on the western frontier. The activity of Spain in making a boundary investigation, which was carried on even during the Napoleonic occupation, has not previously received adequate notice. Historians have usually accepted the view that the claim to Texas was given up in exchange for Florida. The writer believes that the purchase of Florida was a foregone conclusion from early in 1818, and thereafter Adams yielded the claim to Texas and advanced a claim to the Oregon country; it would perhaps be more correct then to say that Texas was given up in exchange for Spanish claims to the Oregon country.

The writer disagrees fundamentally with the views of some historians regarding the purity of Andrew Jackson's motives concerning Texas. The operations of General Edmund P. Gaines on the Sabine frontier in 1836 have never before been examined critically. Lastly, the Sabine boundary question during the period of the Texan republic has heretofore been dismissed without comment.

Thanks are due to the officials of the Bancroft Library, to Mr. Joseph C. Rowell, Librarian of the University of California, and to Mr. George T. Clark, Librarian of Leland Stanford Junior University, for many courtesies extended. Acknowledgments are also due to Professor Eugene C. Barker of the University of Texas, who read the proof and offered many valuable suggestions, to Professor Eugene I. McCormac of the University of California, and to Mr. Tom P. Martin for calling attention to important materials; to Dr. William Tappan Lum for structural criticisms, to Mr. William E. Dunn of the University of Texas, who gathered materials in Mexico, to Mr. E. W. Winkler,

Preface

State Librarian of Texas, who furnished copies of important documents, to Mr. A. H. Allen of the University of California Press for many valuable suggestions, and to my wife, who aided in innumerable ways. The writer above all wishes to express his sincere appreciation of the assistance rendered by Professor Herbert E. Bolton, who gave him unstinted use of his collection of documents, who guided him when guidance was most necessary, who encouraged him in the hours of discouragement, and who unselfishly gave of time he could little afford to lose.

THOMAS MAITLAND MARSHALL.

ALAMEDA, CALIFORNIA, September 28, 1914.

CONTENTS

CHAPTER I

THE LOUISIANA PURCHASE

⚹At the close of hostilities in the Revolutionary War, the partitioning of the Mississippi Valley was a vital question to England, France, Spain, and the United States. France and Spain wished to confine the new nation to the east of the Alleghanies. Vergennes, the French minister, voicing the Spanish views, proposed that the territory between the Ohio and the Floridas be erected into an Indian territory, the northern part to be under the protection of the United States and the southern under that of Spain. It was also intimated that France would support England's claim to the territory north of the Ohio. But by an arrangement with England the American commissioners defeated the plan, and the powers finally agreed that the entire territory east of the Mississippi, extending from the Floridas to the Great Lakes, should pass into the possession of the United States.

France, however, did not abandon her designs on the Mississippi Valley. Various schemes were launched in the succeeding years to regain French control. Whether the object was ·a retrocession of Louisiana or the setting up of one or more republics, which might curb English expansion and extend French commerce, is still a debatable question.[1] Several proposals were made to Spain, but each in turn was rejected.

It was, then, no new policy which France inaugurated when, in April, 1800, Napoleon sent General Berthier to Madrid to

---

[1] Turner, in *The Atlantic Monthly*, XCIII, 679–689, 807–815; Turner, in *The American Historical Review*, X, 249–279; Van Tyne, in *The American Historical Review*, XVIII, 605. Phillips (*The West in the Diplomacy of the American Revolution*) argues that Vergennes was honestly working for the best interests of the United States.

enter into a retrocession treaty. The *projet*, drawn by Talleyrand, contained the following significant statement: ''Spain . . . pledges herself to retrocede to the French Republic the colony of Louisiana, with the same extent it actually has in the hands of Spain and such as it should be according to the treaties subsequently passed between Spain and other States. Spain shall further join in this cession that of the two Floridas, eastern and western, with their actual limits.''[2]

Thus was renewed Napoleon's great scheme of colonial empire which had languished since the Egyptian campaign. He hoped to gain control of San Domingo, Louisiana and various islands of the Antilles, and at the same time regain Mauritius and Reunion, colonize Madagascar, reopen the coasts of Pondicherry and Chandenagor to French trade, and establish ascendency in the Punjab.[3]

Berthier's proposal did not meet with the entire approval of the King of Spain, who refused to alienate the Floridas. On October 1, 1800, was signed the secret treaty of San Ildefonso by which Louisiana passed into French possession. The boundaries were left indefinite, the wording of the treaty being ''the same extent which it has in the hands of Spain, and which it had when France possessed it, and such as it should be according to the treaties passed between Spain and other states.''[4] The treaty was confirmed by a public agreement on March 21, 1801, Lucien Bonaparte being the French representative who completed the transaction.[5]

---

[2] Henry Adams, *History of the United States*, I, 366–367.

[3] Fournier, *Napoleon I*, I, 311.

[4] Henry Adams, *History of the United States*, I, 368–370; De Villiers du Terrage, *Les dernières années de la Louisiana française*, 375; De Garden, *Histoire générale des traités de paix*, VIII, 46–49. The French text of the article reads: ''Le dit territoire, avec tous ses droits et appurtenances ainsi et de la manière qu'ils ont ete acquis par la république française en vertu du traité susdit conclu avec sa Majeste Catholic.'' *En vertu du traité susdit conclu* has been frequently mistranslated as ''after the treaties, etc.'' Martens, *Recueil des principaux traités*, VII, 708.

[5] Martens, *Recueil des principaux traités*, VII, 336–339.

In the founding of Napoleon's colonial empire, the first actual occupation occurred in San Domingo. General Leclerc at the head of twenty-five thousand men defeated Toussaint l'Ouverture, who surrendered on May 2, 1802. Shortly after, yellow fever broke out in the French army, and by July only eight thousand men were left. Before the news of this calamity reached him Napoleon had fully intended to occupy Louisiana. Orders were issued for the gathering of troops, which were to sail under command of General Victor in the latter part of September.[6] Information concerning the situation in San Domingo began to arrive and the order for departure was withheld.

At this time public opinion in England was growing hostile. A war was probably not wanted by Napoleon, who desired to carry out his colonial policy, but he realized that it could not long be averted; in case of hostilities, if he could not hold San Domingo, he foresaw that Louisiana would be a vulnerable point. If it could be disposed of to some power which would find it to its interest to protect it, he would extricate himself from an unpleasant situation. In the event of war, the sale would furnish some ready money. Such appear to have been the considerations which determined Napoleon to sell Louisiana.

This decision was reached earlier than has been supposed. In an interview between the First Consul and his brothers, Lucien and Joseph, his determination was announced. This interview, the well-known bath-tub scene, has been made famous by Henry Adams, but wrongly dated by that author, who placed the incident in 1803, relating it as if it occurred about the time of Monroe's arrival in April. It occurred in 1802, probably between the latter part of September, 1802, when Victor's orders to depart were withheld, and October 28. On that day Livingston, the American minister, wrote to Jefferson that Victor's expedition was ready, but might not sail. He stated that he had had a

---

[6] Napoleon I, *Correspondance*, VII, 617–618, VIII, 5–6.

conversation with Joseph Bonaparte, who had asked whether the United States would not prefer Louisiana to the Floridas. Livingston replied that there was no comparison in value, that his government had no desire to extend its boundary across the Mississippi, but sought only security. The fact that Joseph Bonaparte, rather than Talleyrand, addressed Livingston is deeply significant. It is not reasonable to suppose that Joseph would have introduced the subject without authority. It would appear, then, that Napoleon had made up his mind to sell Louisiana and that Joseph had been designated to ascertain the attitude of the United States.[7]

Napoleon's plan to part with Louisiana was thus frustrated for the time being by the flat refusal of the American minister. The First Consul had only one alternative, namely, to continue to reinforce the army of San Domingo and prepare for Victor's occupation of Louisiana. Instructions for that general were prepared; in regard to boundaries they read:

> The extent of Louisiana . . . is well determined at the south by the Gulf of Mexico. But bounded on the west by the river called Rio Bravo, from its mouth to the thirtieth degree, its line of demarcation has not been traced beyond the latter point and it appears that no convention has ever been held concerning this part of the frontier.

---

[7] Livingston to Jefferson, October 28, 1802, *State Papers, Foreign Relations,* II, 525–526. Further proof of the date may be gathered from *Lucien Bonaparte et ses mémoires,* (Th. Iung, ed.) II, 121–192, the authority on which Henry Adams based his narrative. The date is not given in the body of the memoir, but Iung, who was a very careful editor, dated the interview in 1802. The order of events before and after the interview corresponds with Bourrienne, *Memoirs of Napoleon.* There is also internal evidence. In the interview Napoleon referred to his brother-in-law, Leclerc, as a ''bon diable.'' Leclerc died in the autumn of 1802, and Napoleon would hardly have referred to his relative in that manner after his demise. The return of Pauline is also given much later in the narrative. Hosmer (*The History of the Louisiana Purchase,* 74) has made much of the fact that the actor, Talma, who was mentioned in the memoir, played Hamlet at the Theatre Français in April, 1803. This argument has no weight, as the name of the play is not given in the text; Talma was a regular actor at the theatre, and a reference to the files of the *Moniteur* shows that the plays were frequently changed. For further proof, see Barbé-Marbois, *The History of Louisiana,* 261–264.

The contents of these instructions were also made known to Laussat, the French prefect of Louisiana.[8]

It has been argued that Victor's instructions settled the question of the true boundary of Louisiana,[9] but such does not seem to be the case. The instructions show that Napoleon did not take the trouble to fortify himself by consulting the principal French geographers. The De Lisle map of 1707 traced the western boundary to 38° 30′. Le Page du Pratz printed a map in 1758 on which the western boundary was defined, according to French claims, to 41°. Moreover, the fact that an arbitrary order was given could not be considered of weight in determining the ownership of territory which had belonged to Spain by right of settlement for nearly a century.[10]

In spite of the instructions, the Louisiana expedition did not sail. The death of Leclerc, the incompetency of his successor, and the increasing danger of war with England, appear to have been the main factors in preventing the departure of the troops.[11]

At this time Robert R. Livingston was the American minister at Paris. He was instructed by Madison in September, 1801, to obtain definite information concerning the cession of Louisiana to France, and to try to obtain the Floridas, if they were included in the cession. Livingston, however, was unable to obtain definite information. His letters were frequently contradictory and show that his diplomacy in no wise affected the policy of France. On September 1, 1802, Livingston informed Madison that on the previous day he had made several propositions to Talleyrand with a view of obtaining the Floridas and New Orleans. Talley-

[8] Decrés to Victor, November 26, 1802, Robertson, *Louisiana under Spain, France and the United States*, I, 361–362; Decrés to Laussat, December 7, 1802, *ibid.*, I, 375–376.

[9] Henry Adams, *History of the United States*, II, 4–7.

[10] For De Lisle's map see French, *Historical Collections of Louisiana*, II, frontis. The Du Pratz map is printed in his *Histoire de la Louisiane*, I, op. p. 138.

[11] Livingston to Madison, December 20, 1802, *State Papers, Foreign Relations*, II, 528; *Le Moniteur*, 17 nivôse, an. 11, no. 107, p. 429; Henry Adams, *History of the United States*, II, 15–19; Fournier, *Napoleon I*, I, 313–319; Rose, *The Life of Napoleon I*, I, 335–337.

rand told him frankly that every offer was premature, as the
French government was determined to take possession of the
ceded territory before anything else was done. Nothing definite
occurred again until October 28, when Joseph Bonaparte sounded
Livingston on the subject of the United States acquiring
Louisiana instead of the Floridas.[12]

  ✳ Events were occurring in America at this time which caused
Jefferson to send James Monroe on a special mission to France.
✳ In 1795 Spain and the United States had entered into a treaty
which defined the boundaries between their territories, guaranteed
the free navigation of the Mississippi to American citizens, and
gave them the right to deposit merchandise at New Orleans for
a period of three years, with the privilege of exporting the goods
without paying duty, a privilege which was to continue unless
the King of Spain found it prejudicial to his interests.   For
seven years Americans enjoyed the right of *entrepôt* without
interruption, but in October, 1802, Morales, the Spanish intendant, arbitrarily closed the port.   The news of the closing of
the Mississippi created a great sensation in the United States.
In Kentucky and Tennessee there was talk of war, and the
New England Federalists, ascribing the action of the Spanish
intendant to the French, clamored for war with France.   On
January 7, 1803, the House of Representatives passed a resolution expressing its determination to maintain the former rights
of navigation on the Mississippi.   The uncertainty of affairs in
France, the closing of the port of New Orleans, and the desire
to silence the war party determined Jefferson to send a special
envoy.   Monroe sailed on March 9, 1803, arriving in Paris on
April 12.[13]

---

[12] The correspondence covering the first year of Livingston's mission
is printed in *State Papers, Foreign Relations*, II, 510–526.

[13] *Treaties, Conventions* (Malloy, ed.), II, 1640–1649; Lyman, *The
Diplomacy of the United States*, 328–329; Chadwick, *The Relations of the
United States and Spain, Diplomacy*, 51; Henry Adams, *History of the
United States*, I, 421–422; *Annals of Cong.*, 7 Cong., 1 Sess., 339–343;
Monroe, *Writings*, VII, 298–300; *ibid.*, IV, 8; *ibid.*, VII, 303.

Before Monroe's arrival, Napoleon had definitely settled upon disposing of Louisiana. Barbé-Marbois, to whom the final negotiation was intrusted, says:

Bonaparte . . . well knew that colonies could not be defended without naval forces; but so great a revolution in the plan of his foreign policy was not suddenly made. It may even be perceived, from the correspondence of the Minister of foreign affairs at this period, how gradually and in what manner the change was effected. M. Talleyrand renewed, after a long silence, his communications with Mr. Livingston. Bonaparte had only a very reduced navy to oppose to the most formidable power that has ever had the dominion of the ocean. Louisiana was at the mercy of the English, who had a naval armament in the neighboring seas, and good garrisons in Jamaica and the Windward Islands. It might be supposed that they would open the campaign by this easy conquest . . . He concluded . . . that it was requisite to change without delay his policy in relation of St. Domingo, Louisiana, and the United States. He could not tolerate indecision; and before the rupture was decided on, he adopted the same course of measures, as if it had been certain.

✳ On April 10, 1803, Napoleon called Marbois and another councillor to him, and informed them that he was thinking of ceding Louisiana to the United States to keep it from falling into the possession of England. The conference ended without a final decision, but at dawn on the following day the arrival of dispatches from England, stating that naval and military preparations were progressing rapidly, determined him. He immediately directed Marbois to interview Livingston without awaiting the arrival of Monroe. He closed by remarking, "I require a great deal of money for this war, and I would not like to commence it with new contributions."[14]

On April 13 Livingston was definitely informed that Napoleon had decided to sell the whole of Louisiana. Monroe, who had arrived upon the scene on the previous day, and Livingston, soon decided to accept the offer. After a few days spent in haggling over the price, an agreement was reached; on May 2 the treaty of cession and a convention regarding price, and on the eighth

---

[14] Barbé-Marbois, *The History of Louisiana*, 261–264, 274–275.

or ninth a claims convention were signed, all being antedated to
April 30.[15]

⚑In respect to boundaries, the words of the treaty of March 21,
1801, between France and Spain were incorporated—''Louisiana
with the same extent it now has in the hands of Spain, and that
it had when France possessed it; and such as it should be after
[according to] the Treaties subsequently entered into between
Spain and other states.''[16]   The American ministers attempted
to have the boundaries more definitely stated, but when it was
brought to the attention of Napoleon, he replied, ''If an obscurity
did not already exist, it would perhaps be good policy to put
one there.''[17]

While the negotiations were in progress at Paris, Jefferson
was considering the project of exploring the Missouri and
Columbia rivers.   He had long been interested in the region
beyond the Mississippi.   As early as 1783 he had suggested to
George Rogers Clark the exploration of an overland route to the
Pacific.   While minister to France he had induced John Ledyard·
to attempt to cross Siberia and open communication from the
Pacific by way of the Missouri, an effort which was frustrated
by Catherine II.   Early in Washington's administration he had
determined to obtain French aid to induce Spain to cede the
island of New Orleans and the Floridas to the United States,
a project which came to naught through the Anglo-Spanish
alliance of 1790.   Later the French botanist, André Michaux,
interested him in a scheme to visit the Missouri and Columbia,
but this was dissolved by the intrigues of Genet.   In 1798 Jefferson wrote to Philip Nolan inquiring about the wild horses on
the plains east of New Mexico, and in the following years communicated with Daniel Clark, James Wilkinson, and William

---

[15] Livingston to Monroe, April 13, 1803, *State Papers, Foreign Relations,* II, 552–554; Monroe, *Writings,* IV, 12–19, 34–36; *ibid.,* VII, 250;
Henry Adams, *History of the United States,* II, 42.

[16] *Treaties, Conventions* (Malloy, ed.), I, 508–509.

[17] Barbé-Marbois, *The History of Louisiana,* 283–286.

Dunbar concerning the Southwest. In 1801, when a negro insurrection occurred in Virginia, he suggested to Governor Monroe the possibility of obtaining lands beyond the limits of the United States where the malefactors might be placed, observing, "However our present interests may restrain us within our limits, it is impossible not to look forward to distant times, when our rapid multiplication will expand it beyond those limits, and cover the whole northern if not the southern continent . . ." The cession of Louisiana to France alarmed Jefferson, and he wrote to Livingston urging that an attempt be made to convince France that the ownership of Louisiana would be inimical to her interests. If this proved futile, he suggested that the island of New Orleans and the Floridas be ceded to the United States.[18]

A few days after the appointment of Monroe, the President sent a confidential message to Congress advising that an expedition be sent out "to enlarge the boundaries of knowledge," "for other literary purposes," and "to explore this the only line of easy communication across the continent."[19] In consequence Lewis was selected to guide the expedition for which Congress provided the funds, Clark being associated with him later. Lewis' instructions stated that the object of the expedition was the exploration of the Missouri and such tributaries as might communicate with rivers emptying into the Pacific, which might serve for purposes of commerce. Information was to be gathered concerning the Southwest, especially regarding the Rio Grande or Colorado.[20]

These instructions were signed before the purchase of Louisiana was known to Jefferson. In July he received the

[18] Thwaites, *Rocky Mountain Exploration,* 68; Thwaites, *Original Journals of the Lewis and Clark Expedition,* I, pp. XX–XXII; Turner, in *The Atlantic Monthly,* XCIII, 679–683; various letters, in Texas State Historical Association, *The Quarterly,* VII, 308–317; Jefferson, *Writings.* (Washington, ed.) IV, 419–422; *ibid.,* IV, 431–434.

[19] Richardson, *Messages and Papers of the Presidents,* I, 353–354.

[20] Coues, *The History of the Lewis and Clark Expedition,* I, pp. xxiv-xxxiii.

treaty.   Regarding the extent of the territory, to a friend he wrote:

> The territory acquired, as it includes all the waters of the Missouri and Mississippi, has more than doubled the area of the United States . . . I presume the island of N. Orleans and the settled country on the opposite bank, will be annexed to the Mississippi territory . . . The rest . . . will probably be locked up from American settlement, and under the self government of the native occupants.[21]

It would appear from this that Jefferson had no idea at this time that Texas might be included in the purchase. In the light of its future importance in the negotiations, it is also worthy of note that this is the first suggestion of a neutral ground.

Jefferson immediately took steps to obtain information concerning the size of Louisiana, submitting a series of questions regarding boundaries to Ephraim Kirby, a land commissioner for the district east of the Pearl River, to William Dunbar, Daniel Clark, and Claiborne. He also made inquiries of the scientist, Humboldt. Madison wrote to Livingston to investigate the boundary question.[22]

On August 9 Jefferson stated his views as follows:

> The *unquestioned* bounds of Louisiana are the Iberville and Mississippi, on the east, the Mexicana [Sabine] or the Highlands east of it, on the west; then from the head of the Mexicana gaining the highlands which include the waters of the Mississippi, and following those highlands round the head springs of the western waters of the Mississippi to its source where we join the English or perhaps to the Lake of the Woods . . .✷ We have some pretensions to extend the western territory of Louisiana to the Rio Norte, or Bravo; and still stronger the eastern boundary to the Rio Perdido between the rivers Mobile and Pensacola.

---

[21] Jefferson, *Writings*, (Ford, ed.) VIII, 199–200, note; *ibid.*, VIII, 249–251.

[22] Jefferson, *Writings*, (Ford, ed.) VIII, 252–256, note; Jefferson, *Writings*, (Washington, ed.) IV, 497–498; Cox, *The Early Exploration of Louisiana*, 36; Cox, in *The Southwestern Historical Quarterly*, XVII, 13; *State Papers, Foreign Relations*, II, 566.

A few days later he wrote in similar vein to John C. Breckenridge. In this letter he observed, "These claims will be a subject of negotiation with Spain, and if, as soon as she is at war, we push them strongly with one hand, holding out a price in the other, we shall certainly obtain the Floridas, and all in good time."[23]

Jefferson possessed a considerable collection of books on America and he now proceeded to make an investigation of the boundary question. In August he wrote to Madison: "I have used my spare moments to investigate, by the help of my books here, the subject of the limits of Louisiana. I am satisfied our right to the Perdido is substantial, and can be opposed by a quibble on form only; and our right westwardly to the Bay of St. Bernard, may be strongly maintained."[24]

The results of his study Jefferson incorporated in an historical memoir. In this document he argued that because of the explorations and settlements made by La Salle and Iberville, France had actual possession of the coast from St. Bernard Bay to Mobile, and that international law sanctioned the principle that ownership of the coast gave possession to the sources of any rivers which might empty within that coast. The Pánuco, according to Jefferson, was the Spanish frontier in the time of La Salle.[25] France had considered that the Rio Grande, which was half way between the Pánuco and St. Bernard Bay, was the rightful boundary. This claim had not been abridged by any public treaty. It was strengthened by the fact that the French commissioner had stated that his instructions were to take possession to the Rio Grande. The next proof Jefferson based upon the Crozat grant. The Spanish expeditions and settlements in the

---

[23] Jefferson, *Writings*, (Ford, ed.) VIII, 261–263; *ibid.*, VIII, 242–244, note.

[24] Jefferson, *Writings*, (Washington, ed.) IV, 501–503.

[25] This view of course shows that Jefferson's knowledge of the history of New Spain was very imperfect. See Bolton, *The Spanish Occupation of Texas, 1519–1690*, in *The Southwestern Historical Quarterly*, XVI, 11–15.

territory he characterized as "contraband encroachments," which could have no weight against the "solemn establishment of boundary by Louis XIV."[26]

About this time Jefferson began to obtain information in answer to his queries. Claiborne wrote that there were several maps showing portions of the territory, and that Dr. John Sibley was then working on a map of the region between the Mississippi and the Rio Grande, and that he understood [although incorrectly] that before 1763 the Spanish and French planned to run a boundary. Those engaged in running this line had proceeded up the Sabine to a small fort, where they buried some leaden plates. From there they carried the line in an uncertain direction to a point about five leagues northwest of Natchitoches. Clark wrote that the map of the coast made by Don Juan de Langara, published in 1799, gave the Sabine as the boundary. He also observed that the Arroyo Hondo was considered the boundary. Dunbar wrote that he had seen a sketch based upon a chart which represented the boundary as running east-northeast from the Sabine to a point near Red River, where it made a right angle to include the post of Adaes, thence west-northwest nearly parallel to the Red River. He thought that the United States might claim a line parallel to that stream and prolonged to the Rocky Mountains. Sibley agreed with Dunbar and reported that Bayou Pierre was under the jurisdiction of Texas. Wilkinson also presented a memorial on the country between the Mississippi and the Rio Grande, which may have caused Jefferson to instruct the envoys in Spain to insist more urgently on the western boundary claims.[27]

----

[26] Jefferson, *The Limits and Bounds of Louisiana,* in American Philosophical Society, *Documents relating to the Purchase and Exploration of Louisiana.*

[27] Cox, *The Early Exploration of Louisiana,* 36–38; Cox, in *The Southwestern Historical Quarterly,* XVII, 6–8; Cox, in *The American Historical Review,* XIX, 800. For the Arroyo Hondo agreement, see Spanish documents published in Yoakum, *History of Texas,* I, app.

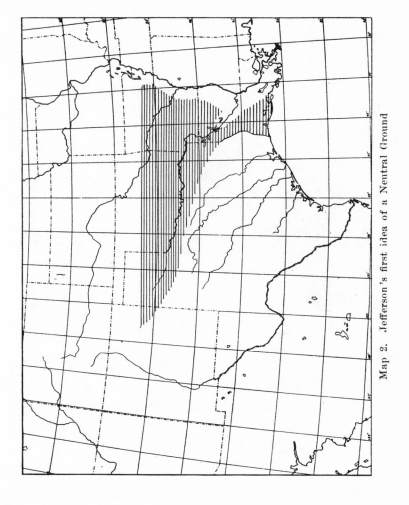

Map 2. Jefferson's first idea of a Neutral Ground

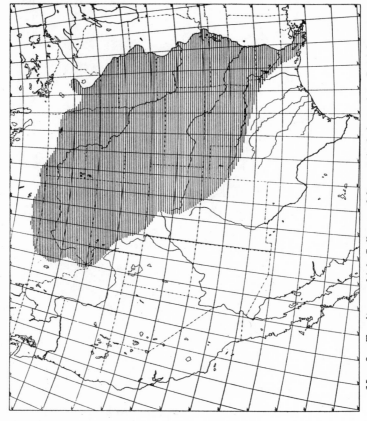

Map 3. Territory which Jefferson felt certain belonged to Louisiana in 1803.

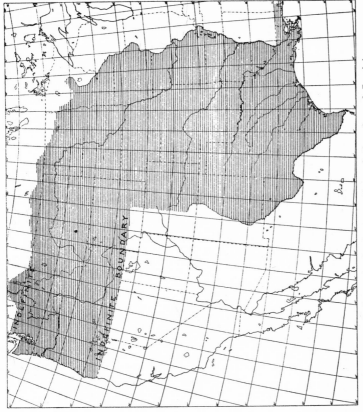

Map 4. Jefferson's final conception of the size of Louisiana.

In November Jefferson submitted to Congress a lengthy description of Louisiana. He admitted that the northern and western boundaries were obscure. He showed clearly that he believed that the territory included the Red, Arkansas, and Missouri rivers, but he did not include Texas in the purchase. His silence in regard to the western boundary is explained in a letter to Dunbar, in which he pointed out that he thought it politic to have explanations with Spain before asserting his belief.[28]

The idea that the Louisiana Purchase extended to the Rio Grande became a certainty with Jefferson early in 1804. On December 27, 1803, Claiborne and Wilkinson wrote to him that Laussat had stated that the French claims extended to the Rio Grande. Livingston was immediately informed and was instructed to obtain a copy of the Crozat charter of 1712 and any other documents that might have bearing.[29]

Up to this time Jefferson had considered the Rocky Mountains as the western boundary of the purchase, but the pretentions of the American government were not to be bound by that range. The views expressed in Congress concerning the size of the purchase showed great diversity of opinion. The majority were willing to accept the views of the President. On March 8, 1804, Samuel L. Mitchell, of the House Committee of Commerce and Manufactures, made a report on the expediency of authorizing the President to employ persons to explore such parts of Louisiana as he might deem proper. In defining the extent the report asserted that it included the lands beyond the Rockies "between the territories claimed by Great Britain on the one side, and by Spain on the other, quite to the South Sea." Although Jefferson's name did not appear in the document, it

---

[28] *Annals of Cong.*, 8 Cong., 2 Sess., 1498–1578; Jefferson, *Writings*, (Washington, ed.) IV, 537–541. Cox (*The Early Exploration of Louisiana*, 39) appears to be in error in assigning reasons for Jefferson's silence.

[29] Robertson, *Louisiana under Spain, France and the United States*, II, 289–291; *State Papers, Foreign Relations*, II, 574–575.

is certain that he had been working with the committee. The report may be taken as evidence of the final conception to which Jefferson had come. The fact that Jefferson considered the Oregon country as a part of Louisiana was made more apparent in 1808 during the discussion of a boundary treaty with England, when he agreed to the 49th parallel, "provided, that nothing in the present article shall be considered to extend to the north-west coast of America or to the territories belonging to or claimed by either party on the continent of America to the westward of the Stony Mountains."[30] Starting with the idea that the purchase was confined to the western waters of the Mississippi Valley, the conception had gradually expanded until it included West Florida, Texas, and the Oregon country, a view which was to be the basis of a large part of American diplomacy for nearly half a century.

To explore the vast acquisition was a pleasing idea to the President and he soon formulated a plan to make known the great interior rivers and the country which they drained.[31] We have already noted the inception of the Lewis and Clark expedition. This was now carried on with added zest.[32] Congress became interested in the idea of exploration. The House Committee of Commerce and Manufactures formulated a plan; after commenting on the authorized Lewis and Clark expedition, it stated that a survey of the upper Mississippi had been ordered, that the lower part of the river had been examined, and that the coast from the Perdido to the Bay of St. Bernard was well known. The committee advised that the channels of the Arkansas and Red rivers be examined, as they were believed to be included in the purchase. It also believed that the Black, White, Sabine

---

[30] *Annals of Cong.*, 8 Cong., 1 Sess., 47, 48, 60, 401, 486, 1124–1126; Jefferson, *Writings*, (Washington, ed.) IV, 515–517; Greenhow, *The History of Oregon and California*, (4th ed.), 281–282.

[31] Jefferson, *Writings*, (Washington, ed.) IV, 515–517.

[32] Wheeler, *The Trail of Lewis and Clark*, I, 43–44.

and other rivers should be explored. A small appropriation was voted to begin the work.[33]

The actual work of exploration was actively carried on for three years. The Dunbar-Hunter expedition of 1804-1805 explored the Red River as far as the mouth of the Washita and up that river to the Hot Springs. Dr. John Sibley, the Indian agent for Orleans Territory, in 1805 sent to the War Department a detailed description of the Red River district and the country as far as Santa Fé, a large part of which regions he had examined. In 1806 the Freeman expedition ascended the Red River but was stopped by a Spanish force at a point not far from the western boundary of the present state of Arkansas.[34]

In the northwest the efforts of Jefferson met with better success. In May, 1804, Lewis and Clark began their ascent of the Missouri; and on November 7, 1805, came in sight of the Pacific at the mouth of the Columbia. Upon their return Clark explored the Yellowstone, and the entire party reached St. Louis in September, 1806.[35]

In 1805 Pike explored the upper Mississippi, but did not discover its source. In 1806 he was sent out by Wilkinson to explore the Arkansas and Red rivers. Wilkinson's son accompanied the expedition and was sent back by way of the Arkansas. Pike discovered the peak which bears his name, and in 1807 was captured in Spanish territory by Melgàres' expedition. The prisoners were taken to Santa Fé, afterward to Chihuahua,

---

[33] *Annals of Cong.*, 8 Cong., 1 Sess., 1124–1126; Cox, *The Early Exploration of Louisiana*, 41.

[34] Cox, *The Early Exploration of Louisiana*, 40–53, 78–87; Dunbar, *Journal*, in American Philosophical Society, *Documents Relating to the Purchase and Exploration of Louisiana;* a summary of the journal is in *Annals of Cong.*, 9 Cong., 2 Sess., 1106–1146; *Annals of Cong.*, 9 Cong., 2 Sess., 1076–1106; James, *Account of an Expedition from Pittsburgh to the Rocky Mountains*, II, 303–314.

[35] Thwaites, *Rocky Mountain Exploration*, 92–187; Wheeler, *The Trail of Lewis and Clark;* Coues, *History of the Expedition under the Command of Lewis and Clark; Original Journals of the Lewis and Clark Expedition* (Thwaites, ed.).

and returned to the United States through Texas, arriving at Natchitoches on July 1, 1807.[36]

Thus within four years from the time when the purchase of Louisiana became known to Jefferson, the President's efforts had brought forth a general knowledge of the vast interior regions. The greater part of the courses of the rivers which he conceived to be within the purchase had been explored. It remained for the diplomats to wrangle over the boundaries, and for the settlers to make good the pretensions of the President.

---

[36] Coues, *The Expeditions of Zebulon Montgomery Pike.* The confiscated papers of Pike were found in the archives of Mexico by Professor Herbert E. Bolton and were partly published in *The American Historical Review,* XIII, 798–827.

CHAPTER II

THE OPENING OF THE BOUNDARY QUESTION

Spain was greatly alarmed and incensed by the sale of Louisiana to the United States. For many years it had been in her possession, and furthermore she had carried on a succession of intrigues to obtain possession of the territory between the Mississippi and the Appalachians. In 1785 and 1786 the attempt of the state of Georgia to extend its jurisdiction over the Natchez district resulted in much ill-feeling and suspicion. Governor Miró, through the instrumentality of James Wilkinson, exerted his influence to get Kentucky to separate from the Union.[37] Every advance of the Americans alarmed the Spanish; the settlements on the Yazoo and the Tennessee especially aroused the fears of De Lemos, the Spanish representative at Natchez.[38] Baron Carondelet, in a military report of 1794, stated that the Americans were attempting to occupy the entire region north of the Floridas and east of the Mississippi, forcing the Indian nations back upon the Spanish, at the same time demanding the free navigation of the Mississippi. He believed that in time they would demand the possession of the rich mines of the Interior Provinces.[39] The granting of the right of deposit at New Orleans in 1795 was met by the Spanish officials with a stubborn refusal to carry out the stipulations of the treaty, but they later acquiesced.[40]

---

[37] Houck, *History of Missouri*, II, 336–342, 347; Winsor, *Westward Movement*, 518, 553, 567, 573; *Papers Relating to Bourbon County, Georgia, 1785–1786*, in *Am. Hist. Review*, XV, 66–111, 297–353; Shepherd, *ibid.*, IX, 490–506, 748–766.

[38] Robertson, *Louisiana under Spain, France and the United States*, I, 276–283.

[39] *Ibid.*, I, 298.

[40] *Treaties, Conventions*, (Malloy, ed.) II, 1640–1649; Houck, *History of Missouri*, II, 345.

During the closing years of the Spanish régime the officials were on the alert.[41]   In 1799 the Bishop of Louisiana advised that Americans be prevented from settling in the province, claiming that they had penetrated even to New Mexico.[42]   Among those who caused suspicion was Philip Nolan, an employee of Wilkinson, who made frequent trips into Texas to obtain horses; it is probable that he also had political designs.   The Spanish were fearful that he meant to stir up a revolution.   In 1800 an order was issued for his arrest and on March 21, 1801, he was killed and his followers captured.[43]   The same feeling of distrust led Morales to issue in 1802 the proclamation suspending the right of deposit at New Orleans.[44]

The acquisition of Louisiana by the United States increased the fears of the Spanish, for by it the Americans removed the buffer between their territory and Mexico.   To prevent the occupation was the first idea of the Spanish officials; but soon realizing the futility of this, the government at Madrid determined to restrict Louisiana to as narrow bounds as possible.   To save the Floridas, Texas and the Oregon country was the difficult task that confronted the enfeebled Spanish monarchy.   A well-defined plan of defense was soon developed, and though there were occasional difficulties between officials, their efforts were united in carrying out a policy which for the time being saved the provinces.[45]

Yrujo, the Spanish minister at Washington, took the initiative in the attempts to save Louisiana.* He protested against the sale on the grounds that France had promised not to alienate

---

[41] For a statement of the attempts of Spain to hold back the Anglo-American frontier after 1770, see Bolton, *Athanase de Mézières and the Louisiana-Texas Frontier, 1768–1780*, I, 66–122.

[42] Gayarré, *History of Louisiana*, III, 456–457.

[43] *Texas Almanac, 1868*, 60–64; Garrison, *Texas*, 111–116; Wilkinson, *Memoirs of my own Times*, II, app. II; Texas State Historical Association, *The Quarterly*, VII, 308–317.

[44] Gayarré, *History of Louisiana*, III, 456–457.

[45] This interpretation is at variance with Cox (*The Early Exploration of Louisiana*, 66).

the territory without the consent of Spain. Madison, the secretary of state, replied that the United States "can address themselves to the French government to negotiate the acquisition of territories which may suit their interests."[46]

Finding that he could get no satisfaction from the American government, Yrujo wrote to Casa Calvo, the recently appointed Spanish boundary commissioner at New Orleans, that in case he had received a royal order to suspend the transfer, he was to prepare to defend the province. Shortly after, he sent to his government a plan for the defense of the colony; but on the following day, being frightened by a threat of an attack on the Floridas if Louisiana were not delivered, he wrote that he did not think the province was worth a war if the Floridas could be preserved.[47]

The government at Washington was fully alert to the danger and a considerable military force was placed at Fort Adams to assist in occupying the province if necessary. The territory, however, was surrendered without violence. The French representative received the title from the Spanish commissioners on November 30, 1803, and on December 20 Claiborne and Wilkinson were given possession.[48]

In January, 1804, Yrujo was instructed to renounce his declaration against the alienation of Louisiana, the object of the Spanish government being to secure a better result in the demarcation of boundaries.[49] The Spanish policy now entered upon its second stage, namely, to restrict Louisiana to the narrowest bounds possible.

Early in 1804 a *junta* at Madrid considered the boundary question. They concluded to attempt to restrict the United States

[46] *State Papers, Foreign Relations,* II, 569–570.

[47] Robertson, *Louisiana under Spain, France and the United States,* II, 93–122.

[48] *State Papers, Foreign Relations,* II, 572, 581–582; Richardson, *Messages and Papers of the Presidents,* I, 367; McMaster, *History of the People of the United States,* III, 10–11.

[49] Robertson, *Louisiana under Spain, France and the United States,* II, 128–129.

to the Red River and the lower Mississippi, except Natchitoches, which was to be left to the United States. Cevallos later expressed himself as favoring a simple boundary rather than a neutral ground.[50]

The boundary commissioner, the Marqués de Casa Calvo, now became the central figure. He arrived at New Orleans early in 1803, and began to collect information regarding the boundaries of the province. From Nemesio Salcedo, the commandant-general of the Interior Provinces, he learned that the only map professing accuracy was that of Joseph de Evía, who had explored the coast in 1785, and that the boundaries of that captaincy-general had been reckoned from a point between the mouths of the Calcasieu and Mermento rivers in a straight line through the vicinity of Natchitoches to the Red River and north beyond the Missouri, which was as far as the Indian tribes had been subdued.

Manuel de Salcedo, the governor of Louisiana, also carried on an investigation, and ascertained, though probably incorrectly, that engineers of Spain and France had once established a line between the Spanish and French possessions beginning near Natchitoches and running due south to the sea, and that the Red River to its source had also been agreed upon. Later, owing to the Spanish withdrawal from Adaes, the French had considered that their jurisdiction extended to the Sabine.[51]

Soon after the delivery of the province to the Americans, Casa Calvo wrote to Cevallos, the Spanish Minister of State, that he foresaw difficulties regarding the western boundary, which both the French and American commissioners believed to be the Rio Grande. He stated that inventories and appraisals were to be made in New Orleans before all the edifices and archives could be delivered. This work he proposed to hinder, because, when completed, he foresaw that "inconveniences" would arise over boundaries. He also feared the commercial schemes of the

[50] Cox, in *The Southwestern Historical Quarterly,* XVII, 20–21.

[51] Robertson, *Louisiana under Spain, France and the United States,* II, 139–145, 150–156.

Americans. His conclusion was that Spain must keep control of Louisiana.[52]

Salcedo and Casa Calvo next proposed to Laussat that they run the boundary near Natchitoches. The Frenchman was too astute to be thus entangled and refused on the grounds that his government had not expected him to proceed to a demarcation. He then stated that he believed that Louisiana extended along the Rio Grande to the thirtieth degree, beyond which point it was indefinite.[53] Wilkinson and Claiborne, when approached by Casa Calvo, declared that it was not their intention to investigate Spain's rights to territory nor to state their opinion of the boundaries.[54]

The commissioner employed a French traveler named Robin to explore the Red and Washita rivers. Upon his return he pointed out the danger of the American occupation. After a second exploration he presented a memoir on the country.[55] While carrying on his investigations, Casa Calvo continued his policy of delay. He wrote to Cevallos that he was determined not to begin the demarcation except at the Sabine, and that he would endeavor to gain time to ascertain the true position of the Rio Grande and Sabine, making use of the observations of the commander-in-chief of the revenue vessels of the Gulf.[56] The following day he sent a protest to Laussat, asking him to inform the French government that he would oppose any attempt to place the boundary beyond the Sabine.[57]

During 1804 a considerable number of Spanish officers and troops remained in New Orleans, and Claiborne believed that they fomented the undercurrent of discontent. Madison re-

---

[52] Robertson, *Louisiana under Spain, France, and the United States*, II, 162–167.

[53] *Ibid.*, II, 171–173.

[54] Robertson, *Louisiana under Spain, France and the United States*, II, 183–184

[55] Cox, *The Early Exploration of Louisiana*, 62–63.

[56] Robertson, *Louisiana under Spain, France and the United States*, II, 240–243; *ibid.*, II, 261–262; *ibid.*, II, 167–168.

[57] *Ibid.*, II, 184–185.

quested that they depart, but they did not comply. The order
would probably have been more stringent had it been known that
Casa Calvo was sending information both to the governor of
Texas and to Cevallos concerning American exploring expeditions. The commissioner sent Juan Minor of Natchez to visit
Bahía and San Antonio. After examining the coast and rivers,
he was to proceed to Natchitoches to commence demarcation of
the boundary. Owing probably to the fact that he did not present any documents, Minor was not allowed to enter Texas.[58]

The commissioner continued his policy of delay. Quarrels between Morales and Casa Calvo were referred to Claiborne, but the
governor refused to interfere. He again requested the Spaniards
to depart; the troops were accordingly sent to Pensacola but the
officers remained, Casa Calvo among them, claiming that he
expected shortly to be employed in defining the boundary, but
later assuring the governor that he intended to set out soon on an
excursion through the Interior Provinces. Nevertheless he continued in New Orleans during the summer of 1805. At this time
a rumor became current that Louisiana had been retroceded to
Spain. In answer to Claiborne, who asked the commissioner if
he knew on whose authority it was circulated, he replied in the
negative, adding that he understood that Monroe's mission to
Spain had failed and that the King desired to make the Mississippi the boundary.[59]   Soon after Claiborne asked the commissioner for a passport for the Freeman party. With the greatest reluctance he granted it, but neutralized it by immediately
informing the captain-general of the Interior Provinces, who
stopped the expedition.[60]

Finally, on October 15, Casa Calvo set out on his long-
promised journey. He gave notice that he would proceed to

---

[58] Gayarré, *History of Louisiana*, IV, 24; Cox, *The Early Exploration of
Louisiana*, 56–57, 63–64. The writer is at variance with Cox, regarding
the refusal to admit Minor.

[59] Gayarré, *History of Louisiana*, IV, 29–32, 69–76, 83–85.

[60] Cox, *The Early Exploration of Louisiana*, 57–58; Coues, *The Expeditions of Zebulon Montgomery Pike*, II, 612–613.

Adaes where he expected to find some stone posts which were on the old Spanish and French line. He consented to a proposal of Claiborne that Captain Turner be allowed to join him from Natchitoches,[61] but succeeded in eluding the American officer. While the commissioner was absent, orders arrived from Jefferson urging the departure of the Spaniards. Captain Ross of the New Orleans volunteers was sent to inform Casa Calvo of his dismissal from the province, and orders were sent to Major Porter at Natchitoches to prevent the commissioner's return. After proceeding as far as the Trinity, Casa Calvo went to Nacogdoches, and later to Natchitoches; Captain Ross failed to find him nor was he detained by Porter, and on February 4, 1806, he arrived in New Orleans. There he was informed that all who held Spanish commissions must leave, and though protesting, on the fifteenth he made his departure. He afterwards wrote to Yrujo that he had examined the records of the Mission at Adaes, which proved that Spain had been in possession of that region for more than eighty-five years. He also found that the dividing line between Louisiana and Texas had always been the Arroyo Hondo near Natchitoches.[62]

As soon as the cession of Louisiana became known, the Spanish representatives in America believed that war was inevitable. Thinking that the United States intended to occupy the Floridas, Yrujo sent warnings to Casa Calvo, to the captain-general of Cuba, to the consul at Charleston, to Enrique White, the governor of East Florida, and to Vicente Folch, the governor of West Florida. Instructions were also sent to Havana to prepare a squadron to blockade the mouths of the Potomac, the Delaware, and the Mississippi, and American ports.[63]

Governor Folch also submitted a plan, advising that the fortifications of West Florida be strengthened, and that Ship Island

---

[61] Gayarré, *History of Louisiana*, II, 86–87.

[62] Cox, *The Early Exploration of Louisiana*, 67–71; Gayarré, *History of Louisiana*, IV, 130–132.

[63] Robertson, *Louisiana under Spain, France and the United States*, II, 109–114.

and Nacogdoches be fortified and a fort be erected on the Sabine. He suggested that three thousand men be placed in West Florida, eight hundred at Nacogdoches and fifteen hundred on the Sabine. He also urged that settlements be made at the mouths of the Teche and Sabine, or, if the latter were impracticable, at Matagorda Bay. He advised that Spain should set aside twenty thousand pesos to be used among the discontented tribes which the United States was driving across the Mississippi. These Indians he hoped to use to check the extension of American settlements, and if necessary, to destroy them. To protect the frontier, he believed that troops should be sent from Chihuahua and Santa Fé to intercept Lewis and Clark. Boone's advance into central Missouri he considered dangerous, for he and his followers might quickly explore the right path to Santa Fé.[64]

The Spanish plan of defense on the southwestern frontier, as carried out, appears to have been fourfold: all foreigners were to be forbidden to cross the frontier, Texas was to be colonized, garrisons established, and expeditions were to be sent out to gain control of the Indians, impede the advance of American settlement, and intercept exploring expeditions. Instances of foreigners being stopped are furnished by the refusal of entrance to Minor in 1804 and the arrest of Baptiste Lalande in New Mexico.[65] It was reported that during the same year three thousand settlers for Texas were gathered in Spain; that the expedition was on the point of sailing from Cadiz when the Spanish frigates were captured, and that, in spite of this, a few families arrived at San Antonio with a considerable detachment of troops.[66] For the defense of Texas, forts were established on

---

[64] Robertson, *Louisiana under Spain, France and the United States*, II, 339–345. I. J. Cox has revealed the fact that Folch's recommendations emanated from Wilkinson. See *The Southwestern Historical Quarterly*, XVII, 28–32. Cox has given a more extended treatment of this and has also shown that Wilkinson engaged in intrigues with Casa Calvo at this time. See *The American Historical Review*, XIX, 794–802.

[65] Bancroft, *History of Arizona and New Mexico*, 291.

[66] Ward, *Mexico in 1827*, I, 556; *Annals of Cong.*, 9 Cong., 1 Sess., 1206-1207. Sibley reported that there were five hundred families, probably an exaggeration.

Matagorda Bay and at Orcoquisac at the mouth of the Trinity. When Cordero arrived at San Antonio to take up his duties as governor, he brought a considerable reinforcement for Orco-quisac, Nacogdoches, and Adaes.[67]

The Spanish frontiers were guarded with the greatest care; during 1804–1807 several expeditions were sent northward for the double purpose of pacifying the Indian tribes and preventing American encroachment. In 1804 the governor of New Mexico sent a force of fifty-two men among the tribes south of the Platte. They were attacked near the Arkansas by a large force of Indians and compelled to return. The following year another expedition from New Mexico under Lucero visited the Kiowas and Comanches, and succeeded in making an alliance with them. In 1806 two expeditions left the Interior Provinces to intercept American explorers and control the border Indians, one from Nacogdoches under Viana, the other from New Mexico under Melgares. Viana's force penetrated the Caddo villages and inter-cepted Freeman's expedition, forcing it to turn back. Melgares visited the Pawnees, Kansas, and other plains tribes, kept a close watch for Freeman or Pike, and eventually captured the latter.[68] In 1808 under Amangual a military expedition of three com-panies from Nuevo Leon, Nuevo Santander, and Texas, left San Antonio, passed through the Comanche country, and reached Santa Fé. Conferences were held with the Comanche tribes to obtain information regarding the Americans and to warn the Indians against them.[69]

While the Spanish were vigorously preparing to defend their frontiers, the United States was equally active. As we have seen, a thousand men were gathered to take forcible possession

---

[67] *State Papers, Foreign Relations*, II, 690–692.

[68] Cox, *The Early Exploration of Louisiana*, 65–66, 85–87; Coues, *The Expeditions of Zebulon Montgomery Pike*, II, 410–414, 508–510, 597. Pike misspelled Melgares' name, and the misspelling has been followed by historians.

[69] Bolton MS notes, based on the diary of Amangual. See Bolton, *Guide to the Archives of Mexico*, 277.

of Louisiana if necessary. After the transfer, the troops were
stationed at New Orleans, Fort Adams, and other points. Captain Turner was sent to Natchitoches to watch the border, where
considerable friction developed over land titles and fugitive
slaves. Sibley made his headquarters there and kept informed
regarding activities in Texas by collecting information from
Indians and traders.[70] Governor Claiborne also busied himself
in organizing the militia.[71]

Alarming news from the border in 1805 and rumors of a
rupture with Spain caused Claiborne to increase his exertions.
In August he journeyed through the territory to assist personally
in the organization. Hearing of continual reinforcements in
Texas, he later wrote to Madison asking for troops, and advised
that Forts Plaquemines and St. Johns be placed in a state of
defense, that troops be moved from Fort Adams to Point Coupée,
and that the soldiers then posted at New Orleans be placed
above and below the city. In December he made a second inspection of the provinces, commissioning many military officers.
Alarmed at the activities of Casa Calvo, he took measures to
remove him. At this time he was surprised and chagrined to find
that Wilkinson had ordered one full company of the troops at
New Orleans to repair to Fort Adams. This left barely a
hundred effective men in the city. Strictures on American trade
through West Florida and conditions on the western border
further alarmed him, and in March, 1806, the governor again
asked Madison for troops, recommending that twelve hundred
men be stationed on the western border.[72]

In the latter part of 1805 the Spanish established posts at
Bayou Pierre and Nana, east of the Sabine, and at Adaes.

---

[70] Robertson, *Louisiana under Spain, France and the United States*, II,
289–291; *State Papers, Foreign Relations*, II, 690–691; Cox, in *The Southwestern Historical Quarterly*, XVII, 35–42.

[71] Gayarré, *History of Louisiana*, IV, 15–16; Robertson, *Louisiana under
Spain, France and the United States*, II, 225–231, 267–268, 272.

[72] Gayarré, *History of Louisiana*, IV, 85–86, 90–91, 122–130, 136–137.

Accounts were current that Cordero had marched from San Antonio with several hundred troops and at the Trinity had beén joined by reinforcements from Monterey. In January, 1806, Major Moses Porter, then commanding at Natchitoches, received an order from the War Department that he should require the commandant at Nacogdoches to give assurance that no acts of violence would be committed east of the Sabine. Porter was to patrol the country east of that river, repel invasion, but avoid bloodshed if possible. If the commandant gave proper assurances, the establishment at Bayou Pierre was not to be disturbed. Rodriguez, the commandant, assured Porter that no encroachment had been intended, except to prevent contraband trade and exportation of horses, but that it was his duty to patrol to the Arroyo Hondo. Captain Turner with sixty men was then sent to remove the force at Adaes, which was accomplished without difficulty.[73]

The easy withdrawal of the Spanish is accounted for by the fact that there were only fifty-one soldiers at Adaes. Soon after, however, Herrera led six hundred troops to the frontier, there then being about a thousand soldiers in Texas, seven hundred of whom were stationed near the eastern border.[74]

The American government was equally active; in March orders were issued to Wilkinson to send all the troops in the neighborhood of St. Louis, except one company, to Fort Adams. Colonel T. H. Cushing was ordered to Natchitoches with three companies and two field pieces, to reinforce the two hundred there under Porter. Not until May 6 did Wilkinson obey the order, but shortly after the departure of the troops, an alarming dispatch from Porter caused the commander to send orders to

---

[73] McCaleb, *The Aaron Burr Conspiracy*, 106; Martin, *History of Louisiana*, 330–331; *State Papers, Foreign Relations*, II, 799; Richardson, *Messages and Papers of the Presidents*, I, 400. For further details, see Cox, *The Louisiana-Texas Frontier*, Part II, in *The Southwestern Historical Quarterly*, XVII, 1–42.

[74] McCaleb, *The Aaron Burr Conspiracy*, 108; Jefferson, *Writings*, (Ford, ed.) VIII, 116, 435–436.

Cushing to push forward with all haste. If the Spaniards were again east of the Sabine or assumed a menacing attitude, he was to add to his command the force at Fort Adams. He was to avoid hostilities if possible and was not to cross the Sabine. Cushing arrived at Natchitoches on June 1.[75]

When the news of Turner's expulsion of the Spaniards reached Washington, a cabinet meeting was held at which it was decided to order nine war-vessels to Louisiana, to erect fortifications at New Orleans, and to have the militia drilled. Mobile, Pensacola, and Baton Rouge were to be seized if necessary. On May 6 Wilkinson was ordered to Orleans Territory to take personal command. He was to repel invasion and to warn the governors of Texas and West Florida that the *status quo* must be respected, and that the United States would insist upon the possession of territory east of the Sabine, except Bayou Pierre.[76]

In July additional Spanish troops occupied Bayou Pierre. Cushing demanded that Herrera withdraw them, but he refused on the grounds that that region was a part of Texas. News of the further advance of the Spaniards reached Claiborne; after consulting with Cowles Meade, the acting governor of Mississippi Territory, he issued a proclamation calling upon the people to assist in driving the enemy from Bayou Pierre. Shortly after he proceeded to Natchitoches.[77] There he learned that Viana's expedition had cut down the American flag at a Caddo village, that several slaves had found asylum at Nacogdoches, and that three Americans had been apprehended twelve miles from Natchitoches. Claiborne demanded explanations from Herrera regarding these, and also concerning the stopping of the Freeman party.[78]

---

[75] Wilkinson, *Memoirs of my own Times*, II, App. lxxxvii, lxxxix; McCaleb, *The Aaron Burr Conspiracy*, 107; Martin, *History of Louisiana*, 332.

[76] Wilkinson, *Memoirs of my own Times*, II, App. xc.

[77] *State Papers, Foreign Relations*, II, 801; McCaleb, *The Aaron Burr Conspiracy*, 117.

[78] Martin, *History of Louisiana*, 334.

Herrera replied that he was keeping the territory of the King inviolate, that the citizens were caught spying upon Spanish movements, and that the detention of the negroes was an affair then before the captain-general. Claiborne wished to make an immediate advance and drive the Spanish beyond the Sabine, but was checked by Cushing.[79]

In spite of the orders of May 6, Wilkinson did not arrive at Natchez until September 7, probably, as McCaleb says, because he was waiting for the development of the Burr conspiracy, to which he was a party. At Natchez he met Governor Williams and was informed of the plans formulated by him and Claiborne for the defense of the territory. He wrote that he would discourage the march of the militia "until I have penetrated the designs of the Spaniard, and may find him deaf to the solemn appeal which I shall make to his understanding, his interest, and his duty." He wrote in a grandiloquent style to Dearborn that he would do all in his power to preserve inviolate, by peaceful means, the territory east of the Sabine, but if a blow were once struck, he would "soon plant our standards on the left bank of the Grand river."[80]

After giving orders for the strengthening of the ports adjacent to West Florida, Wilkinson proceeded to Natchitoches, having on the way met Claiborne, who promised four hundred militia, but five hundred responded to the call. From Natchitoches Wilkinson wrote to Cordero that in lieu of a recognized line of demarcation and as Nacogdoches was the easternmost Spanish outpost, the United States had adopted the Sabine as a boundary and demanded the withdrawal of the Spanish to the west side of the river. Cordero simply replied that he had referred the matter to Salcedo. On October 4 Wilkinson warned the Spanish that he would advance to the Sabine, but he did

---

[79] Wilkinson, *Memoirs of my own Times,* II, App. xciii; McCaleb, *The Aaron Burr Conspiracy,* 118–119.

[80] *Annals of Cong.,* 10 Cong., 1 Sess., App., 568–570.

not carry out the threat, for on the twenty-first he had not taken action. On September 27 the Spanish retreated from Bayou Pierre; two weeks later Cordero threatened to advance, but made no offensive move. In the latter part of October he received orders from Salcedo that under no circumstances should the American forces be attacked.[81]

Late in October Wilkinson finally headed for the Sabine. To Cordero he dispatched his aide-de-camp, Burling, with the proposal that the Spanish remain west of the Sabine and the Americans east of the Arroyo Hondo, leaving an unoccupied neutral ground between. A favorable reply was shortly after received, the arrangement thus concluded being familiarly known as the Neutral Ground Treaty. Shortly after Wilkinson returned to New Orleans, where he busied himself in fortifying the city against the insignificant forces of his former co-worker, Aaron Burr.

The period of inaction on the border, the apparent ease with which an agreement was reached, and the fact that Wilkinson suddenly turned against Burr need further explanation. McCaleb believes that in all the early operations Wilkinson was preparing the way for the conquest of Mexico, but that the withdrawal of the Spanish troops from Bayou Pierre destroyed the power of Wilkinson to compel a war.[82] But this does not seem to be the true explanation, in the light of certain evidence which appears to have been overlooked.

Monette quotes the following letter from New Orleans, which was published in the *New York Spectator* of June 10, 1807:

The intendant said that General Wilkinson first communicated intelligence of the general nature of this plot [the Burr conspiracy] to Governor Cordero upon the Sabine, and proposed to him, that if he would withdraw his forces from that river, and prevail upon the vice-king to furnish him (General Wilkinson) with $300,000, he would undertake to

---

[81] McCaleb, *The Aaron Burr Conspiracy*, 123–127, 138; *Annals of Cong.*, 10 Cong., 1 Sess., App., 590; *State Papers, Foreign Relations*, II, 803–804; Wilkinson, *Memoirs of my own Times*, II, App. xciii.

[82] McCaleb, *The Aaron Burr Conspiracy*, 149–150, 159, 170.

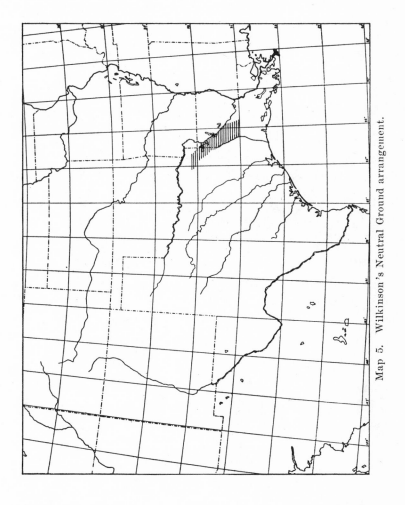

Map 5. Wilkinson's Neutral Ground arrangement.

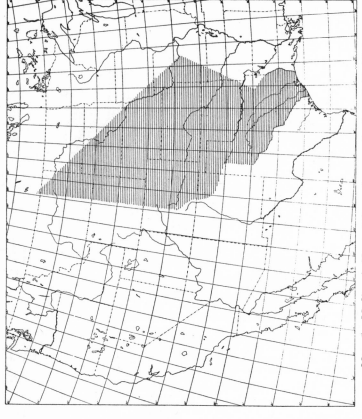

Map 6. Madison's Neutral Ground proposal of April 15, 1804.

frustrate the designs of the conspirators and save the provinces of his Catholic majesty from invasion, employing for that purpose the forces and other resources, naval and military, of the United States. Governor Cordero, knowing Wilkinson to have been for a long time in the interests of his king, lent a favorable ear to his propositions. He immediately consented that both armies should retire from the banks of the Sabine; the Spanish force for the purpose of re-enforcing their posts on the frontiers of New Mexico, and the American troops to defend the passes of the Mississippi. He also dispatched couriers to the vice-king in Mexico, and furnished Wilkinson forthwith with $120,000, *which were sent from St. Antoine upon mules.* The intendant further informed this gentleman that, before the arrival of Cordero's dispatches, the vice-king was by no means inclined to place full confidence in Wilkinson, and refused to transmit $180,000, the balance of the sum which Cordero had undertaken to promise him. Soon after this refusal, the intendant said that Wilkinson had dispatched a confidential aid-de-camp, Major Burling, to Mexico with further proofs of the conspiracy, . . . and with a request for the immediate payment of the $180,000 to General Wilkinson. The vice-king refused to receive the information from Burling, and referred him for the payment of the money to the intendant at La Vera Cruz, for which place he immediately ordered him to depart.

At Vera Cruz Burling received nothing and was sent with a guard to New Orleans. Monette says that he had conversed with some of the militia who had been on the Sabine, and that they corroborated the statement.[83]

From documents in the Mexican archives, McCaleb confirms the statement that Burling went to Mexico, that he demanded a large sum of money and was refused.[84] But apparently not being cognizant of the financial transaction carried on by Wilkinson and Cordero, he did not see the bearing of the evidence on the desertion of Burr, nor upon the Neutral Ground Treaty.

While these events were taking place in America, Monroe and Pinckney were handling the diplomatic side of the question. When Monroe went to France, the intention of the American government was that he was to co-operate with Livingston and

---

[83] Monette, *History of the Discovery and Settlement of the Valley of the Mississippi,* II, 463–464.

[84] McCaleb, *The Aaron Burr Conspiracy,* 168–169. Cox follows McCaleb on this transaction. See *The American Historical Review,* XIX, 802-803.

later to proceed to Madrid to assist Pinckney in the negotiation with Spain. After completing the sale of Louisiana, the French government considered that it would then be inopportune for Monroe to visit Madrid and at the same time the American government found that his presence was needed in England.[85]

Pinckney was thus compelled to carry on the negotiation alone. On January 11, 1804, he addressed a letter to Cevallos in which he stated that there were three subjects for discussion, namely, Louisiana, Florida, and claims. A month later he was informed that Spain withdrew its opposition to the French alienation of Louisiana. This would appear to reduce the pending questions to two, but such was not the case, the Louisiana boundaries being an open question.[86]

Pinckney's diplomacy during 1804 was exceedingly annoying to Spain. The American government, after much delay, had ratified a claims convention with Spain. Soon afterward Yrujo sent to his government a copy of the Mobile Act by which the United States asserted its authority over territory claimed by Spain. At this critical juncture, Pinckney assumed a dictatorial tone in demanding the immediate ratification of the claims convention. The result was that diplomatic relations became so strained that war threatened.[87]

In April Madison instructed Monroe to proceed to Spain. In regard to Louisiana, Madison stated that he might stipulate that beyond a limit not far west of the Mississippi the territory should not be settled for a given term of years, leaving a wide unoccupied tract between the possessions of Spain and American settlements. A *projet* of a treaty was sent which defined the neutral ground as follows:

A limit consisting on one side of the river Sabine . . . from its mouth to its source; thence a straight line to the confluence of the rivers Osage and Missouri; and . . . on the other side, consisting of the river

---

85 Monroe, *Writings*, IV, 36–39, 44–52.
86 *State Papers, Foreign Relations*, II, 583, 616–617.
87 Henry Adams, *History of the United States*, II, 279–287.

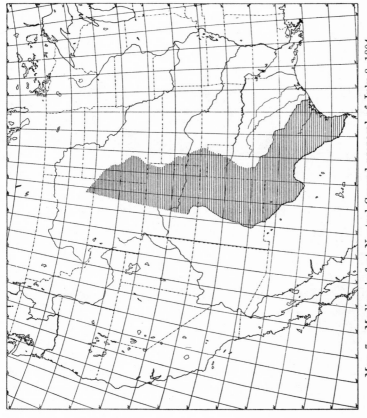

Map 7. Madison's first Neutral Ground proposal of July 8, 1804.

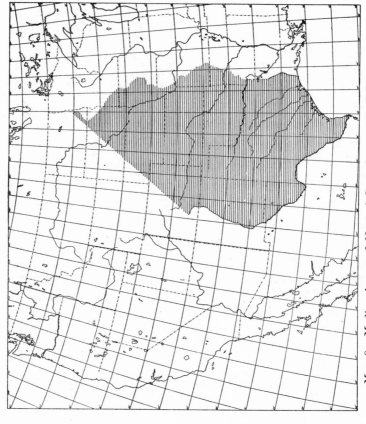

Map 8.   Madison's second Neutral Ground proposal of July 8, 1804.

Colorado, (or some other river emptying into the bay of St. Bernard,) from its mouth to its source; thence a straight line, to the most south-westwardly source of the Red River, with such deflections, however, as will head all the waters of that river; thence along the ridge of the highlands which divide the waters belonging to the Missouri and the Mississippi from those belonging to the Rio Bravo, to the latitude of the northernmost source of that river; and thence, a meridian to the northern boundary of Louisiana.

At whatever place the western limit might commence, a balancing amount was to be demanded east of the Mississippi. A limit as far west as possible was to be obtained, and none would be accepted which did not shut Spain out from the waters emptying into the Missouri and Mississippi. If Spain refused to relinquish West Florida, no agreement was to be made regarding the territory west of the Mississippi. Any arrangement which might be made was not to imply that the United States surrendered her claim as far as the Rio Bravo.[88]

Early in July the cabinet discussed the Spanish negotiation. It was decided that the right to West Florida was a *sine qua non;* that the claim to territory as far as the Rio Grande was not to be surrendered even in exchange for Florida; that a neutral ground should be laid off for a term of years, which should lie between the Rio Grande and the Colorado, or even to the Sabine, and from whatever river was determined upon, the line was to run northwest from its source. Two million dollars was to be the price of all the land east of the Perdido, or less in proportion to the amount obtained. Gallatin, the secretary of the treasury, was of the opinion that the claim to lands beyond the Colorado should be absolutely relinquished, but Jefferson considered that this should not be done except for an entire cession of the Floridas. New instruction were framed which followed the cabinet decision, except that the eastern line of the neutral zone was to run parallel to the Mississippi.[89]

---

[88] *State Papers, Foreign Relations,* II, 626–630.

[89] Jefferson, *Writings* (Ford, ed.), VIII, 309–312, and note on 312; *State Papers, Foreign Relations,* II, 630–631.

In October Monroe left London; he tarried a short time in Paris to urge Talleyrand to take the part of the United States in the difficulties with Spain. There his overtures were fruitless, for the French government had decided to assist Spain in its efforts to restrict the bounds of Louisiana. Talleyrand had already written to Turreau, the French minister at Washington, that the eastern boundary was the Mississippi and the Iberville, but that the western boundary was indefinite. He stated that Spain seemed to fear that the United States might advance into the country north of California. He accordingly instructed Turreau to divert the attention of the United States from any such project. He had also written a letter to the Spanish government in which he laid down the principle that all Spanish settlements should belong to Spain, and all French establishments belonged to Louisiana.[90] Naturally Monroe's attempts proved fruitless, and in December he started for Madrid. Shortly after, Talleyrand wrote to Armstrong, the minister who had succeeded Livingston, emphatically denying that West Florida was a part of Louisiana. No mention was made of the western boundary.[91]

Fearful of the outcome of affairs in Spain, Madison in October instructed Monroe to proceed at once to Madrid. He was informed that no qualifications were to be attached if the claims convention were ratified. The instructions differed from the previous ones in only one particular. If Spain insisted on the Colorado River line, Monroe was to acquiesce.[92]

The negotiations opened in January, 1805. In the first note the American representatives asserted the claim that Louisiana extended from the Rio Grande to the Perdido. Madison's *projet* was submitted, with a suggestion that a neutral ground be established for twenty years, and with an offer to buy East Florida.

---

[90] Monroe, *Writings*, IV, 218–223, 266–274; Henry Adams, *History of the United States*, II, 291–301.

[91] Monroe, *Writings*, IV, 277–297; *State Papers, Foreign Relations*, II, 635–636.

[92] *State Papers, Foreign Relations*, II, 631–632.

Cevallos promptly answered that Casa Calvo would attend to the
eastern boundary. In regard to other questions, he stated that
the King had not decided, and as they were unconnected, he did
not wish to consider them at that time. The commissioners
replied that they were willing to discuss the points of difference
one at a time.

The first question discussed was the eastern boundary,
Cevallos holding firmly to the position that the United States
had no right to West Florida. Finding that they could make no
progress on the question, nor regarding the claims convention,
the commissioners proposed a discussion of the western boundary.
After an aggravating delay, Cevallos finally stated his views. He
laid down the principle that the basis of settlement should depend
upon the territory which each party had occupied and that the
boundary should be run between them by the most natural
points of demarcation. He then gave a brief history of Texas,
pointing out that the Spanish had occupied as far as Adaes. He
said that an attempt to make the boundary the Rio Grande was
based upon illusory and unfounded claims, namely, that the
coast and interior had belonged to France because of the Crozat
grant. He pointed out that the limits were known even when
France possessed Louisiana, for Spanish missions had been
founded in eastern Texas and the French had held Natchitoches.
He thought that the line ought to begin between the Calcasieu
and Mermento, thence run northward between Adaes and Natchitoches to Red River. From this point he considered the limits
doubtful and suggested that its settlement be referred to
commissioners.[93]

Monroe and Pinckney replied that the American claims were
based upon the settlement of La Salle and the Crozat grant.
They laid down the principle that if the coasts belonged to a
country, so also did the rivers which emptied into the adjacent
waters. A second principle was that when two portions were

---

[93] *State Papers, Foreign Relations,* II, 638–649, 657–662.

occupied by different nations and the boundary was unmarked, the middle distance became the boundary. A third principle stated that when an European nation had acquired territory, its rights could never be diminished by virtue of purchases made, by grants or conquests of the natives within the limits thereof. On these principles the commissioners believed that the United States would own Texas.[94]

They backed their argument by citing several authorities, a discussion of which seems pertinent. The De Lisle map of 1707 was cited. This French map shows the western boundary as running up the Rio Grande to the mouth of the Pecos, thence up that river to a point east of Tiguas, thence northeast across the San Marcos [Colorado], then along the mountains in a generally north by northeast direction, crossing the Rio Grande and turning west just above Taos.[95] Reference was also made to page twelve of the first volume of the *Histoire de la Louisiane* by Le Page du Pratz. This citation referred to the expedition of St. Denis to the Presidio of San Juan Bautista on the Rio Grande. But no reference was made to the map, which laid down the boundary practically the same as the De Lisle map with the exception that it turned west at the fortieth degree of north latitude.[96]

The López map of 1763, a Spanish production, was also cited, but it is difficult to understand how the commissioners could consider this as strengthening their case, for no boundaries were marked. The Rio Grande was given in its lower course, but so were Florida, Carolina, and Georgia. The place where northwestern Texas and New Mexico would appear was given up to inscriptions; the coast line of Texas appears to have been added merely for artistic effect.[97]

---

[94] *State Papers, Foreign Relations*, II, 662–665.

[95] A reprint may be found in French, *Historical Collections of Louisiana*, II, frontis.

[96] Le Page du Pratz, *Histoire de la Louisiane*, I.

[97] Reprint in Gayarré, *History of Louisiana*, (1903 edition) I.

The memoir of the Chevalier de Champigny was a fourth authority. On page twelve the French claim is stated as follows: "What remains to France [in 1762] of her vast province of Louisiana comprises a strip eighty leagues from east to west, from the mouth of the Mississippi to Mexico. The Rio Bravo on the west and the Mississippi on the east bounded these possessions, which extended from twenty-nine degrees north latitude to fifty degrees and even beyond." This will at once be perceived to be a ridiculous statement in the light of geography and history. No mention of the Crozat grant appears in the account.[98]

The spurious memoir of Count de Vergennes was a fifth source. On page twenty-six occurs this statement: "It [Louisiana] is inclosed on the south between the possessions of the Spaniards; it extends on the west to the territories of Mexico, and on the east to Florida." Vergennes' description of French activities is fairly accurate, but it is evident from the memoir that he laid great stress on the Mississippi and the region east of it, and paid little attention to the west. In describing rivers, no mention was made of streams in Texas, and a similar omission is found regarding Indian tribes. The La Salle incident he considered the result of a blunder.[99]

As the argument of the American representatives appeared to have no effect, they submitted a statement of the ultimate conditions to which they would consent. If Spain would cede the territory east of the Mississippi and settle claims according to the convention of 1802, they would accept the Colorado as the boundary. They suggested a perpetual neutral zone thirty leagues wide, to run from the Gulf to the northern limit of Louisiana, and offered to relinquish the claim for French spoliations which occurred within Spanish jurisdiction. Cevallos promptly rejected the American proposition, and on May 23

---

[98] De Champigny, *Etat-present de la Louisiane.*

[99] Vergennes, *Mémoire historique et politique sur la Louisiane;* Phillips, *The West in the Diplomacy of the American Revolution,* pp. 30–31, note.

Monroe and Pinckney informed their government of their complete failure.[100]

Two months before the negotiations ended, Monroe had written to Armstrong, that if the United States put on a firm front and a representation was made that an understanding might be made with England, France might be brought to her assistance. The effort, however, was a failure, Armstrong being told that in case of a rupture France would side with Spain. Armstrong saw clearly that Texas could be acquired only by war. Monroe hastened to Paris to consult with him and soon came to the same conclusion.[101]

As early as March Jefferson foresaw the probable failure of the Monroe mission. A change of diplomats, it was hoped, might bring happier results, and James Bowdoin was accordingly sent as minister to Spain. In a letter to Bowdoin, Jefferson expressed the wish that peace might be maintained but said that he had ceased to expect it.[102]

In May Madison wrote to Armstrong that he still hoped that France might support the American claim to the Rio Grande, but realized that the present temper and view of France was such that failure ought to be anticipated.[103] In June other dispatches arrived from Armstrong acquainting the government still further concerning the hostile attitude of France. Madison answered that her position might force the United States to the side of Great Britain.[104] In the month of July Madison still clung to the hope that France would eventually assist the United States.[105]

---

[100] *State Papers, Foreign Relations,* II, 665–669.

[101] Henry Adams, *History of the United States,* III, 30–31, 39–40; *State Papers, Foreign Relations,* II, 636.

[102] Henry Adams, *History of the United States,* III, 54–55; Jefferson, *Writings* (Ford, ed.), VIII, 350–351.

[103] *Annals of Cong.,* 8 Cong., 2 Sess., App., 1353–1356.

[104] Madison, *Writings,* VII, 183–190. Henry Adams, (*History of the United States,* III, 58–62) represents Madison as a man without a policy, and credits the conception of the British alliance to Jefferson, a conception, which, according to that author, did not take definite shape until August.

[105] Madison, *Writings,* VII, 187, note.

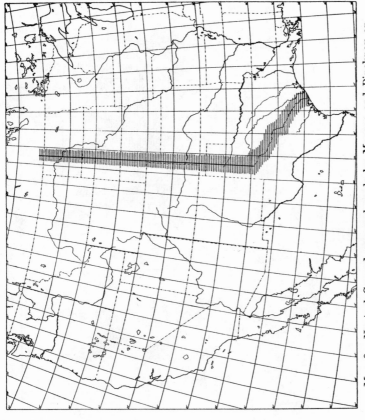

Map 9. Neutral Ground proposal made by Monroe and Pinckney on
May 12, 1805.

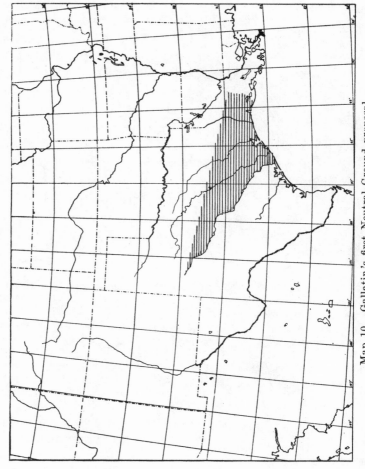

Map 10. Gallatin's first Neutral Ground proposal.

In August it was definitely learned that the Spanish negotiations had failed. Jefferson decided that the failure to settle boundaries or the withholding of a ratification was not sufficient cause for war, but he believed that an alliance with England would be necessary, a view which increased in strength in the succeeding days. Madison, however, calmly viewed the situation, aware that an English alliance was a doubtful expedient.[106]

Gallatin was opposed to the policy which had been adopted toward Spain and in September addressed a long argument to Jefferson in which he pointed out the flimsy basis of the claim to Texas, and counseled strongly against war with Spain, lest it should force the United States into an alliance with England. He urged that the negotiations be reopened with a modified demand and that the first overtures be made to France. He suggested that the Sabine and Perdido be accepted as the boundaries of Louisiana, but that a temporary arrangement first be made, by which neither party should establish any military post in advance of what it then had:

> If Spain shall insist that not only new military posts, but also new settlements be precluded, the precise lines must be defined, and so save the pride of Spain, by abandoning our rights to settle for the present some part of what she acknowledges to be ours; the river Mermento or Calcasieu, at her choice (both lie a little east of the Sabine), might be fixed on our side, and the Colorado on hers; but it would be preferable to say nothing about settlements, for it must be recollected that the offer of a desert for fifteen years was intended, in case the western boundary could not be settled, as an inducement for a relinquishment on the part of Spain of her claim to the country between Perdido and the Mississippi.

On the following day he again wrote to Jefferson counseling peace,[107] but Jefferson was in a somewhat bellicose state of mind, having received Armstrong's letter which urged the occupation of Texas. Soon after, Jefferson wrote to Madison, asking him to consider the following points before the next cabinet meeting:

---

[106] Jefferson, *Writings* (Ford, ed.), VIII, 374–378; Henry Adams, *History of the United States*, III, 62.

[107] Gallatin, *Writings*, I, 241–255.

An alliance with English, an act of Congress authorizing the suspension of intercourse with Spain at discretion, the dislodgement of the new establishments in Texas, and the appointment of commissioners to consider spoliation claims.[108] Before the meeting, Madison answered that he thought that the United States ought not to go so far into an understanding with England as would preclude an adjustment, if attainable, with Spain. Bowdoin, having heard of Monroe's failure, had gone from Spain to France, and later to England. Bowdoin's withdrawal Madison thought fortunate, believing it to be wise to deal with France or else with Casa Calvo at New Orleans.[109]

Madison was not present at the cabinet meeting, and no decision was reached. In writing to him Jefferson spoke as if war were already in progress:

> The . . . questions . . . for decision are whether we shall enter into a provisional alliance with England to come into force only in the event that *during the present war* we become engaged in war *with France?* leaving the declaration of the casus federis ultimately with us. Whether we shall send away Yrujo, Casacalvo, Morales? Whether we shall instruct Bowdoin not to go to Madrid until further ordered?

The first he considered of prime importance. Madison advised delay in opening overtures with England, that the Spanish representatives be ordered from the country, and that Bowdoin remain in England.[110]

Shortly after, Jefferson wrote to Madison that European war was imminent, and that this would ease the situation for the United States, giving time to make another effort for a peaceful settlement. France should be asked to mediate, the price of the Floridas being the means. An enlargement of the sum might be

---

108 Jefferson, *Writings* (Ford, ed.), VIII, 379–380.

109 Henry Adams, *History of the United States,* III, 70–72. The writer believes that Adams has underestimated the importance that Napoleon would have attached to an Anglo-American alliance.

110 Jefferson, *Writings* (Ford, ed.), VIII, 380–382; Henry Adams *History of the United States,* III, 74. Adams considered Madison's course a sign of weakness. To the writer it seems a safe rather than a weak policy.

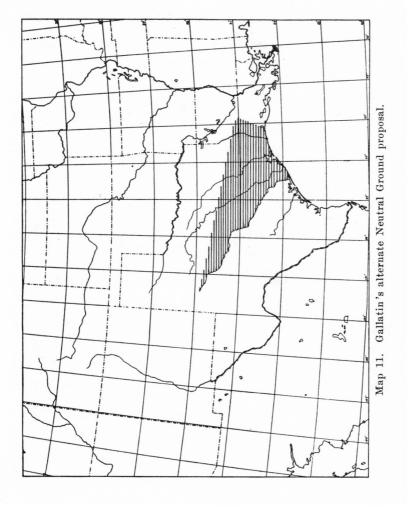

Map 11. Gallatin's alternate Neutral Ground proposal.

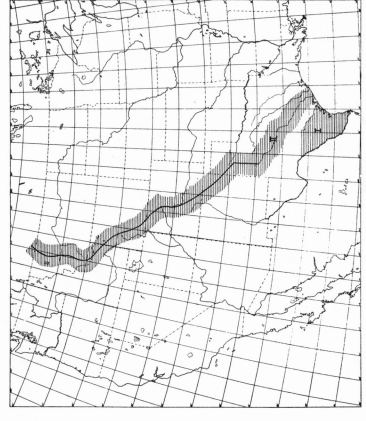

Map 12.   I. Proposal of lands to be hypothecated to satisfy claims.
II. Talleyrand's idea of a Neutral Ground.

the bait to France and the Guadalupe as the western boundary might satisfy Spain. In the meantime, if Spain attempted to change the *status quo*, force would be repelled by force. Gallatin and the Secretary of the Navy were similarly informed. At a cabinet meeting of November 12 this policy was adopted. It was also decided that for the claims, amounting to about four million dollars, Spain should be asked to hypothecate the lands between the Guadalupe and Rio Grande.[111]

In the meantime events were occurring in Europe which were destined to affect the decision. One of Talleyrand's secret agents presented to Armstrong a plan for the adjustment of difficulties with Spain. It was suggested that Godoy be urged to refer matters to Napoleon. If Spain would then consent to the alienation of the Floridas, France would suggest the line of the Colorado with thirty leagues on each side to remain unsettled forever, the upper part of the line to include the headwaters of all streams emptying into the Mississippi; claims against Spain, exclusive of French spoliation, to be paid by bills on the Spanish colonies, and ten millions to be paid to Spain by the United States. These proposals Armstrong rejected, but a few days later the suggested amount was reduced to seven million. This proposal he submitted to his government.[112] Armstrong's letter arrived in Washington on November 13, and on the following day the cabinet again met. It was agreed that five millions should be paid for the Floridas, and the boundary placed at the Guadalupe, if possible; if not, at the Colorado, and a neutral zone should be established.[113]

But the condition of affairs at this time made it impolitic to make known the intended policy. Pitt had begun his strictures on American commerce, New York then being blockaded by English frigates. The cruisers of Spain had captured American

---

[111] Jefferson, *Writings* (Ford, ed.), VIII, 380–382, notes; Henry Adams, *History of the United States*, III, 78–79.

[112] Henry Adams, *History of the United States*, III, 103–105.

[113] Jefferson, *Writings* (Ford, ed.), VIII, 383–384.

vessels, and her troops showed a menacing attitude in Florida and Texas. France, the ally of Spain, was demanding that the United States government prevent trade with the rebellious portions of San Domingo.[114] No step was taken to continue negotiations with France until the meeting of Congress. Jefferson's message of December 3 described the situation; he expressed the hope that peace might be maintained, but recommended that preparation for war be made. This recommendation was intended to satisfy the public and warn the foreign powers. But the President had no intention of appealing to force except as a last resort. On December 6 he sent a special message which was received behind closed doors. He detailed the course of negotiations with Spain, explained the attitude of France, and advised that negotiations be reopened. He stated that war was improbable but that force, interposed to a certain degree, might contribute to advance the object of peace.[115]

Congress was thus placed in an ambiguous position. If war were declared, the President would get the credit, and war was popular with the public. If the policy of further negotiation were adopted, Congress would be blamed. Randolph, the Democratic leader of the House, proved factious. He proposed to humble Madison, and began a policy of obstruction. In spite of his powerful opposition, the administration rallied enough votes to obtain an appropriation of two million dollars to be used in the coming negotiations.

Events both in America and Europe seemed to conspire to defeat the policy of Jefferson. A violent quarrel broke out between Yrujo and Madison. The adventurer Miranda was received by the Secretary of State to the great anoyance of the Spanish government. Burr's schemes were also known to Spain. The three incidents, following the Pinckney embroglio and the

---

[114] Henry Adams, *History of the United States*, III, 91; McCaleb, *The Aaron Burr Conspiracy*, 105–106; *State Papers, Foreign Relations*, II, 726.
[115] Richardson, *Messages and Papers of the Presidents*, I, 382–390.

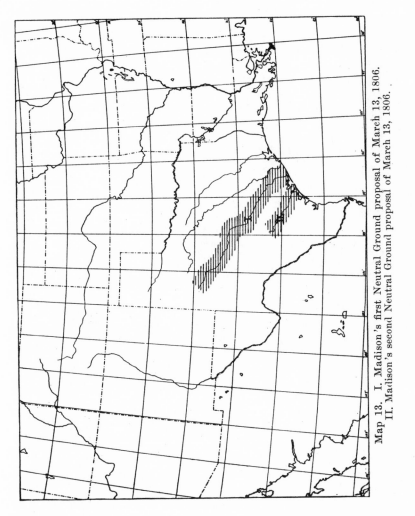

Map 13. I. Madison's first Neutral Ground proposal of March 13, 1806.
II. Madison's second Neutral Ground proposal of March 13, 1806.

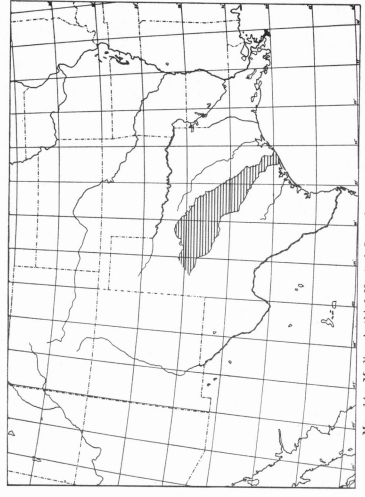

Map 14. Madison's third Neutral Ground proposal of March 13, 1806.

Monroe mission, were most unpropitious for the reopening of negotiations. Furthermore, conditions on the border and the high seas were closely akin to war. On the continent the war against the third coalition had broken out. Ulm had capitulated and the battle of Austerlitz had been fought. But the French and Spanish fleets had been defeated at Trafalgar, leaving Napoleon helpless on the sea. In May, 1806, England declared the coast from the mouth of the Elbe to Brest in a state of blockade. In October Prussia was defeated at Jena, and immediately after Napoleon issued his Berlin Decree. In February, 1807, he was checked at Eylau, but in June the decisive victory of Friedland humbled Russia, resulting in the peace of Tilsit. England's Orders in Council were answered by the Milan Decree, by which Napoleon hoped to throttle his enemy.[116] No assistance could be expected from France unless the United States complied with her commercial decrees, and this meant war with England. From this dilemma Jefferson saw but one way out, namely, a non-intercourse policy.[117]

For over six months Armstrong was kept in suspense. Finally in March, 1806, Madison wrote to him and to Bowdoin that the government had determined to appeal to France. A *projet* of a treaty was enclosed. The first article was to the effect that Spain was to acknowledge the American claim to West Florida and to cede East Florida and the adjacent islands; or, if Spain objected to the acknowledgment of this claim, both Floridas were to be ceded. The third article dealt with the western boundary. If possible, the Guadalupe was to be the line, but if unattainable, the Colorado to its source, thence a right line directly or indirectly to the Mississippi or Missouri,

---

116 Henry Adams, *History of the United States*, III, 132–139, 184–189; Robertson, in Am. Hist. Assoc., *Ann. Rpt., 1907*, I, 361–375; McCaleb, *The Aaron Burr Conspiracy*, 39–40; Fournier, *Napoleon I*, I, 340–465; Sloane, *The Life of Napoleon Bonaparte*, II, 354–467; *Cambridge Modern History*, IX, 208–293, 360–368.

117 Henry Adams, *History of the United States*, IV, 152–177.

and thence along the highlands as far as they bordered on the Spanish possessions. A neutral ground was to be established, thirty leagues on either side of the Guadalupe or Colorado, or thirty leagues on the American side only, or extending from one of those rivers to some river between the Colorado and the Sabine. If all these were rejected, the eastern boundary of the neutral zone might commence at the Sabine and run from the source of that river to the confluence of the Osage and Missouri rivers, thence parallel with the Mississippi to the latitude of its most northerly source, and thence following a meridian to the northern boundary of Louisiana.[118] Jefferson contemplated sending Wilson C. Nicholas to assist in the negotiations, but Nicholas refused the appointment and affairs were left in the hands of Armstrong and Bowdoin.[119]

The instructions reached Armstrong on May 1, and he immediately communicated their contents to Talleyrand. Unknown to his minister, the Emperor had been conducting a secret negotiation with Spain. Napoleon immediately informed Talleyrand that Charles IV would not dispose of the Floridas. The minister communicated this to Armstrong, at the same time telling him that Godoy had informed him that Bowdoin had betrayed certain confidential proposals of the previous year. The result was a quarrel between the American negotiators which destroyed unity of action. A few weeks later Armstrong made a second attempt. Talleyrand assisted him by writing to the French representative at Madrid, ''If Spain is not bent on preserving this colony, she may listen to the American propositions.'' For the time being, Armstrong believed that affairs had taken a favorable turn. On September 30 he wrote to Yzquierdo, a Spanish agent at Paris, that he understood that Charles IV had appointed him to treat with the Americans. But his fancied

---

[118] *State Papers, Foreign Relations,* III, 539–541.
[119] Jefferson, *Writings* (Ford, ed.), VIII, 434–435 note. 436–438.

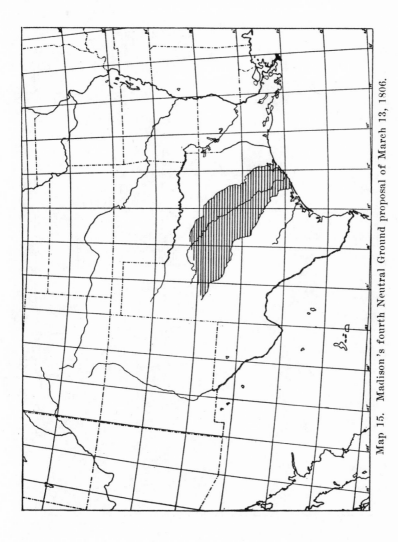

Map 15. Madison's fourth Neutral Ground proposal of March 13, 1806.

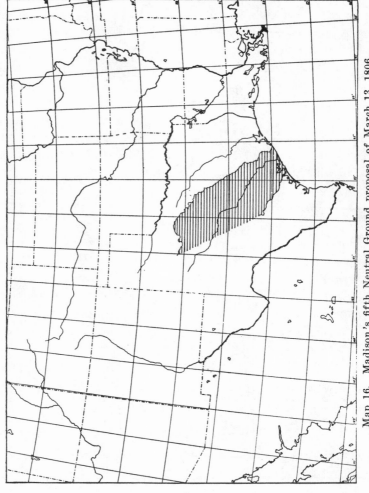

Map 16. Madison's fifth Neutral Ground proposal of March 13, 1806.

progress vanished when the Spaniard informed him that this was beyond his powers.[120]

The reply of Yzquierdo was but the sequel to the resolve which Napoleon had made not to act as mediator. He was then developing his great continental plans, and American interests were lost in the labyrinth of his policy. Spain acquiesced in the continental system by issuing a proclamation of blockade against England. The affair of the "Leopard" brought England and the United States to the verge of war. Realizing that nothing could be done without French assistance and knowing that funds would be needed in case of war, Madison instructed the commissioners to suspend negotiations unless Spain agreed that the payments might be deferred until one year after the suspension of hostilities.[121]

There was no possibility, however, that the negotiation would succeed. Napoleon was already looking forward to the occupation of Spain, a plan which was carried out in 1808. Armstrong was informed that whenever the United States declared war on England and made an alliance with France Napoleon would intervene with Spain to obtain the Floridas and a convenient western boundary. The United States government, having adopted the embargo policy, rejected the proposal, and in spite of the efforts of Turreau, the French minister at Washington, Jefferson held to his policy. The negotiations for the Floridas and the Rio Bravo were necessarily at an end for the time being, and were not resumed until after the battle of Waterloo.[122]

---

[120] Henry Adams, *History of the United States,* III, 376–378, 380–383; Jefferson, *Writings* (Ford, ed.), VIII, 460–462; *State Papers, Foreign Relations,* III, 541.

[121] *State Papers, Foreign Relations,* III, 290, 293, 541–542.

[122] Napoleon I, *Correspondance,* XVI, 281–282, 301; *State Papers, Foreign Relations,* III, 252; Henry Adams, *History of the United States,* IV, 307–310.

CHAPTER III

THE TREATY OF 1819

While Spain was in the throes of the Peninsular War, her grasp upon her colonial possessions became weaker and weaker. In South America Bolívar, San Martín and others revolted, and in Mexico Hidalgo started a war of independence. By 1812 Texas had become a battle-ground for warring factions. The Mexican refugee, Gutiérrez, and Magee, who had formerly been a lieutenant in the United States army, raised the standard of revolt at the head of several hundred men, many of whom were enlisted in the United States. After considerable fighting around La Bahía, the royalists were defeated at Rosillo, Governor Salcedo was captured, and in 1813 San Antonio capitulated. The governor and thirteen others were murdered. Magee had died at La Bahía and Major Kemper had succeeded him. The acts of atrocity at San Antonio caused the Americans to abandon the revolutionists. Gutiérrez was soon after deposed and Toledo became the moving spirit. In August Toledo's forces were almost annihilated and Texas was again in royalist hands.[1]

In 1815 Captain Perry, a former follower of Magee, published a proclamation in New Orleans that a thousand men were ready to invade Texas. Madison issued a proclamation prohibiting such enterprises, but Perry eluded the authorities and crossed the Sabine with a small party, making their way to Galveston Island, where in 1816 they joined forces with the

---

[1] Bancroft *North Mexican States and Texas*, II, 17–31. For the first period of the revolt see McCaleb, in Texas State Historical Association. *The Quarterly*, IV, 218–229. Arredondo's official report of the battle of Medina was obtained by Herbert E. Bolton from the archives of Mexico and is translated by Mrs. Hatcher in Texas State Historical Association, *The Quarterly*, XI, 220–232.

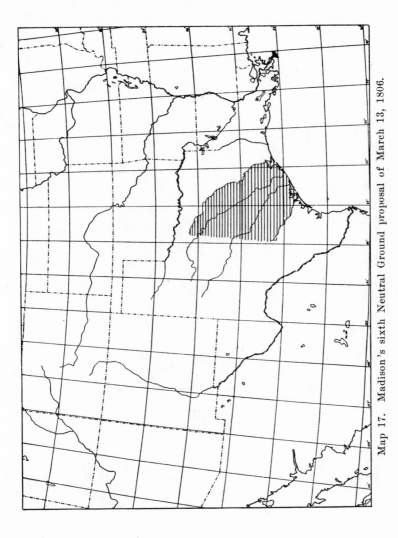

Map 17. Madison's sixth Neutral Ground proposal of March 13, 1806.

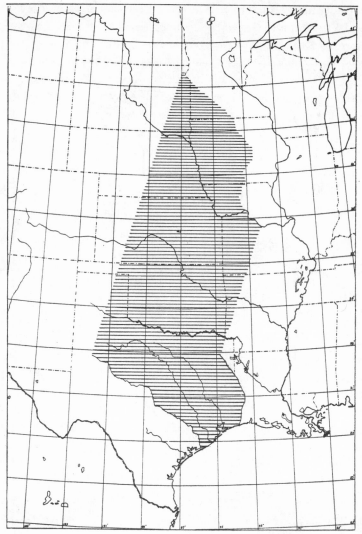

Map 18.   Madison's seventh Neutral Ground proposal of March 13, 1806.

revolutionists, Herrera and Aury. Freebooters from Barataria and a band under General Mina augmented the force. Privateers were sent out, at least a dozen vessels sailing under the flag of the revolutionists. Mina wished to invade Mexico, while Aury desired to confine his operations to Texas. Mina's plan was followed and a descent made on Soto la Marina, where Aury abandoned the enterprise and retreated by sea to Galveston. Perry also started back but his force was surrounded and annihilated. After erecting temporary fortifications at Matagorda Bay, Aury joined forces with Gregor MacGregor at Amelia Island.[2]

No sooner did Aury abandon Galveston Island than it was occupied by Jean Lafitte at the head of a lawless band of Baratarian pirates. In 1817 a thousand men had gathered and the commerce of the Gulf was jeopardized by their operations. The United States was not in a position to dislodge them, because of the complications which might arise with Spain over ownership of that region. Further difficulties appeared when in 1818 a party of Napoleonic exiles under General Lallemand moved from the Tombigbee River to lands along the Trinity. Their presence gave concern to Spain, France and the United States, furnishing a further reason for an immediate settlement of territorial ownership.[3]

In spite of the difficulties of Spain, efforts were made to obtain complete data concerning the boundaries of the Spanish provinces with a view to a future adjustment with the United States. By a royal order of May 20, 1805, the King had requested the viceroy of Mexico to furnish documents concerning the province of Texas to assist in determining the true western boundary of Louisiana, and to send copies to the First Secretary

---

[2] Bancroft, *North Mexican States and Texas*, II, 34–39; Fuller, *The Purchase of Florida*, 231–233.

[3] Bancroft, *North Mexican States and Texas*, II, 39–42; Reeves, in *Johns Hopkins University Studies in Historical and Political Sciences*, Series XXIII, pp. 531–656.

of State, to Casa Calvo, and to the commandant general of the Interior Provinces at Chihuahua. The viceroy, Yturrigaray, on January 27, 1807, appointed Padre Dr. Fr. Melchor Talamantes y Baeza, of the military order of Merced, as chief commissioner to carry on the work.

Talamantes planned an elaborate report which was to consist of five parts: (1) A collection of authentic documents covering the history of Texas from 1630 to 1790; (2) documents concerning Texan and Louisiana history of interest in the discussion; (3) documents relative to the boundary between the provinces; (4) royal *cédulas* and orders, and viceregal reports concerning the rights of Spain to Texas and points north and west; (5) a discussion of the territorial rights of Spain and the principles which should be observed in marking boundaries. Talamantes planned an extensive search, collected bibliographies, and made lists of libraries to be consulted; he wrote to various officials for information and documents. But it remained for another to complete the work. Talamantes died in 1807 and Padre José Antonio Pichardo was appointed. Pichardo's report is to be found in the Archive of the Departamento de Relaciones Exteriores in the City of Mexico, where it was filed in 1812. It covers over four thousand small folio pages, and consists of an introduction and four main parts. The introduction contains memoranda of documents and information collected for the investigation. The first part of the body of the report deals with the boundary between Louisiana and Texas; the second with the explorations of Coronado and De Soto; the third treats of permission given the French to remain in the territory of the King of Spain; the fourth states the objections to the proposed line of D'Arelle.[4]

---

[4] Bolton, *Guide to the Archives of Mexico*, 234–235; Bolton, in Texas State Historical Association, *The Quarterly*, VI, 106–107, VII, 202–203; Robértson, *Louisiana under Spain, France and the United States*, II, 156–158. The papers of the boundary commission were first brought to the knowledge of scholars by Bolton.

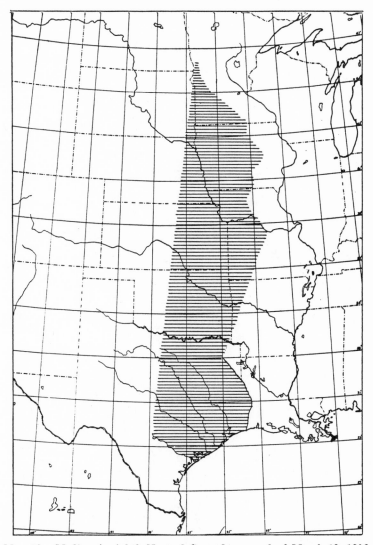

Map 19.   Madison's eighth Neutral Ground proposal of March 13, 1806.

The map which accompanies the report may be found in the cartography department of the Secretaría de Fomento. On this map four lines were marked, showing the views of persons employed in the work, namely Puelles, Navarrete, Talamantes, and Pichardo. Puelles was a priest at Nacogdoches when Pichardo was working and he made a report on the boundary of Texas. The line of Puelles starts at the mouth of the Red River, runs straight west to 93° 30′ west longitude, thence due north to the Red River, and from there in a straight line to the mouth of the Missouri. The line as laid down by Navarrete, a former governor of Texas, commenced at the mouth of the Red River, followed that stream to the Washita, thence up that stream to about 95° west longitude, thence due north to the Missouri and up that stream to an indefinite point. On the map, the lower course of the Red River bears more to the south than it does in reality, causing the Washita to empty about three degrees too far east. 'The line as proposed by Talamantes began at the mouth of the Arkansas and followed that stream to its head-waters, which were represented as being in longitude 110°; from that point it followed the meridian to an indefinite point northward. The line of Pichardo, which was officially adopted by the commissioner, was far more liberal. It started in the Bayou of Atchafalaya, bore north by northwest in a gradual compound curve, passing to the west of Natchitoches, crossing the Red River in west longitude 99° 30′, the Arkansas half a degree farther west, and crossing the Missouri at 102° 30′; from that point the line ran an indefinite distance northward.[5] The report of Pichardo was not received with entire favor by the Spanish government and none of the lines were followed with exactness in the proposals during the negotiation of the treaty of 1819, but several of them followed the general direction of the Pichardo line.

---

[5] A photograph of this map is in the collection of Herbert E. Bolton and is reproduced as the frontispiece in this volume. For reference to Puelles see Bolton, *Guide to the Archives of Mexico*, 50, 235, 395, 400, 403, 414.

During the period when Napoleon was struggling for the mastery of Spain, the United States refused to recognize either the French power or Ferdinand VII, and it was not until after the Congress of Vienna that diplomatic relations were resumed. Monroe was then the secretary of state and De Onis the Spanish minister. In January, 1816, the question of boundaries was taken up. As in 1805, the claim was made that Louisiana extended from the Perdido to the Rio Grande; De Onis answered with a general denial, claiming that the entire territory had belonged to Spain "from the time of the discovery and conquest of Mexico, without ever having passed by treaty to any other nation."[6]

In March George W. Erving was sent as minister to Spain, but was not given full instructions before departing. Before they were sent, De Onis suggested that his government "might be willing to cede its territory on the eastern side of the Mississippi in satisfaction of claims and in exchange for territory on the western side." Following the suggestion of De Onis that the negotiations take place in Madrid, the government determined to entrust the matter to Erving, but two months passed before full instructions were sent and they did not reach him until August. The American position was as before, the claim being reasserted to the territory between the Perdido and Rio Grande. Before Erving was able to accomplish anything, he was informed that the King had decided to transfer the negotiations to Washington. This Erving believed was done to delay the business, but the Spanish minister claimed that it was to facilitate it.[7]

When the negotiations were resumed at Washington in January, 1817, De Onis stated that Spain would not cede her territory east of the Mississippi unless the United States would relinquish her claims to the lands west of that river, and that

---

6 *State Papers, Foreign Relations*, IV, 422–429.

7 *Ibid.*, IV, 433, 435–437.

even then he was restricted to a recommendation to that effect
to his government. Monroe answered that it was useless to
prolong the negotiations on the subject of limits, as it was impossible to comply with his proposition. The discussion, however, continued. In a previous interview Monroe had suggested
that the United States might cede the lands between the Colorado
and the Rio Grande for the Floridas. De Onis replied that that
territory was a portion of Texas, the eastern boundary of which
was "a line by the river Mermento . . . towards the Presidio
of Adais, and from thence by the Arroyo Onda towards Natchitoches." In view of the justice of this, he proposed two courses,
one of which he hoped the United States might adopt: (1) a
discussion upon reciprocal rights and pretensions; (2) that each
government adopt as a basis the *uti possidetis* either of 1792 or
1763. Monroe was unmoved by the suggestion and repeated his
assertion that the United States had no motive to continue the
negotiation on that subject.

Shortly after, De Onis informed Monroe that he felt it necessary to wait for further instructions. He then proceeded to
state the position of the United States in the following terms:

Let us suppose . . . that you and I are intimate friends; you have
purchased an estate joining one of mine . . . ; and, be it because some
officious person said so, or because you thought so, you were of opinion
that there was included in this purchase a part of my estate . . . As
soon as you had made this purchase, and observed that possession was
not given you of the land I worked and which you believed to belong
to you, you asked me to give it up to you. I observed to you that it was
mine; that the land which you had purchased had also belonged to me
formerly; that I had ceded it to him who had sold it such as he had
delivered it, and in no greater extent; and that, consequently, he could
not transfer to you more than I had given to him. You and I refer to
the seller. and he tells us that he never sold the land to you which you
require, and never obtained it from me, nor had an intention of acquiring
it. Notwithstanding this declaration, . . . I from motives of friendship
. . . and to do away all doubt . . . propose . . . that we should discuss
the affair in a friendly manner, and . . . if you present to me unquestion-
able documents to prove that it belongs to you, I am ready to give it up

. . . I, who am anxious to accommodate you, because you are my friend and a good neighbor, knowing that you desire to get part of my territory to round out yours, and to facilitate the exportation of your produce, as tnere is a navigable river running through it, carry my friendship and condescension so far as to say that we will agree between ourselves, by a friendly investigation, what belongs to each; and, this being settled, I am ready to cede to you the lands you desire for an equivalent founded in equity, justice and reciprocal convenience, fixing the limits between us in such a way that our servants should not engage us in quarrels and contests . . . Will you say to me that the friendly propositions are inadmissable? I believe not.

He proposed that provisional limits be arranged, and, if the United States desired that this arrangement should apply only to lands north of the Missouri, the question might be left to commissioners. Monroe did not attempt to answer this argument, but asked if he were to understand that De Onis did not consider himself authorized to conclude a treaty; if not, he considered further negotiation useless until such authority arrived. De Onis responded by sending his secretary of legation to Madrid for more definite powers.[8]

In July, Pizarro, the Minister of Foreign Affairs, proposed to Erving a discussion of the disputed points. Erving replied that if the new instructions to De Onis were submitted to him, he would say whether or not he could accede to them. After some discussion, Pizarro made proposals for the basis of a treaty. He stated that the King was willing to cede the Floridas if the United States would give up its claim to all lands west of the Mississippi, making that river the boundary between their possessions; that the King preferred that near its mouth the main channel of the river, which flowed by New Orleans, should be the separating line, but, to facilitate the arrangement, he would accept the La Fourche as the boundary. This proposal Erving would not consider and soon after he was informed that the

---

[8] *State Papers, Foreign Relations,* IV, 437–441; Fuller, *The Purchase of Florida,* 272.

Spanish government had determined to hasten the departure of the secretary of legation to the United States.[9]

When negotiations were resumed at Washington, Monroe had become President and had chosen John Quincy Adams as Secretary of State. Adams arrived at the seat of government in September, 1817, where he found the negotiation with Spain the most important matter pending. In his first annual message to Congress, Monroe had spoken of the piratical establishment at Galveston, which he described as "within the limits of the United States, as we contend, under the cession of Louisiana," stating that steps had been taken to correct the abuse. De Onis protested against the position taken by Monroe, asserting that Galveston was in Spanish territory and that as such it ought to be respected until the government of the United States produced documents which proved its claims.

Shortly afterward De Onis informed the Department of State that he was ready to resume the negotiation and to pursue it until its final termination. In defining the Spanish position, he presented the views set forth by Pizarro. Being informed that this would not be considered by the United States, he next pointed out that the first step necessary was to free the question of boundaries from all obscurity and to establish the true division points. Shortly after, he presented an historical review of the western boundary; he stated that Spain owned all of the Gulf region and the Californias by right of discovery and exploration, and New Mexico and Texas by right of settlement; he claimed that Texas extended to the Mississippi and that the French never had gone west of that river except by permission or suffrance of the Spanish governors. He asserted that Spain owned as far as the Missouri by right of priority. He considered the French pretensions concerning the size of the Crozat grant as ridiculous, pointing out that the French had been allowed to occupy Natchitoches, and when they had violated their trading privileges,

---

[9] *State Papers, Foreign Relations*, IV, 443–450.

the Spanish officers had made an arrangement that the Arroyo Hondo should remain the dividing line until the matter was decided by the sovereigns. As the boundary had never been formally run, he suggested that the line of the Mermento and Arroyo Hondo, passing between Natchitoches and Adaes, and extending across the Red River toward the Missouri, should be adopted temporarily, leaving the final fixing of exact points to a joint commission. In other words, Spain was ready to yield a large part of the present state of Louisiana and the lands along the western side of the Mississippi.[10]

Adams replied that the United States was willing to accept the line of the Colorado, from its mouth to its source, and from there to the northern limits of Louisiana, or to leave the upper part of the boundary for future arrangement. De Onis dryly commented that he presumed the Colorado of Natchitoches was meant rather than the Colorado in Texas, which was "still farther within the limits of the Spanish provinces." He proposed that the Floridas be ceded to the United States, and that the boundary be established in one of the mouths of the Mississippi; if this were not approved, he proposed that the state of possession in 1763 form the basis, and that the western line be established between the Calcasieu and the Mermento, thence by the Arroyo Hondo till it crossed the Red River between Natchitoches and Adaes, thence northward to a point to be fixed by commissioners.[11]

Adams did not reply to this proposal, as the President was then considering an offer of mediation made by Great Britain to settle the difficulties between Spain and the United States. In a cabinet meeting on January 31, 1818, it was decided to refuse acceptance of the offer, on the grounds that public sentiment would be averse to the interposition of a third party.[12]

---

[10] Adams, *Memoirs*, IV, 7; Richardson, *Messages and Papers of the Presidents*, II, 14; *State Papers, Foreign Relations*, IV, 450–460.

[11] *State Papers, Foreign Relations*, IV, 463–467.

[12] Adams, *Memoirs*, IV, 49–52.

From this time it was evident to the authorities at Washington that Spain was willing to cede the Floridas but was obdurate regarding Texas. Henceforth the negotiations took a different course; after reasserting the claim of the United States to the territory as far as the Rio Grande, Adams gradually gave way in his demands for Texan territory, and as he did so, demanded compensating territory in the Oregon country.

On February 10 De Onis repeated his proposal and suggested that he would consider any modification, if it did not detract from acknowledged principles of justice and reciprocal convenience, and came within his instructions; if beyond his powers, he would send to Madrid for broader instructions. On March 12 Adams replied at length. No mention was made of the Colorado and the claim to the Rio Grande was reasserted. He presented a line of proof to show that France had owned to that river. He based his views on historical facts, on narratives of French explorers and letters of French officers, and on the authority of historians and geographers; of the latter he cited two English, one German, one French, and two Spanish. He stated three principles which were recognized by European nations: (1) That when any European power had taken possession of the seacoast, that possession extended to the contiguous river systems; (2) that when a European nation had discovered and taken possession of any portion of the continent, and another afterward did the same at some distance from it, the middle distance between them became the boundary; (3) that when such rights had been acquired, they could not be affected by purchases, grants or conquests made with nations within those limits. By those principles the United States was willing to settle the question of the western boundary of Louisiana, and until Spain was prepared to abide by them, it would be of little avail to pursue the discussion.[13]

---

13 *State Papers, Foreign Relations*, IV, 467–480.

This was one of the most critical periods in the course of the negotiations. In Congress Clay was arguing for the recognition of the independence of the South American colonies and Forsyth was making frequent utterances hostile to Spain; the executive was obdurate.[14] In spite of this De Onis did not yield; he replied methodically to the arguments of Adams, pointing out that the line between Adaes and Natchitoches had always been acknowledged by Spain and France as far as the Red River; the only thing which seemed necessary, then, was to fix the line above that stream. He then reverted to Adams' communication of January 16 in which he proposed the line of the Colorado; he observed that he had at first supposed the river mentioned was the Red, but had since been informed that Adams meant the San Marcos. As the acceptance of this was beyond his instructions, it would be necessary for him to send a messenger to Madrid; in the meantime the negotiations on other points might continue.[15]

Jackson's invasion of Florida brought a new element into the controversy, and it was not until July that the question of boundary again received attention, when, through the medium of Hyde de Neuville, the French minister, intelligence was conveyed to De Onis that the United States would accept the Trinity, and a line from its source to the Red River, up that stream to its source, thence crossing to the Rio Grande and up that stream, or following the summits of the mountains northward and parallel to it; then stop, or take a line west to the Pacific. Affairs in Florida, however, prevented the Spanish minister from stating his views.[16]

---

14 Adams, *Memoirs*, IV, 65–67.

15 *State Papers, Foreign Relations*, IV, 480–486.

16 Adams, *Memoirs*, IV, 110. It would appear from the above that Jackson's invasion of Florida had two important results as far as the western boundary was concerned: (1) it caused the government to weaken in its demands in Texas; (2) it caused Adams to look to the Oregon country for corresponding compensation. This view is strengthened by subsequent events.

During the summer, Erving in Spain attempted to bring the powers closer together, suggesting that a neutral zone thirty leagues wide and open to the settlement of neither be established. Pizarro put forth two objections: (1) that such a territory would be a gathering-place for banditti; (2) that there might be difficulty in determining the line of division. He stated that he understood that Erving thought the zone should be fixed to the eastward of the St. Bernard Bay, and he asked for a written explanation. The American minister replied that his proposition was based upon the supposition that Spain would consent to the Colorado River boundary. He later explained that he thought the zone should extend fifteen leagues on each side of the river. If Spain did not consider that it should be so broad, she might diminish it on her side as much as she saw fit. Settlers should be excluded, but military posts might be established to keep off intruders.[17]

The proposal of Erving was of no avail, for news of Jackson's invasion reached Spain unofficially in July, and officially in August. The King immediately made a protest and requested that the *status quo* before the invasion be maintained, and that reparation be made. While this matter was pending, the boundary question could not be settled, and in order to free his government from possible complications later, Erving withdrew his neutral zone proposal.[18]

In October De Onis informed the government that he had received new instructions, which, however, were issued before the Spanish government had made its views known regarding the Jackson invasion. The Spanish minister presented a long memorial in which he again reviewed the history of the disputed territory. He proposed that the boundary should be between the rivers Mermento and Calcasieu, pass between Adaes and Natchitoches, cross the Red River at the 32d degree of latitude,

---

[17] *State Papers, Foreign Relations*, IV, 512–517, 520–522.
[18] *Ibid.*, IV, 518, 522–524.

and the 93d of longitude west from London according to Melish's map, and thence run directly north to the Missouri, and up that river to its source. He proposed that the navigation of the Missouri, Mississsippi, and Mermento rivers should remain free to subjects of both powers, and that each should appoint a commissioner and surveyor who, within a year of the ratification of the treaty, should meet at Natchitoches.

Adams replied that he could not accept the proposed line and offered as a substitute another, which he claimed was a final offer:

> Beginning at the mouth of the river Sabine, on the Gulf of Mexico, following the course of said river to the thirty-second degree of latitude, the eastern bank and all the islands in said river to belong to the United States . . . ; thence, due north, to the northernmost part of the thirty-third degree of north latitude, and until it strikes the Rio Roxo, or Red river; thence, following the course of the said river, to its source, touching the chain of the Snow mountains, in latitude thirty-seven degrees twenty-five minutes north, longitude one hundred and six degrees fifteen minutes west, or thereabouts, as marked on Melish's map; thence to the summit of the said mountains, and following the chain of the same to the forty-first parallel of latitude; thence, following the said parallel of latitude forty-one degrees, to the South sea. The northern bank of the said Red river, and all the islands therein, to belong to the United States, and the southern bank of the same to Spain.

Adams thought that commissioners might be needed to run the line from the Sabine to the Red River and to ascertain the point where the forty-first parallel crossed the Snow Mountains.[19]

With this proposal a policy which had been foreshadowed was fully disclosed. In the early stages of the negotiations, Texas had been balanced against Florida. In January, 1818, Spain had offered to relinquish Florida, but not the west. Jackson's invasion, to the writer, appears to have proved a source of strength and of weakness. It assured Florida, but, in turn, the claim to

---

[19] *State Papers, Foreign Relations*, IV, 525–531. Fuller (*The Purchase of Florida*, 305–306) wrongly credits the proposal to De Onis, but two pages later quotes from that portion of Adams' diary in which the secretary states that he was the author.

Texas was abandoned. As compensation, the Oregon country was demanded. The abandonment of Texas was not due to Adams, who asserted, in 1836, that he was the last member of Monroe's cabinet to consent to the relinquishment of it. Senator Benton claimed that it was due to the southern members of the cabinet who were candidates for the presidency, and who yielded to the northern repugnance to territorial aggrandizement and slavery extension to the southwest, in order to gain northern support.[20]

De Onis replied that he would admit the Sabine, on condition that above the Red River the line should run due north until it reached the Mississippi, and thence along the middle of that stream to its source.[21]

Affairs had reached this point when it became known that Spain had determined to break off negotiations until satisfaction was given for the invasion of Florida. After sending a dispatch to Erving, in which he attempted to justify the invasion on the grounds of the exigencies of the war against the Seminoles, Adams informed De Onis that, as he had rejected the offer of boundary, the proposal was no longer obligatory upon the United States, which reserved the right to all the territory to the Rio Grande.[22] De Onis replied that he was at a loss to explain the

---

[20] Benton, *Thirty Years' View*, I, 14–18; *Congressional Debates*, XII, Pt. 3, pp. 3579–3580. Benton's view that Texas was traded for Florida, ignoring the fact that Oregon was gained, has frequently been accepted by historians. See Schouler, *History of the United States*, IV, 97; Smith, *The Annexation of Texas*, 5–6. In a debate in the House on April 13, 1846, regarding Oregon, Adams denied that Texas was relinquished as a means of obtaining Oregon, and added these astonishing statements: ''Texas was not a question at the time of the negotiation of that treaty [1819], or until years afterwards, . . . That negotiation was for the purpose of Florida; and as to the boundaries of-Louisiana, they had been considered as settled long before.'' *Congressional Globe*, 29 Cong., 1 Sess., I, 663.

[21] *State Papers, Foreign Relations*, IV, 531–533.

[22] *Ibid.*, IV, 539–546. This, at first sight, may seem to controvert the writer's view that Jackson's invasion was the cause of the relinquishment of Texas, but such is not the case. Adams was aware of the questionable position in which Jackson had placed the United States. He was re-asserting the claim to more than he could obtain, hoping eventually to get better terms thereby. A bold front was necessary to justify the Jackson episode.

peremptory declaration of the American government. He found it necessary to state that any offers he may have made were no longer binding upon his own government.

A month later, in January, 1819, De Onis informed Adams that he had received instructions in regard to running the line to the Pacific.[23] This had already been made known to Adams through the medium of Hyde de Neuville, who had attributed the changed attitude to the fact that Pizarro had retired in favor of Casa Yrujo. The French minister had urged that the United States ought to yield something of the western line which went within a few leagues of Santa Fé, to accept the forty-third parallel, and take an upper chain instead of the Snow Mountains. Adams had replied that the line which he had offered was an ultimatum.[24]

Shortly afterward De Onis stated that the King would agree to a boundary extending from the source of the Missouri westward to the Columbia, and along the middle of that stream to the Pacific. This Adams refused, repeating his former proposition and intimating that, if the powers of De Onis were incompetent, the President thought it useless to pursue the discussion further. This, however, did not express the true temper of the government, for the same day Monroe directed Adams to confide to De Neuville that the United States would accept a modification of the line. The offer was to run a line due north from the Pawnee Bend of the Red River to the Arkansas, thence up that river to its source in latitude forty-one, and along that parallel to the sea, but on condition that Spain would form no settlements north of the Snow Mountains. De Neuville proposed that the western end of the line be left to the settlement of commissioners, but Adams objected. De Neuville, however, consented to sound De Onis on the last proposition without disclosing the fact that the United States would accept that line.

---

[23] *State Papers, Foreign Relations*, IV, 612–615.
[24] Adams, *Memoirs*, IV, 208–209.

At a cabinet meeting on the following day it was discovered that Adams had erred, and that instead of the Pawnee Bend, which was between the ninety-sixth and ninety-seventh degrees, he had intended the bend at longitude one hundred and one. De Neuville was summoned and assured the secretary that he had not thought of even suggesting such a line as that at Pawnee Bend. Adams states that the difficulty was entirely removed, but such does not appear to have been the case.[25]

That Adams was misled by the suavity of the French minister is evident from the proposal which came the next day from De Onis; he suggested that from the source of the Sabine the line should follow the ninety-fourth meridian to the Red River, thence up that stream to the ninety-fifth, and north along that line to the Arkansas, which it was to follow to its source; thence due north till it reached the source of the San Clemente River, or Multonomah,[26] in latitude 41°, and along that river to the ocean. Finding that Adams would not accept this, De Neuville proposed that the line should follow the course of the Red River to the hundredth degree, then north to the Arkansas, up it to its source, thence to the Multonomah, and along it to the forty-third degree of latitude, and on that parallel to the sea. According to the *Memoirs,* Monroe was favorable to an acceptance of this line, but Adams thought that a better one might be obtained. Accordingly he presented the following *projet:*

Beginning at the middle of the river Sabine, on the Gulf of Mexico; following the course of said river to the thirty-second degree of latitude, the eastern bank and all the islands in the river to belong to the United States, and the western bank to Spain; thence, due north, to the northernmost part of the thirty-third degree of north latitude, and until it strikes the Rio Roxo, or Red River; thence, following the course of said river, to the northernmost point of the bend, between longitude 101 and 102 degrees; thence, by the shortest line, to the southernmost point of the bed

---

25 *State Papers, Foreign Relations,* IV, 615–616; Adams, *Memoirs,* IV, 234–237.

26 The Multnomah is identified as the Willamette by Greenhow, *The History of Oregon and California* (4th ed.), 287, but from Adams' *Memoirs,* IV, 237, it is evident that the Snake River was intended.

of the river Arkansas, between the same degrees of longitude 101 and 102; thence, following the course of the river Arkansas, to its source, in latitude 41 degrees north; thence, following the same parallel of latitude 41 degrees to the South sea . . . . But, if the source of the Arkansas River should fall south or north of latitude 41 degrees, then the line from the said source shall run due north or south, as the case may be, till it meets the said parallel of latitude, and thence, as aforesaid, to the South sea.

It further stipulated that the northern banks and adjacent islands in the Red and Arkansas were to belong to the United States, that Spain was to make no settlement on those rivers or their tributaries, or east of the Snow Mountains between the thirty-first and forty-first degrees, and that the navigation of the Arkansas and Red should belong to the United States exclusively.[27]

De Neuville was consulted regarding the *projet* and pointed out that De Onis would never accept such stipulations. Adams answered that if the Spanish minister would accept the balance of the draft, he would give up the obnoxious exclusions, and refer the matter to the President with a recommendation that, if De Onis accepted the line of the forty-first degree, the United States would agree to the hundredth meridian.[28]

On February 9 De Onis made a counter proposal: the lower part of the line followed that of Adams, but left the Red River at the hundredth meridian and ran north to the Arkansas, thence along the middle of that stream to the forty-second degree of latitude, then west on that parallel to the source of the Multnomah, following the course of that river to the forty-third parallel, and west to the ocean. It also stipulated that all the islands were to belong to the United States, but both nations were to have free navigation of such parts of the rivers as constituted their frontiers.[29]

[27] *State Papers, Foreign Relations*, IV. 616–617; Adams. *Memoirs*, IV, 239, 244–246.

[28] Adams, *Memoirs*, IV, 246.

[29] *State Papers, Foreign Relations*, IV, 617–619.

The proposed treaty was discussed in cabinet meeting and a decision was reached to accept the proposal of the hundredth meridian and forty-third parallel, if no better could be obtained. Adams, however, drew a more grasping *projet*. He proposed that the line follow the hundred and second meridian between the Red and Arkansas, then along the southern bank of the latter to its source in latitude forty-one, and along that parallel to the sea. The islands and both banks of the river were to belong to the United States. This, he told De Neuville, was the last offer which would be made.

To quote Adams' *Memoirs*:

> After a long and violent struggle, he [De Onis] . . . agreed to take longitude one hundred, from the Red River to the Arkansas, and latitude forty-two, from the source of the Arkansas to the South Sea. But he insisted upon having the middle of all the rivers for the boundary . . . ; and he also insisted upon the free navigation of the rivers to be common to both nations.

Adams accepted the forty-second parallel, but held out for both banks of the rivers. De Onis finally conceded this point, and the long drawn out negotiations were ended. On February 22, 1819, the treaty was signed, the sixteenth article stating that the ratifications were to be exchanged within six months, or sooner if possible.[30]

The treaty was unanimously approved by the Senate on February 24,[31] and shortly after Forsyth was sent to Madrid as minister, his chief duty being to secure the ratification by the King.[32] No more unfortunate choice could have been made. In Congress Forsyth had openly advocated the military occupation of Florida; after his appointment as minister, for some time he had kept his seat in the Senate where he had been an adversary

---

[30] Adams, *Memoirs*, IV, 253–255; *State Papers, Foreign Relations*, IV, 619–626.

[31] *Treaties, Conventions* (Malloy, ed.), II, 1651; Fuller, *The Purchase of Florida*, 309.

[32] *State Papers, Foreign Relations*, IV, 650–651.

of Jackson, a fact which may have put him on a somewhat better basis with Spain. In temperament he was blunt and hot-tempered, qualities which unfitted him for the atmosphere of the Escurial.[33]

Soon after his arrival in Spain he informed the government that he was ready to exchange the ratifications, impoliticly adding that the "Hornet" was waiting at Cadiz to carry the document back to the United States. As no reply was forth-coming, two weeks later he sent a second note demanding per-emptorily that the Spanish government cease its delay. A fort-night later Salmon, the Minister of Foreign Relations, answered vaguely that because of the great importance and interest of the treaty, the King found it necessary to examine it with the greatest caution and deliberation before ratifying it.

This angered Forsyth, who answered that the delay would arouse conjectures in the United States, and stated that the attitude of the Spanish government had given rise to monstrous and absurd suppositions in Madrid. He said that the King was being calumniated in his own capital for his attitude. "No wise King," he wrote, "will dare to do an act which would deprive him of the respect of all nations, sully the reputation of his Kingdom in the eyes of the civilized world, and deprive his people of the strongest incentive to virtuous exertions, under every dispensation of Heaven—the confidence in the integrity of their Government . . . " After this piece of ill-advised bombast, it was two months before the Spanish government deigned to reply. The answer sharply criticized Forsyth for exceeding his instructions in doing more than stating his surprise at the delay, and for the style of his expressions. It stated that a final decision could not be made without entering into certain explanations with the United States and intimated that a person had been sent to America to settle the difficulties. Forsyth ex-pressed regret that his words were open to criticism, but never-

<hr>

[33] Adams, *Memoirs*. IV. 262–263.

theless defended them and made other observations on the attitude of Spain.

On August 19 Salmon informed Forsyth that an agent had been dispatched to the United States. The six month's period for the ratification was about to expire, and in view of this, Forsyth's anger increased. On the day before the date of expiration, he informed Salmon that if the ratification were not exchanged by the following day, the situation would be as if the treaty had never been entered into. He accompanied this with another sharp criticism of the Spanish attitude. Naturally no reply was given.[34]

In anticipation of the probable delay, Adams had instructed Forsyth that the time might be extended, if he could get the ratification to Washington before the first Monday in December. If it did not then arrive, the matter would be referred to Congress. For the expenses incurred by delay, the United States would expect indemnities, and would look to the territory west of the Sabine for payment. Adams claimed that according to the rules of international law, as given by Vattel and Martens, the treaty was binding on Spain as soon as it was signed by De Onis, because that minister had not transcended his powers. On October 2 Forsyth presented these views and also discussed the question of certain land grants in Florida, which had been made in December, 1817, and in January, 1818. Two of these had been given letters patent in February and one in April. It was feared that these grants made to Spaniards were intended partially to annul the value of the Florida cession by placing much of the land in private ownership. An article had been added to the treaty which confirmed all grants made prior to January 24, 1818, but all grants made after January 29, 1818, when the King first proposed the cession of the Floridas, were declared null and void.[35]

34 *State Papers, Foreign Relations*, IV. 654–657.

35 *Ibid.*, IV, 657–660, 668–671; *Treaties, Conventions* (Malloy, ed.), 1656–1658.

The land grants now gave considerable concern to Monroe and Adams. Clay was heading the congressional opposition to the Monroe policies, strenuously opposing the surrender of the claim to Texas. If the Florida grants gave rise to difficulties, it would furnish another argument against the treaty. The administration was also suspicious of De Onis and the Spanish government, believing that De Onis expected personally to profit from the grants, and that his government was pursuing a policy to defeat the ratification of the treaty.[36]

After the treaty was signed, Clay spread a rumor that the grants were made on January 23, 1818. Adams wrote to De Onis insisting that the treaty covered those grants and fully annulled them. De Onis replied that such was the case, but if they had antedated January 24, 1818, he would have insisted upon their recognition.[37]

In August Forsyth had written to Adams that the delay in ratification was supposed to be on account of the grants, but believed that the real reason was to procure an assurance that the United States would not recognize the revolted South American colonies. After receiving Adams' instructions, Forsyth informed the Spanish government that if the Florida grants were considered void, the treaty would still be held valid, if the exchange were made at once. He also presented Adams' views on international law governing ratification.[38] The opening of the question of land grants was a short-sighted action, for in view of the assurance of De Onis the statement of Forsyth could be taken only as an insinuation of bad faith.

The Spanish government defended its action in not ratifying the treaty, claiming that the instructions to De Onis were secret, and that the United States could not know whether or not he had exceeded his instructions. It was also observed that the

---

[36] Adams, *Memoirs,* IV, 276, 287–291, 304–306, 328.

[37] *State Papers, Foreign Relations,* IV, 651–653; Adams, *Memoirs,* IV, 287.

[38] *State Papers, Foreign Relations,* IV, 661–663.

PROPOSALS OF THE UNITED STATES

I	Position on	January	19,	1816	(p. 50)
II	Proposal of	January	16,	1818	(p. 54)
III	"	March	12,	1818	(p. 55)
IV	"	July	16,	1818	(p. 56)
V	"	August	9,	1818	(p. 57)
VI	"	October	31,	1818	(p. 58)
VII	"	January	29,	1819	(p. 60)
VIII	"	January	30,	1819	(p. 61)
IX	"	February	6,	1819	(p. 61)
X 2nd	"	February	6,	1819	(p. 62)
XI	"	February	13,	1919	(p. 63)

PROPOSALS OF SPAIN

1	Proposal of	August	17,	1817	(p. 52)
2	"	December	29,	1817	(p. 53)
3	"	January	5,	1818	(p. 54)
4	"	January	24,	1818	(p. 54)
5	"	October	24,	1818	(p. 57)
6	"	November	16,	1818	(p. 59)
7	"	January	16,	1819	(p. 60)
8	"	February	1,	1819	(p. 61)
9 2nd	"	February	1,	1819	(p. 61)
10	"	February	9,	1819	(p. 62)
11 Final	"	February	15,	1819	(p. 63)

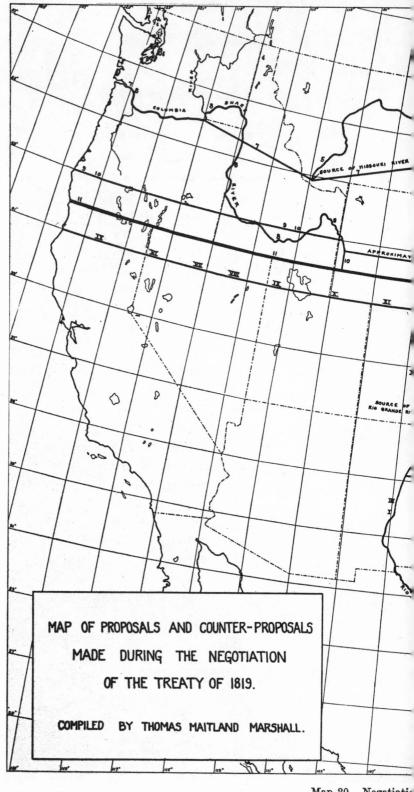

MAP OF PROPOSALS AND COUNTER-PROPOSALS
MADE DURING THE NEGOTIATION
OF THE TREATY OF 1819.

COMPILED BY THOMAS MAITLAND MARSHALL.

Map 20.   Negotiatio

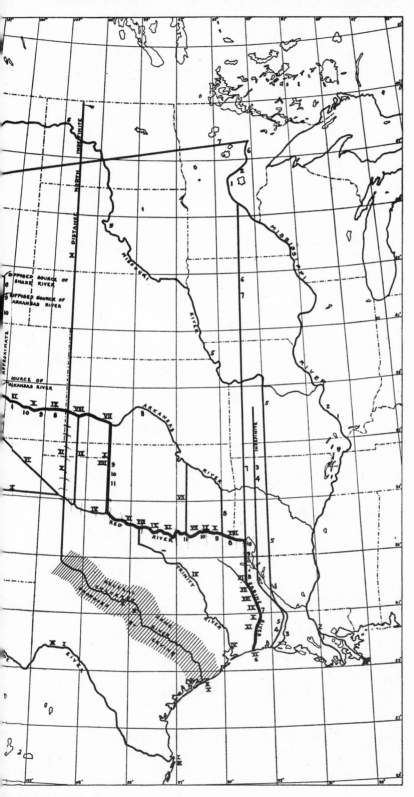

the Treaty of 1819

government had just learned of an expedition against Texas which was tolerated or protected by the United States. This was taken as an act of bad faith.[39]

Forsyth twice demanded copies of the grants, but was refused on the grounds that the minister could not comply without wanting in what was due to the King's dignity. Forsyth insultingly replied, saying that the King's dignity was "so refined and etherial as to be above the comprehension of an American Minister." Two days later another undiplomatic message came from him. In this he reasserted the claim to Texas on the grounds that the treaty had not been ratified by August 22. So inconsiderate was the language of the letter that the minister, San Fernando y Quiroga, returned it without presenting it to the King, offering to receive a communication, if properly worded. Forsyth, however, failed to take advantage of the courtesy, replying that he would have his returned note translated and sent again, a threat which he failed to carry out.[40]

The newly appointed agent to the United States was General Vives. He left Spain while the revolution of 1820 was in progress, and proceeded via France and England. At Paris he was reported as talking rather indiscreetly, saying that the honor of the crown should be saved in the matter of the land grants and that Spain must receive evidence that the United States would remain neutral in the colonial war. It was also said that Vives stated that, though he was not authorized to exchange the ratification, he could consent to the United States taking immediate possession of Florida. This was reported to Adams by Gallatin, the American minister at Paris. The information that Vives did not have the ratified treaty with him was also sent by Forsyth a few weeks later.[41]

---

[39] *State Papers, Foreign Relations,* IV, 663–664; Moore, *A Digest of International Law,* V, 185. The expedition referred to was that of James Long; see Yoakum, *History of Texas,* I, 199–207.

[40] *State Papers, Foreign Relations,* IV, 667–672, 674–675.

[41] *Ibid.,* IV, 678–679. For the revolution of 1820, see *The Cambridge Modern History,* X, 205–217.

The Spanish minister reached Washington in April. In his first communication he demanded that the United States stop piracies against Spanish commerce and have no relations with the revolted provinces. Before replying to the demands, Adams asked for a copy of his full powers, and inquired if he were the bearer of the ratification. In case the United States made suitable explanation of the points raised, he wished to know if Vives were ready to exchange the ratification. The minister immediately sent a copy of his full powers, which were found to be ample to "conclude and sign whatsoever you may judge necessary." He said that he did not have the ratification, as it was not usual to ratify until obstacles had been removed. He promised that there would be no delay, if the results of the proposals were satisfactory.

Adams replied that he was surprised that Vives had not brought the ratification. After making a general criticism of the Spanish policy, he said that explanations would be given, but none were open to discussion. After giving the explanations, if Vives were authorized to order Florida to be delivered and the Senate consented, the President would wait for the ratification; otherwise, it was a waste of time.

Vives answered that there were numerous instances of non-ratification for other reasons than those previously cited. The invasion of Spanish territory, the belief in Europe that ratification of the treaty and acknowledgment of the independence of the South American colonies would be simultaneous, the pretensions of Forsyth concerning land grants and his officious manners, were given as sufficient reasons. Furthermore, Spain delayed in order to obtain correct information. He said that he was not authorized to deliver the Floridas until after ratification.

This appears to have satisfied Adams, who agreed to drop the discussion of delay in ratification. He said that the fears of Spain were unfounded regarding piracies and filibusters, as attempts had been made to suppress them. He repeated his former statement that the land grants must be considered null. He declared that the United States had observed neutrality toward the South American colonies, but could enter into no engagements as to future relations with those provinces. If the ratification were delayed, his government would not accept the Sabine as a boundary, nor so small a sum as five million dollars.

Vives accepted the explanation regarding the suppresssion of piracy and filibustering. Concerning the land grants, he said that the abrogation would cause no trouble, "nor has that been the chief cause for suspending the ratification of the treaty." He was not satisfied with the attitude toward the rebellious provinces, but promised to try to present the case in such a manner that his government would be satisfied. He mentioned that he had heard a rumor of a change in the Spanish government which prevented him from acting with greater latitude.[42]

Adams, in reply, again reviewed the Spanish position and excused Forsyth. He said that the United States had proposed to the European powers the recognition of the provinces, because it was believed that Spain was about to recognize them. He refused to accept the conditional promise of ratification and said that the official correspondence would be submitted to Congress. This course was followed. In his message Monroe stated that a change had occurred in the government of Spain, which prevented Vives from acting. He believed that the differences would be speedily and satisfactorily settled as soon as the Spanish government was completely reorganized.[43] Congress soon after adjourned without taking any action.[44]

---

[42] *State Papers, Foreign Relations*, IV, 681–685. There appears to be no good evidence that Vives' statement was untrue. Chadwick (*The Relations of the United States and Spain, Diplomacy*, 139), however, questions the good faith of Spain in making the land grants.

[43] *State Papers, Foreign Relations*, IV, 685–688; Richardson, *Messages and Papers of the Presidents*, II, 70–72; *Annals of Cong.*, 16 Cong., 1 Sess., II, 2235.

[44] *Annals of Cong.*, 16 Cong., 1 Sess., II, 2229.

Pérez de Castro was the Spanish Minister of State under the new constitution. With him, Forsyth appears to have had no difficulty, although the matter of ratification was before the Cortes for three months before action was taken.[45] In October, Forsyth was officially informed of the determination of the Cortes to cede the Floridas and that the land grants would be set aside. An order was also sent to Vives to cede the Floridas and to deliver them within six months after the ratification, or sooner if possible.[46]

In spite of the opposition of Clay, on February 19, 1821, the Senate again voted to ratify the treaty, and on the twenty-second the ratifications were exchanged, thus ending the negotiations which had been pending for over sixteen years.[47]

---

[45] *State Papers, Foreign Relations,* IV, 691–692.

[46] *Ibid.,* IV, 70.

[47] *Annals of Cong.,* 16 Cong., 1 Sess., II, 1719–1731; Fuller, *The Purchase of Florida,* 321; Chadwick, *The Relations of the United States and Spain, Diplomacy,* 146.

CHAPTER IV

NEGOTIATION OF THE TREATY OF 1828

Owing to the delay in the ratification of the treaty of 1819, the United States had made no move to survey the boundary line when Mexico declared her independence. To the new republic the government at Washington had to look to carry out the stipulations of the treaty. The stability of the Iturbide régime being questionable, the United States proceeded with the greatest caution in opening relations. Instead of sending a regularly accredited minister, Joel R. Poinsett was despatched as an agent to report on conditions.[1]

In 1822 Congress made appropriations to defray the expense of sending ministers to the various Latin American republics, but the executive delayed in making the appointments. At a cabinet meeting in November the matter was discussed; Adams was of the opinion that ministers ought not to be sent except in return for ministers sent by them. Monroe did not agree, but thought that the governments of Mexico, Colombia and Peru were too unstable to warrant the opening of full diplomatic intercourse.[2]

In January, 1823, Monroe determined to send ministers, and asked Adams to offer the Mexican mission to Senator Brown of Louisiana, but Brown declined,[3] whereupon Adams proposed Andrew Jackson;[4] but he likewise refused on the ground that he would not countenance the imperial usurpation of Iturbide.[5]

[1] Bancroft, *History of Mexico*, V, 48; Poinsett, *Notes on Mexico*.

[2] Adams, *Memoirs*, VI, 110–114.

[3] *Ibid.*, VI, 122–123.

[4] *Ibid.*, VI, 128–129.

[5] *Ibid.*, VI, 281.

Two aspirants for the office next appeared, Ninian Edwards, a former governor and at that time a senator from Illinois, and George M. Dallas of Pennsylvania. Edwards had the support of Adams, and Dallas of the Pennsylvania delegation in Congress.[6] Edwards proved to be the successful candidate; in March his nomination was confirmed by the Senate and he made preparations for immediate departure.[7]

At this period the political situation was becoming acute, supporters of Clay, Adams, and Crawford indulging in virulent criticism of the rival candidates. After the appointment of Edwards, Crawford made a report to the House of Representatives that Edwards had made false statements about him before a committee of the House. Edwards retaliated by making several allegations of official misconduct on the part of the Secretary of the Treasury, closing with a broad insinuation that he was guilty of perjury. A committee of investigation was appointed and Edwards, who had started on his journey, returned to Washington.[8] This embroglio proved extremely embarrassing to the administration, and there was considerable difference of opinion as to the course to be pursued, Adams and Monroe agreeing that Edwards ought to resign immediately, Calhoun considering that this would be a confession of guilt.[9] Cabinet meetings were held on June 21 and 22 to discuss the matter, and while the second one was in session, a letter arrived from Edwards, tendering his resignation.[10] Nothing further was done for several months, Adams being fearful that Congress might refuse to vote further appropriations.[11]

In December Obregón arrived at Washington, announcing the establishment of the Mexican constitution and the election of

---

[6] Adams, *Memoirs*, VI, 234; Rives, *The United States and Mexico*, I, 162.

[7] Adams, *Memoirs*, VI, 249–250, 262–263.

[8] *Ibid.*, VI, 296–298.

[9] *Ibid.*, VI, 304–307.

[10] *Ibid.*, VI, 389–395.

[11] *Ibid.*, VI, 413–415.

Victoria and Bravo.[12]   There was no further reason for delay. Adams' principle that a minister should not be sent until one was received could now be applied, and Monroe's fear of the instability of the Mexican government was apparently removed. The mission was offered to Poinsett, but he declined.   Several others were then considered, among them Dallas and Benton,[13] but Monroe finally decided to leave the matter for the incoming President.

In February information was received from Rush, the minister at London, that the British government had determined to recognize immediately the independence of Mexico, Colombia, and Buenos Ayres,[14] a fact which made it desirable that a minister be immediately appointed by the United States.   Clay urged the nomination of General William Henry Harrison, but Adams preferred Poinsett.   To him the offer was made immediately after Adams became President, but Poinsett put forth two objections.   He feared that his successor in Congress might be a troublesome individual; furthermore he had urged the appointment of Benton.   Adams assured him that he would not nominate the Missouri senator, and the following day Poinsett accepted.[15]

Joel Roberts Poinsett was a native of South Carolina, possessed of independent fortune.   He had traveled extensively in Europe, visited Siberia and the interior of Russia, and had declined to enter the service of the Czar.   In 1810 he was appointed as a government agent to South America, his title being "Agent for Seamen and Commerce in the Port of Buenos Ayres," but afterward the title was changed to consul-general. Later he visited Chile, where he joined the revolutionists, leading a brigade of the patriot army against the Spaniards.   He returned to Buenos Ayres and in 1815 came back to the United

12 Adams, *Memoirs*, VI, 456.

13 *Ibid.*, VI, 484–485.

14 *Ibid.*, VI, 498.

15 *Ibid.*, VI, 519–524.

States.[16] In 1817 Monroe offered him a second mission to South
America, but he had entered the legislature of South Carolina
and declined the appointment; later he went to Mexico as special
agent and upon his return was elected to Congress. During the
closing years of Monroe's administration, the United States had
maintained a secretary of legation at Mexico, John Mason acting
in that capacity.[17]

The question of the boundary between the two countries
received the immediate attention of the Mexican government.
In October, 1822, Zozaya, the first representative to the United
States, was instructed to ascertain the views of that government
concerning the limits of Louisiana. He was to proceed on the
assumption that the line of the treaty of 1819 was agreeable to
Mexico. Shortly after his arrival at Washington, he wrote to
his government that he had discovered ambitious designs on the
part of the United States regarding Texas. In August, 1823,
José A. Torrens, the Mexican chargé, wrote to his government
that the public press was averse to the loss of Texas, and advised
against permitting an American population to become pre-
dominant in Texas.

In October, 1823, Alamán, the Secretary of Foreign Relations
after the fall of Iburbide, instructed Torrens to exert himself
to have the boundary, as laid down in 1819, confirmed and
marked.[18] On February 15, 1824, Torrens informed the State
Department that his government desired to fix the limits according to the treaty of 1819, and to appoint commissioners to
run the line.[19] No reply, however, was received. In the summer
of 1824 Obregón was appointed minister. His secret instructions
stated that reports had been received which indicated that the
United States had intentions on the Californias, New Mexico,

---

[16] Paxson, *The Independence of the South American Republics,* 106–112.
[17] Adams, *Memoirs,* VII, 16.
[18] Manning, in *The Southwestern Historical Quarterly,* XVII, 217–220.
[19] Torrens to Adams, February 15, 1824, *Congressional Debates,* XIV,
Pt. 2, App., 126.

and Texas. He was accordingly urged to negotiate a treaty of limits as early as possible.[20]

No move appears to have been made in the matter by the United States until the appointment of Poinsett. In the instructions issued to him on March 25, 1825, the boundary was discussed; the third and fourth articles of the treaty of 1819 were stated in full, and mention was made of Torrens' letter. But it was not the intention to come to an immediate agreement, as was shown by the following statement:

Some difficulties may hereafter arise between the two countries from the line thus agreed upon, against which it would be desirable now to guard, if practicable; and as the government of Mexico may be supposed not to have any disinclination to the fixation of a new line which would prevent those difficulties, the President wishes you to sound it on that subject; and to avail yourself of a favorable disposition, if you should find it, to effect that object. The line of the Sabine approaches our great western mart nearer than could be wished. Perhaps the Mexican Government may not be unwilling to establish that of the Rio Brassos de Dios, or the Rio Colorado, or the Snow mountains, or the Rio del Norte, in lieu of it. By the agreed line, portions of both the Red river and branches of the Arkansas are thrown on the Mexican side, and the navigation of both those rivers, as well as that of the Sabine, is made common to the respective inhabitants of the two countries. When the countries adjacent to those waters shall come to be thickly inhabited, collisions and misunderstandings may arise from the community thus established, in the use of their navigation, which it would be well now to prevent. If the line were so altered as to throw altogether on one side Red river and Arkansas, and their respective tributary streams, and the line on the Sabine were removed further west, all causes of future collision would be prevented. The Government of Mexico may have a motive for such an alteration of the line as is here proposed, in the fact that it would have the effect of placing the city of Mexico nearer the center of its territories. If the line were so changed, the greater part, if not the whole, of the powerful, warlike, and turbulent Indian nation of the Comanches will be thrown on the side of the United States; and as an equivalent for the proposed cession of territory, they would stipulate to restrain, as far as practicable, the Comanches from committing hostilities and depredations upon the territories and people, whether Indians or otherwise, of Mexico.

[20] Manning, in *The Southwestern Historical Quarterly*, XVII, 221–222.

If the Mexican government insisted on the boundary as stated in the treaty of 1819, Poinsett was to acquiesce, but was to insist that an article be inserted providing that each party should undertake to restrain the Indians residing within its territory from committing depredations on the other.[21]

On July 12, 1825, soon after his arrival, Poinsett and Lúcas Alamán, the new Secretary of Foreign Relations, discussed the manner of conducting negotiations of treaties of commerce and limits, and it was decided to treat the subjects separately. Poinsett suggested that though the United States felt bound to carry into effect the boundary as fixed by the treaty of 1819, "it would appear more becoming the independent character of this Government [Mexico] to lay aside that treaty altogether, and to endeavor to establish a boundary which would be more easily defined, and which might be mutually more advantageous." The Mexican secretary suggested that commissioners be appointed to examine the country, to which Poinsett objected, because of the delay which the appointment of commissioners by the United States government would necessitate. The secretary agreed to address a note to Poinsett, stating the views of his government.[22]

Poinsett's apparent desire to hasten matters, however, was not sincere, for a week later he wrote to Clay: "It appears to me that it will be important to gain time if we wish to extend our Territory beyond the Boundary agreed upon by the Treaty of 1819. Most of the good land from the Colorado to the Sabine has been granted by the state of Texas and is rapidly peopling

---

[21] Clay to Poinsett, March 25, 1825, *State Papers, Foreign Relations*, VI, 578–581. In *Congressional Debates*, XIV, Pt. 2, App., 125, the date is given as March 26.

[22] Poinsett to Clay, July 18, 1825, *Congressional Debates*, XIV, Pt. 2, App., 131–132. Before this interview occurred, Alamán had received a letter from Azcárate, a Mexican prominent in diplomatic circles, stating that when Poinsett was previously in Mexico, he had stated that he thought the line of 1819 was undesirable, and with a map before him, had traced a line which showed that he wished to obtain Texas, New Mexico, Upper California, parts of Lower California, Sonora, Coahuila, and Nuevo Leon. See Manning, in *The Southwestern Historical Quarterly*, XVII, 224–226.

with either grantees or squatters from the United States, a population they will find it difficult to govern and perhaps after a short period they may not be so averse to part with that portion of that Territory as they are at present."[23] A few days later he wrote to Clay: "I feel very anxious about the boundary line between the two nations. While it will be politic not to justify their jealous fears on that subject by extravagant pretensions, I think it of the greatest importance that we should extend our territory toward the Rio del Norte either to the Colorado or at least to the Brazos."[24]

Two days later Alamán proposed that the governments proceed at once to enter into a treaty of commerce and that commissioners be appointed to examine "the country within a given latitude, from one sea to the other, who might present exact information upon which the limits might be established . . ." The Congress of the United States had recently appropriated thirty thousand dollars for the survey of a road in the neighborhood of the Santa Fé trail. Alamán stated that his government was pleased with the idea and suggested that the proposed commissioners might also receive instructions respecting the demarcation of this road.[25]

To this Poinsett replied that commissioners had already been appointed to survey the road and were then probably waiting for the treaty of limits to be arranged. The appointment of commissioners, as suggested by Alamán, would mean an embarrassing delay in the Santa Fé trade. He pointed out that at least a year would transpire before anything could be accomplished; nevertheless he agreed to lay the proposal before the American govern-

---

[23] Poinsett to Clay, July 25, 1825, quoted by Rives, *The United States and Mexico*, I, 168.

[24] Poinsett to Clay, August 5, 1825; quoted by Manning, in *The Southwestern Historical Quarterly*, XVII, 227.

[25] Alamán to Poinsett, July 20, 1825, *Congressional Debates*, XIV, Pt. 2, App., 132; Benton, *Thirty Years' View*, I, 41–44; Paxson, *The Last American Frontier*, 58. The surveyors' road was never used, however, as would be supposed from Benton and Paxson. Gregg (*Commerce of the Prairies*, I, 44) says that the traders refused to follow the line of the survey.

ment. The contention that the Santa Fé trade would be embarrassed by the delay is of course of no weight, as the traders followed their own trail across the prairies.[26]

On September 20 Poinsett had an interview with Alamán on the subject of boundaries. He reported the conversation to Clay as follows:

He [Alamán] began by saying that he wished to ascertain the ancient boundaries between the United States and the Spanish possessions, as defined by the treaty of 1795, and asked me to trace them for him in Melish's map. I did so, but observed, at the same time, that the treaty was concluded before the cession of Louisiana. I then inquired his object in wishing to ascertain the former boundaries. He replied, that he thought it would be advisable in the treaty we were about concluding, to specify the ancient boundary until the new line was agreed upon. I replied, he must be aware that, previous to the treaty with Spain concluded at Washington in 1819, the United States of America claimed to the Rio Bravo del Norte, and Spain to the Mississippi; and that treaty was a compromise of various disputed claims made by the contracting parties; that it was binding on the United Mexican States, having been concluded before their emancipation from Spain, and has since been acknowledged by their accredited agents in the United States. There had been ample time to have carried that treaty into full effect, but that the Government of the United States had been withheld from doing so only by motives of delicacy towards Mexico. That the same motives had induced me to propose an entire new treaty, which should not allude to the one formerly concluded with Spain; but that in so doing I did not intend to yield one square inch of land which was included within the limits of the United States according to the boundary line at that time agreed upon. That in my opinion a more advántageous boundary might be drawn between the two countries, but that such a line was not to be sought for east of the Sabine or north of the Red river or the Arkansas; and that, finally, no article such as he proposed could be inserted in the treaty, without my renewing in it the claim of the United States to the country north and east of the Rio Bravo del Norte.[27]

Thus, by a single astute move on the part of Alamán, Clay's house of cards was toppled over and the absurdity of the American position disclosed.

---

[26] Poinsett to Alamán, July 27, 1825, *Congressional Debates*, XIV, Pt. 2, App., 132–133.

[27] Poinsett to Clay, September 20, 1825, *ibid.*, 133.

The reply of the United States government to Alamán's note voiced the disappointment which was occasioned at Washington by the Mexican attitude. Clay observed that there was no connection between the Santa Fé road and the boundary, nor could the United States agree to the proposal of a reconnoitering commission, as that would be a reversal of the usual method of settling limits, the custom being to appoint commissioners after the representatives of the government had come to an agreement. The United States had no objection to Mexico making an examination; but if a commission were appointed for that purpose, it was hoped that it would be done at once to avoid further delay.[28]

The question of boundary was now allowed to rest and Poinsett entered into an extended discussion of a commercial treaty. At this time the Texan Indians were becoming troublesome, Mexican officials attributing this to the fact that the Indians purchased arms and ammunition from citizens of the United States. A question over land grants also arose. In 1824 the Mexican government had reserved twenty leagues bordering on the frontiers of neighboring nations and ten leagues along the seashore to be granted only by the executive. The state of Coahuila and Texas made a grant which included the twenty-league reservation along the Sabine River. Against this Poinsett protested on the ground that no grant should be made there until the boundary was settled, a view with which the Mexican government agreed.[29]

Nothing more was heard of the question until June, 1826, when the Mexican plenipotentiaries, Camacho and Esteva, proposed that the following article be appended to the commercial treaty:

---

[28] Clay to Poinsett, September 24, 1825, *State Papers, Foreign Relations*, VI, 581–582.

[29] Manning, in *The Southwestern Historical Quarterly*, XVII, 230–231; *House Ex. Docs.*, 25 Cong., 1 Sess., Doc. 42, p. 24.

Whereas, it being equally important to the two contracting parties that their boundaries should be definitely settled by means of a solemn treaty, they bind themselves, mutually, to take into consideration this point as early as possible, affording, in their respective territories, the succors that may be required by the Commissioners, or persons sent out by the other party to make scientific observations, reconnaissances, discoveries, and all operations relative to the conclusion of the aforementioned convention, on the basis of justice, and in conformity to the friendly relations which now exist between the two parties, the persons requiring such succors paying for them what is just. Nor shall any acts of possession that may be made in the meantime by the citizens, people, or Indians of the territory of the one party, within the territory of the other, create a right to claims or pretensions to indemnities at the period of concluding the definitive treaty.[30]

To this Poinsett agreed, with the exception that the words "unauthorized by the government" be inserted before the words "acts of possession." In suggesting this, he pointed out that, were either government to authorize such acts while the boundary negotiations were pending, such acts might give rise to claims. He observed that "it ought, likewise, to be distinctly understood that grants, during that period of time, made to individuals, by either Government, of lands so situated as to render it probable that they may be included within the limits of the other, will not be considered valid."

Poinsett stated that this provision was unnecessary to bind his government at once to conclude a boundary treaty, as the treaty of 1819 was considered by his government as binding both upon the United States and Mexico, and that such was the view of the latter, citing Torrens' letter of February 15, 1824, as proof. He said that the United States had been willing to accede to a new line, if Mexico so desired, but he was especially instructed not to insist upon changing the line contrary to the wishes of the Mexican government. He then quoted a large part of Clay's letter of September 24, 1825, which discussed the Mexican pro-

---

[30] Camacho and Esteva to Poinsett, June 19, 1826, *State Papers, Foreign Relations*, VI, 599.

posal of commissioners to examine the country.[31] The suggestion
made by Poinsett, with a slight change, was incorporated into
the original draft of the treaty, the phrase "without the authority
and consent of the Government" being inserted after the words
"within the Territory of the other."[32] Subsequent events made
the entire article unnecessary and it does not appear in the final
draft of the commercial treaty.[33]

On July 12 Poinsett informed Clay that General Terán had
been appointed to examine the country along the frontier and
that Terán had told him that he would set out in September,[34]
although in fact he did not make his visit to northern Texas
until 1828.[35] Before the results of this examination were known,
Clay again showed his hand in a letter to Poinsett in March,
1827. He commented on the ease with which land grants were
obtained in Texas by citizens of the United States, and pointed
out that Americans would never amalgamate with Mexico owing
to their different conceptions of freedom, and that collisions were
sure to arise which would probably lead to misunderstandings
between the countries. He again pointed out that the Sabine
was too close to New Orleans and that perhaps the time was now
auspicious for urging a negotiation to settle the boundary. "The
success of the negotiation," he observed further,

will probably be promoted by throwing into it other motives than those
which strictly belong to the subject itself. If we could obtain such a
boundary as we desire, the Government of the United States might be
disposed to pay a reasonable pecuniary consideration. The boundary
which we prefer is that which, beginning at the mouth of the Rio del
Norte, in the sea, shall ascend that river to the mouth of the Rio Puerco
[Pecos], thence ascending this river to its source, and from its source,

31 Poinsett to Camacho and Esteva, June 26, 1826, *State Papers, Foreign
Relations,* VI, 599–600.

32 *Ibid.,* VI, 613.

33 *Treaties, Conventions* (Malloy, ed.), I, 1082–1084.

34 Poinsett to Clay, July 12, 1826, *Congressional Debates,* XIV, Pt. 2,
App., 133.

35 Obregón to Clay, March 19, 1828; Clay to Obregón, March 24, 1828,
ibid., 140. Garrison (*Texas,* 160), gives the date as 1827.

by a line due north, to strike the Arkansas, thence following the course
of the southern bank of the Arkansas to its source, in latitude 42° north,
and thence by that parallel of latitude to the South sea. The boundary
thus described would, according to the United States Tanner's map,
published in the United States, leave Santa Fé within the limits of
Mexico, and the whole of Red river . . . and the Arkansas, as far up as
it is probably navigable, within the limits assigned to the United States.
If that boundary be unattainable, we would, as the next most desirable,
agree to that of the Colorado, beginning at its mouth, in the bay of
Bernardo, and ascending the river to its source, and thence by a line due
north to the Arkansas, and thence, as above traced, to the South sea.
This latter boundary would probably also give us the whole of the Red
river, would throw us somewhat farther from Santa Fé, but it would
strike the Arkansas possibly at a navigable point. To obtain the first-
described boundary, the President authorizes you to offer to the Government of Mexico a sum not exceeding one million of dollars. If you find it
impracticable to procure that line, you are then authorized to offer, for
the above line of the Colorado, the sum of five hundred thousand dollars.
If either of the above offers should be accepted, you may stipulate for
the payment of the sum of money, as you may happen to agree, within
any period not less than three months after the exchange at the city of
Washington of the ratifications of the treaty.[36]

Poinsett from the first had been cautious about presenting
the views of his government, because he did not wish to aggravate
the distrust which Mexico already felt toward the United States.[37]
Another reason for withholding the proposals was the fact that
a committee of the Chamber of Deputies had recently reported
on the commercial treaty, which had been concluded on July 10,
1826. The report had been discussed in secret session and the
Chamber had disapproved of a portion of it and had expressed

36 Clay to Poinsett, March 15, 1827, *Congressional Debates*, XIV, Pt. 2,
App., 127. In the original draft of the instructions, Clay had included
an offer of ships of war, but at the suggestion of Adams, only money was
offered. Adams, *Memoirs*, VII, 240. Clay's reference to collisions between Americans and Mexicans was probably the result of a recent correspondence concerning the Fredonian war. For a summary of this, see
Manning, in *The Southwestern Historical Quarterly*, XVII, 231–235.

37 Poinsett to Clay, July 27, 1825, *Congressional Debates*, XIV, Pt. 2,
App., 132; Reeves, *American Diplomacy under Tyler and Polk*, 64. A brief
account of the dealings with Mexico during this period will be found in
that book, pp. 58–64.

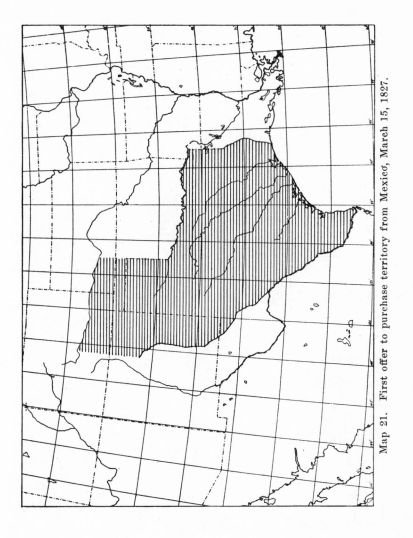

Map 21. First offer to purchase territory from Mexico, March 15, 1827.

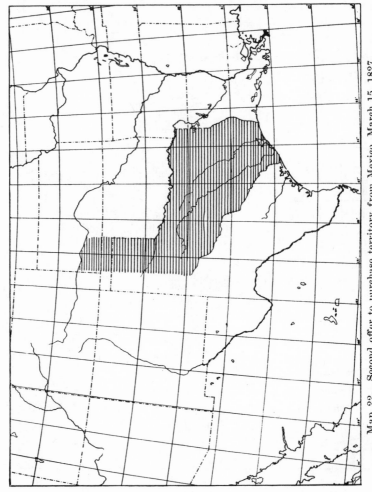

Map 22. Second offer to purchase territory from Mexico, March 15, 1827.

a desire to have inserted an additional article declaring the treaty
of 1819 to be binding upon the two countries.[38] Poinsett considered the sum much too small, and decided not to submit the
proposal at this time.[39] In May he urged that the boundary
question be settled, but he did not suggest the idea of sale.[40]

Nothing more was done toward a settlement of the boundary
question until the fall of 1827, when the Mexican government
appropriated fifteen thousand dollars toward defraying the
expenses of General Terán. The commission had not yet set out
for want of funds and Poinsett tried to dissuade the government
from sending it, but to no avail.[41]

On January 8, 1828, Poinsett reported that ''The negotiations
were renewed this day, and, from the disposition manifested by
the Mexican plenipotentiaries, in the first conference, I have
every expectation of concluding the treaty of friendship, navigation, and commerce, favorably and promptly.'' He then stated
again that the Chamber of Deputies would not consider the treaty
without an article recognizing the validity of the agreement of
1819. He further observed:

The plenipotentiaries, in reply to all my observations on the subject,
and to my proposals to alter the limits, insisted that Mexico had a right
to consider that treaty binding upon the United States, as being invested
with all the rights of Spain, and bound by all the obligations of the
mother country . . . I withdrew my opposition, but observed that, as
the treaty of navigation and commerce was for a limited period, and that
of limits perpetual, it would be better to make them distinct conventions;
to which proposal the Mexican plenipotentiaries consented.[42]

---

38 Poinsett to Clay, April 10, 1827, *Congressional Debates*, XIV, Pt. 2,
App., 134.

39 Rives, *The United States and Mexico*, I, 169.

40 Manning, in *The Southwestern Historical Quarterly*, XVII, 238.

41 Poinsett to Clay, October 6, 1827, *Congressional Debates*, XIV, Pt. 2,
App.. 134.

42 Poinsett to Clay, January 8, 1828, *ibid.*, 134. The text of the protocol of the conference of January 8 is printed in *House Ex. Docs.*, 25
Cong., 1 Sess., Doc. 42, p. 27. The Mexican representatives were Sebas-
tian Camacho and José Ignacio Esteva. Reeves (*Diplomacy under Tyler
and Polk*, 64) gives Poinsett's letter as authority that the treaty was

A second conference was held on the tenth, a protocol being drawn up in which were embodied the principles of the previous one, the obligations of the treaty of 1819 being accepted by the representatives of both governments. The preamble and first article of the treaty were also drawn.[43] Other conferences followed and on the twelfth the document was signed. It provided that the portion of the treaty of 1819 which fixed the limits should have the same force between Mexico and the United States as it had with Spain, and that each government should appoint a commissioner and a surveyor, who should meet at Natchitoches before the termination of a year from the ratification of the treaty, and run and mark the boundary line. It was further provided that the ratifications were to be exchanged at Washington within four months or sooner.[44]

The Mexican government attended at once to the appointment of the boundary commission. On March 19 Obregon informed Clay that the commission would consist of General Mier y Terán, Lieutenant Colonels Tarnaba and Batres, Sub-Lieutenant of Artillery Sanchez R. Chovel as mineralogist, and Luis Berlandier, botanist.[45]

On the twenty-fourth of April, Poinsett was able to inform his government that the Mexican lower house had ratified the treaty and that it was then before the Senate. He deplored the fact that it would be impossible to send the document in time for the ratification to take place within the designated term. The delay he blamed upon the Mexican Secretary of State, who, he claimed, kept it in his office upwards of two months without

concluded. The Mexican commissioners were assisted in their work by two boundary reports; one was that of Puelles, the other extracts from that of Pichardo. See Manning, in *The Southwestern Historical Quarterly,* XVII, 240.

[43] *House Ex. Docs.,* 25 Cong., 1 Sess., Doc. 42, p. 28; Poinsett to Clay, February 7, 1828, *Congressional Debates,* XIV, Pt. 2, App., 134–135.

[44] *Treaties, Conventions* (Malloy, ed.), I, 1082–1084.

[45] Obregón to Clay, March 19, 1828, *Congressional Debates,* XIV, Pt. 2, App., 140.

submitting it to Congress.[46] On the following day the treaty was ratified by the Senate, and Poinsett sent it to the United States with the full knowledge that it could not arrive within the time limit and that it would have to be submitted a second time to the United States Senate.[47]

On April 30 Clay informed the Mexican representative at Washington that the treaty had been ratified by the United States Senate and asked that the ratifications be exchanged,[48] but Obregón was forced to confess that he had not yet received the treaty from his government.[49] On August 2 he informed Clay that he had the ratified treaty in hand and that he was ready to exchange ratifications,[50] but he was informed that, as the time limit had expired, the matter would have to be referred again to the Senate.[51] Soon after, Obregón was taken seriously ill and died on September 10. J. M. Montoya, chargé d'affaires, conducted the Mexican legation,[52] until the arrival of José María Tornel, who was appointed envoy extraordinary and minister plenipotentiary on November 27, 1829.[53] Adams' administration closed without an exchange of ratifications. It was for Jackson's administration to complete the work of his predecessor.

---

[46] Poinsett to Clay, April 24, 1828, *Congressional Debates*, XIV, Pt. 2, App., 135.

[47] Poinsett to Clay, April 26, 1828, *ibid.*, 135.

[48] Clay to Obregón, April 30, 1828, *ibid.*, 140.

[49] Obregón to Clay, May 1, 1828, *ibid.*, 140.

[50] Obregón to Clay, August 2, 1828, *ibid.*, 140.

[51] Brent to Obregón, August 2, 1828, *ibid.*, 140.

[52] Obregón to Clay, August 14, 1828; Montoya to Clay, September 11, 1828, *House Ex. Docs.*, 25 Cong., 2 Sess., XII, Doc. 351, pp. 633–635.

[53] Guerrero to Jackson, November 17, 1829, *ibid.*, 639–640.

CHAPTER V

DIPLOMACY RELATIVE TO THE MEXICAN BOUNDARY AND EFFORTS TO PURCHASE TEXAS, 1829–1835

On March 4, 1829, Andrew Jackson took the oath of office as President of the United States and two days later Martin Van Buren was appointed Secretary of State. On April 16 Montoya, the Mexican chargé, addressed a note to Van Buren in which he informed the secretary that he had been given full power to effect the exchange of ratifications of the treaty of limits. He observed that Adams' objection to the treaty was caused by the expiration of the time limit, which made it necessary to submit it again to the Senate; this he supposed had been done at the recent session and he now desired to know if Van Buren were ready to make the exchange.[1] Van Buren informed him that no action had yet been taken, and that when the commercial treaty was received, both would be submitted to the Senate.[2]

Poinsett remained in Mexico for a time under the Jackson administration. A few days after the President's inauguration, he wrote that the Mexican President and Alamán had formed a plan to negotiate a new treaty by which the United States would be reduced to the margin of the Mississippi, on the grounds that Spain had been unjustly deprived of a large part of her territory. He said that the line of the treaty of 1819 had been secured only by the threat that, if the Sabine were not agreed upon, the United States would assume the Rio Grande

---

[1] Montoya to Van Buren, April 16, 1829, *House Ex. Docs.*, 25 Cong.. 1 Sess., Doc. 42, p. 49.

[2] Van Buren to Montoya, April 22, 1829, *ibid.*, 49–50.

boundary. He said that Congress was wiser than the executive and had compelled the President to confirm the treaty.[3] He again addressed Van Buren in similar vein in July.[4]

Anthony Butler, an old friend of Jackson, who had been interested in Texas lands, appeared in Washington soon after the inauguration as an applicant for office. He talked freely with the President and Van Buren regarding Texan affairs and eventually drew up a statement regarding the geography and productions of the province, and another paper setting forth arguments for the sale of Texas to the United States. In the latter he suggested that the Neches was the stream called the Sabine in the treaty of 1819. The ideas of Butler became the basis of the policy of the Jackson administration.[5]

The American minister was informed that he was to open negotiations for the purchase of a part or practically all of Texas. The reasons assigned were that the frontier and New Orleans must be protected and the inhabitants of the Mississippi Valley must be forever secure in the undisputed and undisturbed possession of the navigation of the great river. It was proposed that the United States purchase all that portion of Texas lying east of a line which should begin at the gulf,

in the centre of the desert or Grand prairie, which lies west of the Rio Nueces, and is represented to be nearly two hundred miles in width, and to extend north to the mountains. The proposed line following the . . . centre of that desert . . . , north, to the mountains dividing the waters of the Rio Grande del Norte from those that run eastward to the Gulf, and until it strikes our present boundary at the 42d degree of north latitude.

For this territory Poinsett was authorized to offer four million dollars, and, if indispensably necessary, five millions.

---

[3] Poinsett to the Secretary of State, March 10, 1829, *Congressional Debates*, XIV, Pt. 2, App., 135.

[4] Poinsett to Van Buren, July 22, 1829, *ibid.*, 135–136.

[5] Rives, *The United States and Mexico*, I, 235–238; Barker, in *The American Historical Review*, XII, 790.

If Mexico objected to selling the region about La Bahia and San Antonio de Bexar, he was authorized to agree to any of the following lines. The second proposal was to run the line along the west bank of the Rio de la Baca to its source, then north to the Colorado, up that stream to its source, and thence up the most direct line that would intersect the forty-second parallel and include the head waters of the Arkansas and Red rivers. The third proposal was for a line along the Colorado to its source, and from this point to follow the line of the second proposal. A fourth and last proposition was for a line following the western bank of the Brazos to the head of its most westerly branch, and then as before to the forty-second parallel. In case that any of these lines were agreed upon, compensation was to be made to Mexico in proportion to the amount of land obtained. In Jackson's memorandum, mention is made of the Trinity as a boundary, but the line was not incorporated in the instructions.

The western limit of Louisiana was also discussed. Van Buren stated that, of the two streams which emptied into Sabine Bay, the western one was the more considerable, and might, with reason, be claimed as the one referred to in the treaty of 1819. He said that the Sabine was navigable only for small craft, that the lands on the east side were poor and those on the Mexican side were good; in consequence, the Mexicans would naturally become numerous in that locality and incessant broils would ensue. It does not seem within the bounds of reason that an American Secretary of State could have been ignorant of the boundary as laid down in the treaty of 1819. The argument that your lands are good, that mine are poor, that therefore I ought to have your lands, could hardly be convincing to Mexico.[6]

The Mexican government was extremely suspicious of Poinsett. He was a prominent York rite Mason and assisted in organizing many lodges in Mexico. The party in power was

_____

[6] Van Buren to Poinsett, August 25, 1829, *Congressional Debates*, XIV, Pt. 2, App., 127–130; Reeves, *American Diplomacy under Tyler and Polk*, 65–67, note.

identified with the Scottish rite lodges, and it was but natural
that Poinsett's masonic activities should arouse suspicions. Open
threats were made against him and the state legislature of Vera
Cruz demanded his recall. Poinsett defended himself as best
he could, proclaiming his innocence in pamphlets and newspapers.[7]

He did not succeed in allaying suspicion; every action of the
American government was studiously watched, and when it was
rumored that United States troops had recently been stationed
along the frontier, Bocanegra, the Secretary of State and of
Foreign Affairs, demanded the reason for such action.[8] Poinsett
declared that no such movement of American troops had taken
place;[9] but if the border Indians were not restrained, it would
be necessary for the United States to pursue and chastise them,
"even under the walls of Mexico."[10]

In view of Poinsett's unpopularity, the Mexican government
determined to ask for his recall, its wishes being communicated
to Van Buren on October 17.[11] The United States government
had already determined upon the recall and on the previous day
had prepared a note informing Poinsett that his mission was at
an end. It was not despatched, however, until after Montoya
presented his request.[12]

The mission was offered to General James Hamilton of
South Carolina, but because of domestic engagements, he was
unable to accept,[13] and Colonel Anthony Butler of Mississippi

---

[7] *Niles' Register*, XXXIII, 13–14; *ibid.*, XXXIII, 23–26; *ibid.*, XXXIV,
140; *ibid.*, XXXV, 155. Poinsett, *Manifiesto de los Principios Politicos;*
Poinsett, *Esposicion de la Conducta Politica de los Estados-Unidos para
con las Nuevas Republicas de America;* Poinsett, *Contestacion del Ministro
Americano, a la Escitativa de la Legislatura del Estado de Mexico.*

[8] Bocanegra to Poinsett, August 20, 1829, *House Ex. Docs.*, 25 Cong.,
2 Sess., XII, Doc. 351, pp. 292–293.

[9] Poinsett to Bocanegra, August 21, 1829, *ibid.*, 293–294.

[10] Poinsett to Van Buren, August 22, 1829, *ibid.*, 291–292.

[11] Montoya to Van Buren, October 17, 1829, *ibid.*, 638–639.

[12] Van Buren to Poinsett, October 16, 1829, *ibid.*, 35–39; Reeves,
American Diplomacy under Tyler and Polk, 68–70, note.

[13] Kennedy, *Texas*, I, 374, note.

was selected as Poinsett's successor. He had already been despatched to Mexico for the purpose of assisting in the negotiations for Texas. Van Buren's letter of introduction read:

Colonel Butler has made himself well acquainted, by actual examination, with the territory in question, its streams and localities. In the belief that he deserves your confidence, and that he may be useful to you in the negotiation by supplying you with facts which might not otherwise be within your reach, he has been instructed to observe your directions in regard to his stay at Mexico, and his agency in the matter whilst there.[14]

Butler was appointed chargé d'affaires in October; his instructions presented a résumé of the diplomatic intercourse with Mexico and warned him against falling into the errors of his predecessor. "A social, open, and frank deportment towards men of all classes and all parties; a proper degree of respect for their opinions, whatever they may be; a ready frankness in explaining the true policy of our Government, without attempting to obtrude your views where they are not desired; and the most guarded care in condemning or censuring theirs, are among the means which the President would suggest as most likely to command the confidence of the people, and to secure for yourself a proper standing in the opinion of their public functionaries." Butler was also ordered to carry out the previous instructions of Poinsett, namely, the negotiations for the purchase of Texas.[15]

Butler had not been long in Mexico before it was noised abroad that the United States was trying to buy the territory. *El Sol* of January 9, 1830, contained the following:

A few days before the departure of Mr. Poinsett from this capital, the American Colonel Butler arrived here, commissioned, as it is said, by the Government of Washington, to negotiate with ours for the cession of the province of Texas for the sum of five millions of dollars. As we are not informed that, so far, the colonel has made any overtures on the

---

[14] Van Buren to Poinsett, August 25, 1829, *Congressional Debates*, XIV, Pt. 2, App., 127–130.

[15] Van Buren to Butler, October 16, 1829, *House Ex. Docs.*, 25 Cong., 2 Sess., XII, Doc. 351, pp. 40–53.

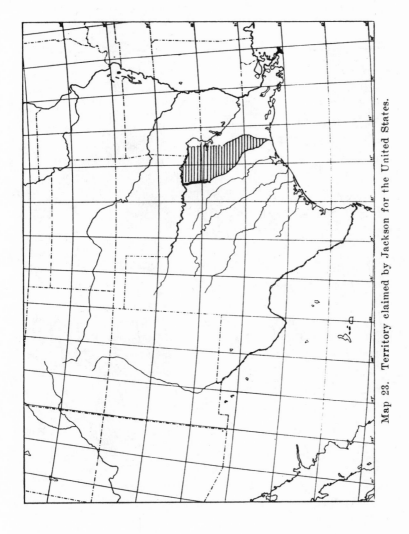

Map 23.   Territory claimed by Jackson for the United States.

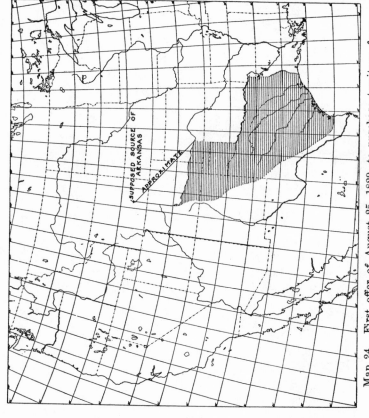

Map 24. First offer of August 25, 1829, to purchase territory from Mexico.

subject, we presume that he does the new administration the justice
to suppose it incapable of lending itself to a transaction as prejudicial
and degrading to the republic as it would be disgraceful to the minister
who would subscribe to it.[16]

A month later Lúcas Alamán, who was again Secretary of
Foreign Relations, presented to the Mexican Congress a report
on Texas, in which he incorporated many ideas furnished by
General Terán. Alamán pointed out that the intentions of the
United States to possess it were clearly manifest and that the
American policy was to colonize and explore. The pioneer settlers stirred up trouble and then the work of the diplomats commenced. He advised that under no circumstances could Mexico
afford to part with Texas. He pointed out that the governor
of Arkansas had demanded territory which clearly belonged to
Mexico. The non-execution of the treaty of limits he considered
as a portion of the American policy of aggrandizement.

This treaty secured to us that part of Texas . . . ; this Government
knows that the new chargé d'affaires of the United States has come with
the special authorization of proposing an arrangement for the sum of five
millions of dollars; and if this is not accepted, it is very probable that
they will propose the appointment of a mediator to determine that affair.
. . . The evil, then, is done; Texas will be lost for this republic, unless
necessary measures are adopted to preserve it.

He then presented a plan for securing the province, which
included military occupation, colonization by foreigners other
than Americans, the suspension of state government, and the
establishment of Mexican colonies. He advised that the laws
in regard to slavery and religion be suspended in justice to the
settlers of Texas.[17]

---

[16] Butler to Van Buren, January 10, 1830, with enclosure, *House Ex.
Docs.*, 25 Cong., 2 Sess., XII, Doc., 351, p. 310.

[17] Alamán's report is given in part in *House Ex. Docs.*, 25 Cong., 2
Sess., XII, Doc. 351, pp. 312–322. For the entire report see Filisola,
Memorias para la Historia de la Guerra de ⊥ejas, II, 560–612. For Teran's
influence upon Alamán's report, see Howren, in *The Southwestern Historical Quarterly*, XVI, 402–404.

Butler sent a copy of the report to his government. ''Had his project been adopted, as recommended,'' he wrote, ''I am confident that a revolution in that province would immediately have followed, and Texas become ours, by a movement among the people themselves, without costing the Government of the United States a dollar.'' He said that the purchase of Texas was a more difficult problem than two years before, as Mexico had become aware of the value of the territory and because of the opposition of the British party. He said further:

> The Secretary himself suggests a probability of our claiming territory as far west as the Rio Grande, and I have so managed as to strengthen that impression on his mind, (without committing myself or the Government,) as one means of facilitating the retrocession when we come to negotiate for the country; and the failure to ratify the treaty of limits has been, in connection with that subject, a most fortunate event for us, that may be turned to good account. I have ascertained . . . that the Mexican Government are becoming anxious on the question of limits and boundary between the United States and Mexico; and I have more than once been approached on that subject, but always found means to evade it, leaving them under the influence of whatever their imagination might create to awake suspicion and alarm their fears.

He then suggested that he be empowered to urge the claim of the United States as far as the Rio Grande, to facilitate the negotiations.[18]

On April 6 the Mexican Congress embodied several of Alamán's recommendations in a law which prohibited the citizens of adjacent states from colonizing; it suspended unfulfilled and unlawful contracts, provided that foreigners should not enter without passports, and prohibited the further importation of slaves. Terán was instructed to occupy Texas with a military force, posts were established at various points, and customs houses were put in operation. These actions led to much dis-

18 Butler to Van Buren, March 9, 1830, *House Ex. Docs.*, 25 Cong., 2 Sess., XII, Doc. 351, pp. 311–312.

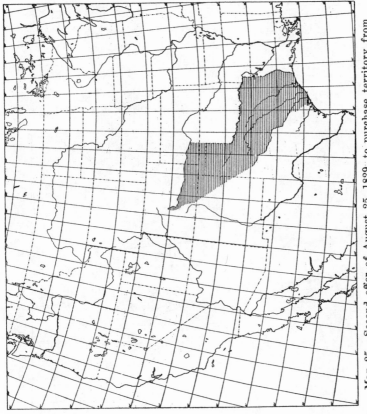

Map 25.   Second offer of August 25, 1829, to purchase territory from Mexico.

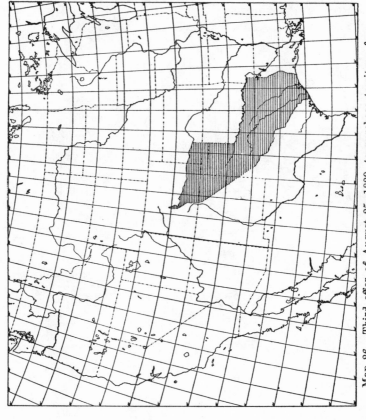

Map 26. Third offer of August 25, 1829, to purchase territory from Mexico.

content in Texas, which gathered into open rebellion in the spring and summer of 1832.[19]

On April 15, 1830, Butler wrote that he believed the time was near at hand when the hopes of the United States would be realized. He based this upon the fact that an invasion from Spain was apprehended; in such an event, Mexico naturally would turn to the United States for assistance, and Texas would be the reward.[20]

Butler's hopes were suddenly checked, however, by his government, which instructed him to drop negotiations for the acquisition of Texas for the time being. "The unsettled state of affairs in Mexico, and the excitement growing out of it . . . have induced an apprehension on the part of the President that the present is not an auspicious moment for the successful opening of the negotiations."[21]

A clash of authority soon occurred on the Arkansas frontier to disturb the diplomats. General Terán ordered Colonel Bean to prevent adventurers entering in the neighborhood of Punta Pacana [Pecan Point]. This carried him into the disputed district between the Neches and Sabine rivers, over a portion of which Arkansas claimed jurisdiction. Pope, the governor of Arkansas Territory, demanded by what authority Bean claimed jurisdiction in that region. Benjamin R. Milam, joint empresario with Arthur G. Wavell, informed Pope that he was about to survey a tract of land under a grant from the Mexican government.[22]

Pope informed Van Buren of the proceedings, who replied that he greatly regretted the occurrence and advised him to adopt a conciliatory course. He stated, however, that the jurisdiction

---

[19] Bancroft, *North Mexican States and Texas*, II, 114–124; Garrison, *Texas*, 173–180; Barker, in Texas State Historical Association, *Quarterly*, IV, 190–202.

[20] Butler to Jackson , April 15, 1830, *House Ex. Docs.*, 25 Cong., 2 Sess., XII, Doc. 351, pp. 323–324.

[21] Van Buren to Butler, April 1, 1830, *ibid.*, 59–63.

[22] Reynolds, in Arkansas Historical Association, *Publications*, II, 232.

over the disputed territory was not to be relinquished while the boundary remained undecided, but the governor was not to resort to force without receiving permission from the President.[23] Van Buren immediately protested to Tornel, the Mexican minister, against the actions of Milam.[24]

Tornel replied that he would write to General Terán, if Van Buren so desired, to induce him to order a suspension of proceedings on the part of Bean and Milam until the Mexican government could decide on the case. He recommended that Van Buren instruct Governor Pope to refrain from violent measures until the decision might be made. At the same time he urged that the treaty of limits be ratified at the next session of Congress.[25] Shortly after, he wrote to Terán[26] and Van Buren wrote to Pope.[27] The prompt action allayed the difficulty.

In his annual message of December 6, Jackson said:

> There was reason to fear in the course of the last summer that the harmony of our relations might be disturbed by the acts of certain claimants, under Mexican grants, of territory which had hitherto been under our jurisdiction. The cooperation of the representative of Mexico near this Government was asked on the occasion and was readily afforded. Instructions and advice have been given to the governor of Arkansas and the officers in command in the adjoining Mexican State by which it is hoped the quiet of that frontier will be preserved until a final settlement of the dividing line shall have removed all ground of controversy.[28]

The hope expressed by Jackson was fulfilled by the action of Terán, who ordered the suspension of the activities of Milam. Terán maintained, however, that Bean and Milam were both operating on Mexican soil. He observed that many Americans were entering that district, and he thought it only just that,

---

[23] Van Buren to Pope, September 28, 1830, *House Ex. Docs.*, 25 Cong., 2 Sess. XII, Doc. 351, p. 68.

[24] Van Buren to Tornel, September 28, 1830, *ibid.*, 650–651.

[25] Tornel to Van Buren, October 2, 1830, *ibid.*, 652–653.

[26] Tornel to Terán, October 8, 1830, *ibid.*, 653.

[27] Van Buren to Pope, October 11, 1830, *ibid.*, 69.

[28] Richardson, *Messages and Papers of the Presidents*, II. 507.

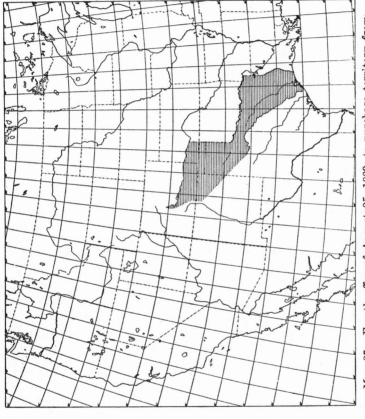

Map 27. Fourth offer of August 25, 1829, to purchase territory from Mexico.

if the governor of Arkansas opposed Mexican settlements, he should also oppose the introduction of Americans until the boundary had been run.[29]

In March a change occurred, José María Montoya being appointed to take the place of Tornel.[30] Montoya began his official work in June.[31] Van Buren retired from the office of Secretary of State on March 23, Edward Livingston being appointed the following day.[32]

On April 5, 1831, a commercial treaty was concluded between the two powers. The same day additional articles to the treaty of limits were also signed, providing that the treaty of 1828 be ratified in the city of Washington on or before April 5, 1832.[33] It is evident that Butler's policy of delay had been interrupted by the action of the Mexican government; it remained for the Mexican Congress to act upon the treaties before sending them to the United States.[34]

Jackson had not given up his idea of acquiring Texas; he wrote to Butler urging that he press the matter. In May Butler wrote that he believed the time was at hand to reopen the negotiations,[35] but nothing was done, and in August he was still making excuses for his inactivity.[36] In October he approached the Minister of Foreign Relations on the subject, but was informed that the sale of Texas would violate the constitution and would meet with the opposition of the states. In spite of this, in December Butler expressed a hope that he might shortly communicate something on the subject of Texas.[37]

[29] Terán to Tornel, February 2, 1831, *House Ex. Docs.*, 25 Cong., 2 Sess., XII, Doc. 351, pp. 660–661.

[30] Alamán to Livingston, March 8, 1831, *ibid.*, 664–665.

[31] Brent to Montoya, June 1, 1831, *ibid.*, 666.

[32] Moore, *A Digest of International Law*, I, p. vii.

[33] *Treaties, Conventions,* (Malloy, ed.) I, 1084–1085.

[34] Butler to Van Buren, April 8, 1831, *House Ex. Docs.*, 25 Cong., 2 Sess., XII, Doc. 351, pp. 375–376.

[35] Butler to Jackson, May 25, 1831, *ibid.*, 381.

[36] Butler to Livingston, August 11, 1831, *ibid.*, 390–391.

[37] Rives, *The United States and Mexico*, I, 248–249.

At this time a piece of diplomacy was being carried on in Spain, one purpose of which was evidently intended to serve the interests of the United States in dealing with Mexico. Spain had never recognized the independence of her former colonies; this action was urged upon her by the American minister, but the Spanish government courteously replied: ''As this American question is fully present to his royal mind, his Majesty will take it into consideration, when the opportunity may be favorable, in such a manner as may be most suitable to the interests of his crown.''[38]

The solicitude of the United States was made known to Montoya,[39] who replied: ''The undersigned trusts that the mediation which the President offers to exert on every convenient occasion will have the desired effect; whatever may be the issue, the United States will always be grateful for his philanthropic wishes and endeavors to establish peace.''[40]

The treaties which were signed on April 5 were before the Mexican Congress until December. The Senate committee on foreign relations in October reported favorably upon the article respecting limits,[41] but the commercial treaty met with considerable opposition, due mainly to provisions regarding fugitive slaves; but it was finally ratified.[42]

In February the treaty was placed in the hands of Livingston, but no immediate action was taken by the Senate. Montoya commented upon the delay, saying, ''The undersigned says nothing of the unfavorable impression which this delay will produce upon the Mexican nation, and ventures to hope that when the Secretary of State thinks proper to exchange the ratification

---

[38] Salmon to the American Minister, June 10, 1832, *House Ex. Docs..* 25 Cong., 2 Sess., XII, Doc. 351, p. 668.

[39] Livingston to Montoya, October 1, 1831, *ibid.*, 668.

[40] Montoya to Livingston October 7, 1831, *ibid.*, 669.

[41] Butler to Livingston, October 25, 1831, with enclosure, *ibid.*, 402–404.

[42] Various letters, protocols, and a copy of the commercial treaty are to be found, *ibid.*, 407–428.

of the treaty of friendship, commerce, and navigation, he will likewise exchange those of the treaty of limits at the same time.''[43]

Livingston immediately replied, stating that the Senate had ratified the commercial treaty, but had not yet acted upon the one involving boundary, a galling state of affairs as far as Mexico was concerned, as only five days remained before the time limit would expire.[44] Montoya replied that, according to his instructions, he was not to exchange the ratification of the commercial treaty without that of boundary.[45] The difficulty was obviated by the favorable action of the Senate on April 5, 1832, the last day of the time limit; the ratifications were immediately exchanged and the treaties proclaimed the same day.[46]

On July 3 an act of Congress was approved for carrying the treaty into effect. It provided that a commissioner, surveyor, and commissioner's clerk, be appointed; the salary of the commissioner was fixed at two thousand five hundred dollars per year, the surveyor's at two thousand, and the clerk's at twelve hundred; ten thousand dollars was appropriated for instruments, wages and other contingencies.[47] William McRee of Missouri was appointed commissioner, Robert Love of North Carolina surveyor, and Samuel O. Bayard of Ohio, clerk.[48] Love declined and John Donelson, Jr., of Tennessee filled the vacancy.[49]

In July Livingston informed Montoya of the action of Congress, and made inquiry as to whether Mexico had made any arrangement to carry out her part of the agreement; if not,

---

[43] Montoya to Livingston, March 31, 1832, *Congressional Debates*, XIV, Pt. 2, App., 142.

[44] Livingston to Montoya, March 31, 1832, *ibid.*, 142–143. The commercial treaty was ratified by the Senate March 23, 1832. *Treaties, Conventions*, (Malloy, ed.) I, 1085.

[45] Montoya to Livingston, April 3, 1832, *Congressional Debates*, 25 Cong., 2 Sess., XII, Pt. 2, 143.

[46] *Treaties, Conventions*, (Malloy, ed.) I, 1084–1085.

[47] *Congressional Debates*, VIII, Pt. 3, App., *Acts of the 22 Cong.*, p. xxxi.

[48] *Niles' Register*, XLII, 387.

[49] *Ibid.*, XLIII, 330.

Montoya was requested to ask his government to give immediate attention to the matter.[50]

It is time to turn again to Butler's attempts to acquire Texas. On June 23, 1831, he had written that he thought that seven million dollars should be offered, but it was decided that the original offer of five millions should not be exceeded. In February of the following year he wrote that the Mexican government was much in need of money, and that he had suggested that arrangements might be made for getting several millions from the United States, a suggestion which Jackson considered very judicious.[51]

On July 2, 1832, he found an opportunity of broaching to Alamán the subject of a new boundary. He presented the matter as follows:

I stated to the Secretary the desire which my Government entertained to negotiate for a new boundary between the two republics. That the present, as established by the treaty of 1819, it was believed would produce difficulties, and that great benefit might accrue to both nations by the accomplishment of such an event as placing the line farther west. That on our part it would leave entirely disembarrassed a portion of territory now in the occupation of our citizens, which, in the opinion of some affecting accurate knowledge of the geography of the country, would be included the province of Texas, as the line would in all probability now go. That in such an event, a novel, important, and doubtful question would be presented, viz: Whether the General Government of the United States possessed the power of transferring any portion of the citizens of the United States to a foreign government, without their consent? That I felt assured the assent would not be given, and equally certain that the inhabitants of the territory referred to would not relinquish their property, unless the Mexican Government consented to make ample compensation for the improvements made and money expended by the settlers on the land they had purchased and occupied. That these lands covered two counties in the Territory of Arkansas, including several thousand of inhabitants, and many hundred thousand acres of land. That my knowledge of the exhausted state of the Mexican treasury forbade the expectation of the Government being able to command the means for

---

[50] Livingston to Montoya, July 20, 1832, *Congressional Debates,* XIV, Pt. 2, App., 144.

[51] Barker, in *The American Historical Review,* XII, 791–792.

making compensation either at the present moment, or within any defined period; and that I should suppose Mexico would herself be desirous of avoiding so heavy a pecuniary responsibility. That an extension of the boundary west would obviate every difficulty; the United States would be relieved from the embarrassment presented by the question of transfer already spoken of, and Mexico saved from the heavy pecuniary responsibility involved in the payments for land and improvements.

He then commented upon the revolution in progress in Texas, pointing out the probability of its success, in which case it would be better to dispose of the province to the United States. He spoke also of the expense that would be incurred to bring Texas again into the Mexican state, even though success were attained.

Alamán replied that he desired to adopt any measures that would obviate future jealousies between the United States and Mexico, but thought there were many practical difficulties in the way. He made an appointment for July 10, at which time Butler was to bring his maps on which they might trace the line as it then stood, "and see to what limit it might prudently be extended west."

On the appointed day they met and traced the line, Alamán following the Sabine and Butler contending for the Neches. The American minister used this discrepancy as an argument for establishing a new line. He now pointed out to Alamán that there were two rivers in Texas called Sabine, the easterly one emptying into Sabine Lake.

That another river, now known, and also heretofore known to all Mexicans and others as the Sabine river, nad its rise west of the Nueces, and discharged itself above Loredo, on the Rio Grande, and which, if it were established as the true boundary, would give us more than we ask by the new line; and the question may, perhaps, be fairly made hereafter by the commissioners, which is the Sabine river meant as the boundary under the treaty of 1819. . . .

We then proceeded to examine the map, and to determine on a proper location for the new boundary west. I at once pointed to the Desert, or

Grand Prairie, as the spot that seemed designed by nature as the boundary
between the two nations. . . .

The Secretary thought it was going too far west, and besides included
a portion of the population of Texas purely Mexican. . . .

Alamán now suggested that Butler put his proposals in writing.
that they might be laid before the government.[52]

Butler was of the opinion that Alamán could be bribed, for
shortly before the interview above related he had written to
Jackson that he thought he held the key to unlock Alamán's
heart and the means of enlightening his understanding. Two
days after the interview he wrote that, although Alamán had
apparently withdrawn from the cabinet, he still directed the
department of foreign affairs and that part of the sum which
would be offered for Texas would probably be applied to facilitate the negotiation.[53]

A few days later Butler called the attention of the Mexican
government to the fact that the United States was ready to carry
out the boundary treaty by appointing commissioners. He again
pointed out that the line was unsatisfactory and stated that he
had received instructions to negotiate for a new boundary.[54]
Butler's proposals, however, appealed to deaf ears. Alamán had
retired from office and Francisco Fagoaga had taken his place.[55]
Revolutionary disturbances were occurring, Bustamente and
Santa Anna struggling for supremacy. At the close of 1832
they came to terms, agreeing to recognize Pedraza as president
until April 1, 1833. Early in the year elections were held, and
on March 30 Congress declared Santa Anna president.[56]

Naturally during such a period nothing was accomplished.

---

[52] Butler to Livingston, July 16, 1832, with inclosures, *House Ex. Docs.*,
25 Cong., 2 Sess., XII, Doc. 351, pp. 442–445.

[53] Rives, *The United States and Mexico*, I, 250.

[54] Butler to Monasterio, July 25, 1832, *Congressional Debates*, XIV,
Pt. 2, App., 136.

[55] Butler to Livingston, August 12, 1832. *House Ex. Docs.*, 25 Cong.,
2 Sess., XII, Doc. 351, p. 46. Fagoaga to Butler, September 12, 1832, *ibid.*,
451.

[56] Butler to Fagoaga, November 29, 1832, *ibid.*, 459–460.

No political party dared to broach so delicate a subject as the ceding of a portion of Mexican soil. The public mind was inflamed by the appearance of handbills, probably issued by governmental sanction, which charged the people and government of the United States with secret designs upon Texas; asserted that that province would be seized whenever a fit occasion offered and that the United States was watching the progress of the revolution in Texas with this in view.

Butler bided his time until February, 1833, when he imagined that Texas might be acquired by loaning money to Mexico. He wrote to Jackson:

My views are these: Suppose it is perceived that an absolute sale at this time will not be made, but that a mortgage on the territory of T—— would be given as security for the repayment of money advanced on loan: then, I ask, would it be expedient to advance as a loan that sum which we are willing to pay for the purchase, and secured by a lien on the territory as far west as the middle of the desert; and if so, shall the lien be accepted *with* or *without* receiving possession of the country? I am convinced that a loan on such terms would be tantamount to a purchase, because, in the present condition of the public treasury, years must elapse . . . before they will be in a state to meet existing engagements; and this loan would no doubt be considered, and intended from the beginning, to be extinguished by a surrender of the hypothecated territory; and, therefore, neither be a thought bestowed upon or a single effort made for its repayment, but the country suffered quietly to fall in to us. Should the proposal be made to me, as expected, I shall endeavor to simplify the transaction, by negotiating an absolute sale, if possible. Yet I confess that my hopes of success are more faint from knowing that some large grants have been recently made to persons, some of them friends of General Santa Anna, evidently with a view to the New York market; and those grantees, by uniting their influence, might have great weight in arresting the negotiation, should they discover that it was pending, because its consummation would convert all their golden prospects into moonshine. There is besides another difficulty I can forsee, which would interpose itself against an *absolute unconditional* transfer of the territory at the present moment, in the use which might be made of such an event against the party in power by their adversaries; whilst against a contract in which the territory was merely pledged for repayment of money loaned to meet the public exigency, no solid objection could be sustained.[57]

[57] Butler to Jackson, February 10, 1833, *House Ex. Docs.*, 25 Cong., 2 Sess., XII, Doc. 351, pp. 466–467.

The idea of Butler did not meet with the approval of Jackson, who sent the letter to Livingston with instructions to inform Butler that he was to bring the negotiations to a close. The thoughts in Jackson's mind were disclosed by the endorsement on the back of the letter which said, in part: "The Convention in Texas meets the 1st of next April to form a constitution for themselves. When this is done, Mexico can never annex it to her jurisdiction again, or control its legislature. It will be useless after this act to enter into a treaty of boundary with Mexico."[58]

On March 20 Livingston wrote to Butler instructing him to reject any proposal of a loan. Jackson's decision to end the negotiations regarding a new boundary, however, appears to have changed, for the instruction said: "No new instructions on the subject of the proposed cession being deemed necessary, the President has directed me to refer you to those already given on that subject."[59]

It is significant that about this time occurred the entry of Sam Houston into Texas. Houston had been in Washington and his long-standing friendship with Jackson brought them into close relationship. Dr. Robert Mayo, in his book entitled *Eight Years in Washington,* is authority for the statement that Houston was projecting a filibustering expedition into Texas of which Jackson was cognizant.[60] He entered Texas and immediately took part in the revolutionary movement then in progress.[61] He also communicated directly with Jackson at this time.[62]

It is time to return to events in Mexico. On February 14 Gonzales, the recently appointed secretary, addressed Butler on

---

[58] Quoted by Reeves, *American Diplomacy under Tyler and Polk,* 72, and by Rives, *The United States and Mexico,* I, 251.

[59] Livingston to Butler, March 20, 1833, *House Ex. Docs.,* 25 Cong., 2 Sess., XII, Doc. 351, pp. 95–96; *Congressional Debates,* XIV, Pt. 2, App., 130.

[60] Parton, *Life of Andrew Jackson,* III, 653–656.

[61] Garrison, *Texas,* 184–185; Williams, *Sam Houston,* 79–81.

[62] Crane, *Life and Select Literary Remains of Sam Houston of Texas,* 46–47.

the subject of the treaty of limits. He said that the revolution
had hindered the publication of the treaty, but it would soon be
done and commissioners would be appointed to fix the limits.[63]
Butler replied at once, urging that the treaties be promulgated
as soon as possible, as an injustice was done to American citizens
in Mexico by its being withheld.[64] On the twenty-first and again
on the twenty-seventh Butler was assured that the matter would
soon receive attention,[65] but in spite of this it was not until
September that a commissioner and surveyor were appointed.[66]

The attempts to acquire Texas met only with rebuffs and
silence. In March, Gonzales informed Butler that the government had received credible advices that Texas intended to secede
and unite with the United States;

and in order to realize this project, it appears that they are favored and
encouraged by the inhabitants of the adjacent parts of said States. His
excellency [the President] commands me to make this communication to
you, in order that your Government, in taking corresponding measures,
may adopt such precautions as will prevent any steps being taken on
the part of said inhabitants for the purpose of dismembering the national
territory. . . .[67]

In July Butler wrote to his government as follows:

I can obtain no answer to my several communications on the subject
of Texas, although I adopted the course of addressing the President an
unofficial note, calling his attention to the subject, and urging the propriety, nay, the necessity, of a prompt decision of that question; and
during all this delay we are calumniated and misrepresented to this
administration as entertaining views towards Texas of a character hostile
to the territorial integrity of Mexico, and of secretly abetting and en-
couraging the citizens of that country to throw off their allegiance to
Mexico.[68]

---

[63] Gonzalez to Butler, February 14, 1833, *Congressional Debates*, XIV,
Pt. 2, App., 136.

[64] Butler to Gonzales, February 16, 1833, *ibid.*, 136–137.

[65] Gonzales to Butler, February 21 and 27, 1833, *ibid.*, 137.

[66] García to Butler, September 25, 1833, *ibid.*, 138.

[67] Gonzales to Butler, March 2, 1833, *House Ex. Docs.*, 25 Cong., 2
Sess., XII, Doc. 351, pp. 470–471.

[68] Butler to McLane, July 26, 1833, *ibid.*, 483.

Disgusted with his failure, Butler urged that the United States occupy the territory between the Neches and the Sabine. In October he suggested that two or three hundred thousand dollars would be required to obtain the support of a certain important personage to gain his ends. Jackson refused to resort to bribery; he urged haste in the negotiations, and stated that if there were no possibility of arranging a boundary, the United States would run the line and take possession of Nacogdoches.[69]

Butler's conduct does not appear to have been such as would raise either him or his government in the opinion of the Mexicans. James S. Wilcocks, the United States Consul in Mexico City, preferred charges against him "to show that the said Butler is unworthy of and a disgrace to the office he now holds, and ought to be recalled by his Government." He charged him with immorality, seduction, usury, refusal to pay debts, assault, interference with the consular duties, and lastly,

for being a mean and despicable character; inasmuch as he himself has confessed that, before the election of General Andrew Jackson for President of the United States of America, he was in favor of Henry Clay, Esq., a candidate for that office; and seeing that General Jackson was likely to gain the election, he left Mr. Clay's party and went over to that of the General—a base, sordid and dishonorable act.[70]

Butler was informed of these charges by the Secretary of State, that he might make such explanations as he could. Without taking the trouble to investigate or waiting for Butler's defense, Jackson decided to dismiss Wilcocks; six days later the charges were sent to Butler and he was asked to find a suitable person to fill the position.[71]

In October Butler wrote to Jackson advising the military occupation of Texas by United States troops. The same month

---

[69] Barker, in *The American Historical Review*, XII, 794–796. The person referred to was Zavala. See Rives, *The United States and Mexico*, I, 253.

[70] McLane to Butler, October 12, 1833, *House Ex. Docs.*, 25 Cong., 2 Sess., XII, Doc. 351, pp. 109–111.

[71] McLane to Butler, October 18, 1833, *ibid.*, 111–112.

he again suggested to the President that several hundred thousand dollars be used in bribes. Jackson replied that he had no intention of bribery and advised Butler to be cautious.[72]

In February, 1834, Butler again expressed his opinion that bribery was the only means of acquiring Texas. A month later he urged that the United States take forcible possession, and suggested that he be placed as chief officer of the territory. On the back of the letter Jackson wrote:

A Butler. What a scamp. Carefully read. The Secretary of State will reiterate his instructions to ask an extension on the treaty for running boundary line, and then recal him, or if he has received his former instructions and the Mexican Government has refused, to recal him at once.[73]

It would appear from this that Jackson was following a straight course and that his motives were entirely above reproach, but a shadow of doubt is thrown upon the case when the fact is taken into consideration that the "scamp" was not recalled for over a year. Jackson was thoroughly aware of his worthlessness; if the President's motives had been sincerely open, the minister should have been recalled as soon as possible.[74]

Several changes were made in the personnel of the diplomatic representations during 1833. In January Augustin Yturbide, secretary of legation at Washington, was advanced to the position of chargé.[75] He held this office until June 25, being succeeded by Joaquin María del Castillo.[76] Edward Livingston retired on May 29, and Louis McLane was appointed as his successor.[77]

---

[72] Barker, in *The American Historical Review*, XII, 796.

[73] Rives, *The United States and Mexico*, I, 254–255.

[74] Barker has made an able defense of Jackson's motives in an article in *The American Historical Review*, XII, 788–809; Smith (*The Annexation of Texas*, 25–28), follows Barker closely.

[75] Gonzales to Livingston, January 25, 1833, *House Ex. Docs.*, 25 Cong., 2 Sess., XII, Doc. 351, p. 682.

[76] Yturbide to McLane, June 5, 1833, *ibid.*, 684.

[77] Moore, *A Digest of International Law*, I, p. vii.

In December Castillo informed McLane that Lieutenant Colonel Don Tomás Ramón del Moral had been appointed boundary commissioner, and Don Castillo Navarro, surveyor. He inquired if similar appointments had been made by the United States.[78]   McLane asked when the commissioners were appointed.[79]   Castillo answered that he had not been informed of the exact date; the despatch bore date of September 25, 1833. The delay, he said, was due to the recent revolution, but Mexico had shown a desire to fulfill its obligations.[80]

The additional article had been ratified on April 5, 1832, and the original treaty stated that the commissioners were to meet within a year from that date.   A commissioner and surveyor had been appointed by the United States on May 30, 1832, and notice had been given to Montoya on July 20.   McLane had learned from a report made by the Minister of Foreign Affairs to the Mexican Congress on May 20, 1833, that no commission up to that time had been appointed.   In consequence he informed Butler that the treaty of limits could not be carried into effect until a new convention was entered into, with the object of again extending the time limit.   Butler was also informed that he was to repair to the United States, and to acquaint the Mexican government with the fact that diplomatic relations would be renewed as early as practicable.[81]   This despatch, however, was delayed in transmittal, and did not reach Butler until sometime in June.[82]

While the instructions were on their way, Castillo communicated with McLane.   He remarked that the delay in the

---

[78] Castillo to McLane, December 2, 1833, *House Ex. Docs.*, 25 Cong., 1 Sess., Doc. 42, pp. 60–61.

[79] McLane to Castillo, December 31, 1833, *Congressional Debates*, XIV, Pt. 2, App., 144.

[80] Castillo to McLane, January 9, 1834, *House Ex. Docs.*, 25 Cong., 1 Sess., Doc. 42, pp. 61–62.   The date is given erroneously as 1835 in the printed document.

[81] McLane to Butler, January 13, 1834, *Congressional Debates*, XIV, Pt. 2, App., 130–131.

[82] Butler to McLane, July 1, 1834, *ibid.*, 138.

fulfillment of the treaty by his government had been unavoidable because of the disturbed condition in Mexico, "but that these circumstances should not, in any way, affect the results of the negotiations concluded; the more so, as the commissioners and surveyor of the United States, although appointed the one on the 31st of July, and the other on the 24th of September last, have not yet proceeded on their journey to the place of operations." He pointed out that nothing remained but to enter into a convention for the extension of the time limit, and that such powers would be forwarded to him on June 1.[83] The promised powers, however, did not arrive by thàt date, and on June 11 McLane sent a duplicate of his despatch authorizing Butler to negotiate an additional article to the treaty of limits.[84]

The powers to negotiate were not sent from Mexico until October 21, the delay being explained by the fact that the commissioners were dismissed and others appointed, who were to proceed without delay to Natchitoches.[85] Castillo, in December, informed Forsyth, now Secretary of State, of the appointment of commissioners, stating that Colonel Don Juan Nepomuceno Almonte had been appointed commissioner, and Lieutenant Colonel Don Pedro García Conde, mathematician.[86] Forsyth replied that the time for the meeting of the Mexican Congress was so near at hand and, Butler having been instructed to conclude the convention, it was unnecessary to reopen the matter at Washington.[87]

This brought forth a critical reply from Castillo which showed the suspicion of the American government felt by Mexico.

---

[83] Castillo to McLane, May 26, 1834, *Congressional Debates*, XIV, Pt. 2, App., 144–145.

[84] McLane to Butler, June 11, 1834, *House Ex. Docs.*, 25 Cong., 2 Sess., XII, Doc. 351, pp. 142–143.

[85] Lombardo to Forsyth, October 21, 1834, *Congressional Debates*, XIV, Pt. 2., App., 145.

[86] Castillo to Forsyth, December 4, 1834, *ibid.*, 145.

[87] Forsyth to Castillo, December 11, 1834, *ibid.*, 145–146.

The significant part of his answer was as follows:

> Now, the undersigned cannot comprehend how it is, that . . . the purpose of his Government having been from the beginning of this year, to carry on the negotiation in this country, the powers and instructions sent by this Government [United States] to Mr. Butler for the same object should, nevertheless, be received at a more advanced period, without any remark. And, even supposing that they were, in fact, received in the month of July, as Mr. Forsyth has been pleased to say, it seems to be in the highest degree extraordinary that, subsequently to this, on the 21st of October last, that is to say, nearly four months later, the positive powers and instructions which the undersigned has received within a few days should have been forwarded to him under the belief that they would not only be promptly recognized by this Government, but that the Secretary of State would see fit to take measures . . . to carry into effect the object of the said instrument. . . .
>
> The Mexican Government, in its last communication to the undersigned of the 21st of October of this year, neither mentions that Mr. Butler had presented any power, nor that he had apprised it that he had received such an instrument for the purpose of setting on foot any negotiation upon the subject of an additional article to the treaty of limits; and this, in the opinion of the undersigned, shows still more clearly that that Government has constantly preferred that the negotiation in question should be begun in this country.

He then suggested that, inasmuch as nothing had so far been done in Mexico, and as the Congress of the United States would adjourn about March 1 and the Mexican Chamber six weeks later, it would be better to conclude the convention at Washington.[88]

No reply was made to Castillo's letter, and on January 12, 1835, he again addressed Forsyth, calling attention to the fact that up to November 26 Butler had not given notice to the Mexican government of his powers to conclude the convention. He stated that this gave added reason for carrying on the negotiation at Washington. His efforts were of no avail and diplomacy continued its sinuous course in Mexico.[89]

---

[88] Castillo to Forsyth, December 15, 1834, *Congressional Debates*, XIV, Pt. 2, App., 146.

[89] Castillo to Forsyth, January 12, 1835, *ibid.*, 147.

On July 1, 1834, Butler had informed his government of the delay in the arrival of the instructions telling him to repair to the United States. In the six months' interval he had received various despatches from his state department, none of which mentioned the matter.[90] Naturally he was in somewhat of a quandary as to what course to pursue. He called attention to the fact that a new convention would have to be ratified by the General Congress, which would assemble January 1, 1835. In the meantime he asked if it would not be best to permit him to return to the United States either on leave of absence or permanently. "I am fully persuaded," he wrote, "that the public service may derive benefit from an interview either with yourself or the President, at which certain communications may be made, and opinions freely exchanged and compared, which it is impracticable to do by any other mode; and after the interview, it may be better determined whether the public interest will be more advanced by my return to Mexico, or by the appointment of a successor to the mission."[91] The request for permission to return was not complied with until the following year. The full meaning of Butler's communication will be disclosed in connection with the account of his visit to the United States.

During 1834 the American government was trying to strengthen its position in Mexico by mediation with Spain. The accession of Isabel II to the throne under the regency of her mother had been considered a favorable opportunity of renewing the offer of mediation.[92] In June affairs appeared to take on a favorable aspect,[93] and Forsyth so informed Butler, instructing him to communicate the matter at once to the Mexican govern-

---

[90] Various letters, *House Ex. Docs.*, 25 Cong., 2 Sess., XII, Doc. 351, pp. 115–142.

[91] Butler to McLane, July 1, 1834, *Congressional Debates*, XIV, Pt. 2, App., 138.

[92] McLane to Butler, April 20, 1834, *House Ex. Docs.*, 25 Cong., 2 Sess., XII, Doc. 351, pp. 118–119.

[93] De la Rosa to Van Ness, June 12, 1834, *ibid.*, 148–149.

ment.[94] Butler naturally made the most of this, dwelling at length upon the friendly and disinterested part played by the United States.[95] In the following February he was able to inform the Mexican government definitely that Spain had at length consented to treat with the various Latin American states.[96]

The intentions of the United States government concerning boundaries were disclosed by Butler in December, 1834, in a letter to Lombardo, the Secretary of State and of Foreign Relations, which said:

> By a communication received recently from the Government of the undersigned, he is instructed to propose to that of Mexico a renewal of the treaty of boundary between the two nations. . . . The undersigned forbears to urge the many cogent reasons for concluding this subject definitely, because they are too obvious to require being stated; he will merely remark that Mexico being in the occupancy of a large portion of territory which the Government of the undersigned conceives respectfully to belong to the people of the United States, and great part of which, it is understood, has already been granted under the authority of Mexico to various individuals, it becomes the more imperiously urgent that this question should promptly be disposed of. The undersigned requests, therefore, that this subject be immediately brought before his excellency, the President of the Mexican United States, with the view of concluding the treaty in time to be acted on by the Senate of the United States of America, which will adjourn on the 4th day of March ensuing.[97]

It is obvious that Butler was not playing a straight game; to speak of his instructions as *received recently* was, of course, intentional deception; he also knew that the time was probably too short to obtain a favorable action from the Mexican Chamber in time to get the matter before the United States Senate before its adjournment. He did not again address the Mexican government on the subject until January 27, 1835, and on February 7 Gutiérrez de Estrada, now Secretary of State, replied that nego-

---

[94] Forsyth to Butler, August 22, 1834, *House Ex. Docs.*, 25 Cong., 2 Sess., XII, Doc. 351, pp. 147–148.

[95] Butler to Lombardo, October 1, 1834, *ibid.*, 540–541.

[96] Butler to Gutiérrez de Estrada, February 9, 1835, *ibid.*, 551–552.

[97] Butler to Lombardo, December 21, 1834, *Congressional Debates*, XIV, Pt. 2, App., 138.

tiations were under way at Washington and he deemed it proper to await the result.[98]

On February 26 Butler wrote to Jackson, reciting the course of events in Mexico and stating that he would return in April, and hoped to bring the papers for the exchange of ratifications.

Whenever I shall have the pleasure of seeing you, it will be in my power to show you clearly that I have not been idle; that all has been done which, under present circumstances, could have been done; that everything is ripe for concluding satisfactorily *the whole subject.* I can prove almost to demonstration that in three months we may consummate every thing; that there is but one stumbling-block in the way, which *you* must remove. The explanation would be too long for a letter, independent of the documents which it is proper to lay before you, in order to command the whole ground; and I am so shortly to be with you myself, when we may confer fully, that I feel it the less necessary to write a written communication; and, moreover, the stumbling-block to whch I allude you cannot immediately remove. It will require a few months to get everything in motion; but I pledge myself to you—mark me—I give you my pledge, that your administration shall not close without seeing the object [Texas] in your possession.[99]

Again, on March 31, he wrote:

By the establishment of the true line, a door will be opened to us, through which we may enter for the satisfactory arrangement of a question of much deeper interest to us than the mere marking of a boundary line. All this will be fully, and unless I am greatly mistaken, satisfactorily explained to you by documents and other information in my possession that can be best communicated at a personal conference.[100]

These mysterious letters will be fully explained in connection with Butler's visit to Washington.

On March 29 Gutiérrez informed Butler that no steps had been taken in the negotiations at Washington, and that he and José Mariano Blasco, Secretary of the Treasury, had been authorized to negotiate with him. Matters now progressed rapidly and

[98] Gutiérrez de Estrada to Butler, February 7, 1835, *Congressional Debates,* XIV, Pt. 2, App., 138–139.

[99] Butler to Jackson, February 26, 1835, *ibid.,* 139. *House Ex. Docs.,* 25 Cong., 2 Sess., XII, Doc. 351, p. 555.

[100] Butler to Forsyth, March 31, 1835. *House Ex. Docs.,* 25 Cong., 2 Sess., XII, Doc. 351, p. 556.

on April 3 the long-delayed convention was signed, the time for the appointment of commissioners being thereby extended for a year.[101] The State Department at Washington received its information from Castillo, Butler not having informed his government of the consummation of the convention.[102]

---

[101] Castillo to Dickens, June 2, 1835, *Congressional Debates*, XIV, Pt. 2, App., 147–148.   *Treaties, Conventions,* (Malloy, ed.) I, 1099–1101.

[102] Dickens to Castillo, June 4, 1835, *Congressional Debates*, XIV, Pt. 2, App., 148.

CHAPTER VI

THE LAST YEAR OF BUTLER'S MISSION

Butler appeared in Washington in June, 1835, bringing with him the signed convention.[1] He now explained what was meant by his communication in which he had urged that he be allowed to return to the United States. He laid before the government a scheme for the acquisition of Texas by bribery, the agent to be employed being Hernández, a priest who was influential with Santa Anna. He hoped that a series of treaties might be arranged by which New Mexico and both the Californias could be acquired. Butler brought with him copies of the correspondence which he claimed to have had with Hernández; he had gone on the assumption that five million dollars was the price for Texas; but a shadow of doubt as to the recipient appears when Hernández was quoted as replying that half a million would bring the desired result.

The idea of bribery was not well received by Jackson. He was anxious to get Texas, was willing to pay for it, and would probably have winked at what was done with the money after it was paid into Mexican hands; he was at that time willing to take advantage of a revolutionary movement to obtain it, but bribery was outside of his code of ethics.[2] Nevertheless Butler was retained in the service. In replying to Butler's bribery proposal, Forsyth said:

With an anxious desire to secure the very desirable alteration in our boundary with Mexico, the President is resolved that no means of even an equivocal character shall be used to accomplish it. It is due to the occasion to say to you also, that on the examination of your communications

---

[1] Butler to Forsyth, June 9, 1835, *House Ex. Docs.*, 24 Cong., 1 Sess., VI, Doc. 256, p. 5.

on this subject, connected with your verbal explanations, no confidence is felt that your negotiation is likely to be successful; but as you entertain a confident belief that you can succeed in a very short time, it is deemed proper to give you the opportunity of benefiting your country by your exertions and of doing honor to yourself. The President, however, instructs me to say that the negotiation must be brought to a close at once, so that the result may be known by the meeting of Congress, as provision must be made, in case it is successful, for carrying it into execution. You will be expected in the United States as soon as it is closed, to report the result, whatever it may be, by December.[3]

As may be plainly seen from this, one more attempt was to be made to acquire Texas. There was to be no bribery; the government was to purchase it; but if the Mexican officials were dishonest, that was no concern of the United States. If Jackson and Forsyth were entirely sincere, they should have at once dismissed Butler and sent a man of integrity to Mexico.

In August additional instructions were sent to Butler, which read as follows:

It having been represented to the President that the port of St. Francisco, on the western coast of the United Mexican States, would be a most desirable place of resort for our numerous vessels engaged in the whaling business in the Pacific, far preferable to any to which they now have access, he has directed that an addition should be made to your instructions relative to the negotiation for Texas. The main object is to secure within our limits the whole bay of St. Francisco. If you can induce the Mexican Government to agree to any line which will effect this, you are authorized to offer a sum of [blank] in addition to the sum you were directed to offer for the first line mentioned in your original instructions upon the subject. You are to endeavor first to obtain the following boundary, which is considered the most eligible:

Beginning at the Gulf of Mexico, proceed along the eastern bank of the Rio Bravo del Norte to the 37th parallel of latitude, and thence along that parallel to the Pacific. This line may probably be supposed to approach too near, if not to include, the Mexican settlement of Monterey. If this objection should be urged, you can obviate it by explaining that we have no desire to interfere with the actual settlements of Mexico on

2 Reeves, *American Diplomacy under Tyler and Polk*, 73–74.

3 Forsyth to Butler, July 2, 1835, *Congressional Debates*, XIV, Pt. 2. App., 131.

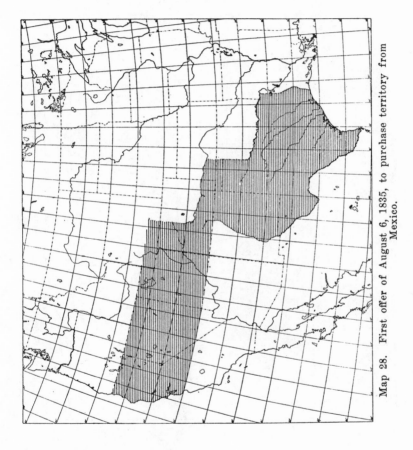

Map 28.   First offer of August 6, 1835, to purchase territory from Mexico.

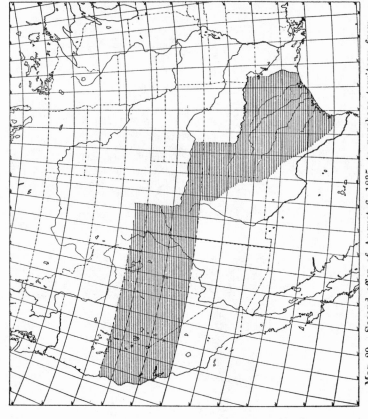

Map 29. Second offer of August 6, 1835, to purchase territory from
Mexico.

that coast, and you may agree to any provision affecting the great object of securing the bay of St. Francisco, and excluding Monterey and the territory in its immediate neighborhood.

As it is not deemed essential to obtain the Rio Bravo del Norte for our western boundary, if any objection should be made to it, you may next propose the western line specified in your original instructions, but stopping at the 37th parallel, or at any other line that would include the bay of St. Francisco, and proceeding along such line to the Pacific . . .

If, however, you cannot obtain a southern line which will include within our limits the whole bay of St. Francisco, you will proceed under your original instructions, and bring the negotiations to a close.[4]

Further evidence of Jackson's intentions is to be found in a confidential communication to Colonel Juan N. Almonte relating to Texan affairs. This document contains a letter from David Lee Child of New Rochelle, dated September 15, 1835. Child wrote to Almonte that certain slaveholding countrymen cherished the intention of wresting Texas from Mexico and that the Honorable Hutchins G. Burton of North Carolina had purchased 40,000 acres of land in Texas. His letter continued:

Week before last, he [Burton] was in Philadelphia and declared to a *near relative* residing there (a respectable man and an earnest abolitionist) that the reason of his making said purchase, was that Texas was soon to be annexed to the United States, that President Jackson had declared to him at the city of Washington on the occasion of calling as he passed through that city about three weeks ago, that we *must have it* either by *negotiation or force*; that if 10,000 men would not do, 100,000 should, and that it was his intention to make said Burton first governor of the Territory.

Child stated that Jackson had made the same declaration to two other persons within a few weeks.[5]

---

[4] Forsyth to Butler, August 6, 1835, *Congressional Debates*, XIV, Pt. 2, App., 131. Bancroft (*History of California*, III, 400, note 33) says the amount was five million dollars. Reeves (*American Diplomacy under Tyler and Polk*, 75) says, "He [Butler] was finally recalled after he had been instructed to press for a cession of Texas and California as far north as San Francisco." Regarding California this is evidently an error, as the United States wanted the territory north of a line which would reach the Pacific near Monterey Bay—in other words, the northern half of California.

[5] Bolton, *Guide to the Archives of Mexico*, 360. That Burton was offered the governorship of Texas is confirmed by Kennedy, *Texas*, II, 297.

The rapidly developing revolution in Texas and the determined attitude of the Mexican government, however, made
abortive any attempt on the part of the United States to acquire
Mexican territory.[6]

The conduct of Butler had brought him under suspicion and
on October 31 his recall was demanded. The letter in part read:

His excellency the acting President, desiring to remove every motive
that may disturb the good understanding between this republic and those
States, and it being manifest to him that public opinion is very unfavorable towards Mr. Anthony Butler, their chargé d'affaires near this supreme
Government, to whom are imputed intrigues unbecoming a diplomatic
agent, which imputation is strengthened by the present occurrences in
Texas, the revolt there having commenced whilst that gentleman was in
those parts; and it being his excellency's wish that his retirement should
be brought about in the usual and established way, that the obvious
necessity of tendering him a passport may be avoided, I am directed to
instruct you to solicit from those States, in the manner at once the most
prudent and the most compatible with the dignity of the Government,
the recall of the aforesaid Mr. Anthony Butler, with the understanding
that such a measure will be no personal degradation or blemish to the
character of that gentleman.[7]

On December 16 Forsyth informed Butler that his mission
would terminate at the end of the month. The Mexican minister
presented his request for the recall, but was informed that the
United States government had already determined upon the
immediate appointment of a successor.[8]

Powhatan Ellis was the new appointee;[9] he was instructed
to do all in his power to allay the suspicions of the Mexican
government and people concerning the views and intentions of
the United States government. In regard to the boundary convention, he was informed that the United States Senate had
approved it, that it had been ratified by the Mexican government,

---

[6] Bancroft, *North Mexican States and Texas*, II, 152–174.

[7] Secretary of State of Mexico to Castillo, October 31, 1835, *House Ex.
Docs.*, 25 Cong., 2 Sess., XII, Doc. 351, p. 719.

[8] Forsyth to Butler, December 16, 1835, *ibid.*, 158.

[9] Forsyth to Ellis, January 8, 1836, *ibid.*, 159.

and when ratified by the President of the United States, the ratifications would be exchanged at Washington. He was also to press the settlement of numerous claims, many of which were of long standing.[10] Ellis did not arrive in Mexico until some time in April, 1836, and Butler during the interim continued his weird course.[11]

A change also occurred at this time in the Mexican legation at Washington, Manuel Eduardo Gorostiza being appointed in January; the former chargé d'affaires was to continue and Gorostiza was to act in the capacity of envoy extraordinary and minister plenipotentiary. The Mexican government considered that the pending questions, meaning no doubt the question of Texas and American neutrality, required a representative of the highest rank and ability.[12] Gorostiza arrived at Washington in March and was immediately presented to Jackson.[13]

The boundary convention at once became the subject of several diplomatic notes. Forsyth claimed that the wording of the convention was ambiguous; after considerable inconsequential discussion the matter was adjusted,[14] and the ratifications were exchanged on April 20, 1836.[15]

It is time to return to Butler's proceedings in Mexico. He was aware that his tenure of office was short and that he had been returned for the purpose of ending the negotiations for the acquisition of Texas, and if possible a part of California. He had not succeeded and, as the year drew to a close, was uncertain of his standing. While he held out little hope to his

---

10 Forsyth to Ellis, January 29, 1836, *House Ex. Docs.*, 25 Cong., 2 Sess., XII, Doc. 351, pp. 160–162.

11 Ellis to Forsyth, April 30, 1836, *ibid.*, 591.

12 Monasterio to Forsyth, January 19, 1836, *ibid.*, 725–726.

13 Gorostiza to Forsyth, and Forsyth to Gorostiza, March 24, 1836, *ibid.*, 732–733.

14 Gorostiza to Forsyth, March 28, 1836; Forsyth to Gorostiza, April 1, 1836; Gorostiza to Forsyth, April 4, 1836; Forsyth to Gorostiza, April 13, 1836; Gorostiza to Forsyth, April 18, 1836; Forsyth to Gorostiza, April 18, 1836, *ibid.*, 149–152.

15 *Treaties, Conventions,* (Malloy, ed.) I, 1099.

government of acquiring California, he was still willing to continue to try. He wrote that the State Department had

fallen into a geographical error, by supposing the bay of San Francisco to be located as high as latitude N. 38½° where you [Forsyth] have placed it, and north of the town of Monterey, in the Upper California. There are two bays on the Pacific known as la bahia San Francisco; the lower, or most southern, is in latitude 31° N., on the line where the upper and lower California unite. The upper, and most northern bay, is in latitude 32° N., in the higher California. The bay to which you refer, is named *Puerto Antonio Nuevo*, at the head of which is a small town, called San Francisco, and which I suppose, caused the error. The name of the bay is, however, unimportant, and the error nothing, because comprehending very clearly the object which you desire to attain, my efforts will not be restrained by the mere mistake in names, and I have no doubt of obtaining *the privilege* of using the port as you desire, but at present nothing beyond.

According to this, Butler was striving to gain practically all of California instead of the northern half and wished to acquaint his government with the fact. The acquisition of territory was cloaked in the words, *"the privilege* of using the port as you desire,"* if the writer has correctly interpreted the italics of Butler's letter.[16]

On January 15 Butler informed his government that his letter of recall had been received; he said that it was welcome news and that under no circumstances would he have remained in Mexico longer than April:

Nothing but the deep interest which I felt in seeing the affair of Texas brought to a successful conclusion would have induced me to remain here so long. The affair in so far as regards our Government, may perhaps be considered as at present concluded; and how far my failure in effecting the object may be attributed to the indiscretion of certain persons who affect to be in the confidence of the President, and to retail his opinions and declare his purposes, will be for aftertimes to disclose. I am in possession of all the facts—and a precious collection they are. This and the movement in Texas, suspended for the moment all my operations.[17]

---

[16] Butler to Forsyth, December 27, 1835, *House Ex. Docs.*, 25 Cong., 2 Sess., XII, Doc. 351, pp. 566–567.

[17] Butler to Forsyth, January 15, 1836, *ibid.*, 573–574.

Butler remained as the representative of the United States until the arrival of Ellis in April, shortly after the battle of San Jacinto.[18] The acquisition of Texas could no longer be a subject of diplomatic negotiation or sharp bargaining. Incensed public opinion would not consent to the territory passing into American hands. An attempt to annex it meant war with Mexico.

The withdrawal of Butler was as undignified as his diplomacy. Conscious of his diplomatic failure, he seemed bent on causing trouble. He had ordered a wagon built in the United States which he had intended to use on his return. When it arrived at Vera Cruz, the collector asked that duty be paid on it. According to the Mexican custom, the exemption from registry for diplomatic agents was limited to the goods introduced upon arrival and six months thereafter. Butler objected to paying the duty, whereupon Monasterio, the secretary of foreign relations, inquired of Ellis regarding the usage in the United States respecting the rights of agents whose commissions were at an end.[19] Ellis replied that the agent retained his privileges until he made a report of his embassy to his government,[20] a view in which Monasterio acquiesced, and the wagon was released.[21]

Not succeeding in provoking a quarrel with the Department of Interior and Exterior Relations, Butler next turned upon General Tornel, the minister of war, whom he credited with being the author of an attack upon him which had recently appeared in print.[22] Butler addressed an insulting letter to Tornel, a document which is so remarkable and gives such an insight into the character of Butler that it seems worthy of giving in full.

Sir: After my letter of a few days ago had been delivered to you, I heard that you were confined to your chamber by indisposition; and although it was my intention to address you again, I refrained from doing

---

[18] Ellis to Forsyth, April 30, 1836, *House Ex. Docs.*, 25 Cong., 2 Sess., XII, Doc. 351, p. 591.

[19] Monasterio to Ellis, July 23, 1836, *ibid.*, 595.

[20] Ellis to Monasterio, July 28, 1836, *ibid.*, 596.

[21] Monasterio to Ellis, August 2, 1836, *ibid.*, 597.

[22] Ellis to Forsyth, August 22, 1836, *ibid.*, 597–598.

so until your health was re-established. That time, it seems, has arrived; and I proceed to carry into effect my intention of once more addressing you.

When I despatched my first letter to you, I had two objects in view; one was to apprize you that I had very correct information of your malicious and contemptible proceedings; and the other was to insult you in terms so direct and gross as might excite you to resent them. Your dastardly spirit has disappointed me in the last, and shown you equally destitute of the honor of a gentleman and the courage of a soldier; and could I now imagine any form of insult by which you could be roused into resentment, there are no words, however energetic and offensive, that I would not employ to effect the purpose. I have, however, no hope of success from such an attempt because I feel convinced that you are alike recreant to every sentiment and feeling of the gentleman and the soldier, and that your cowardly heart would quail at the idea of meeting openly and on equal terms him whom you had secretly assailed with all the malice of a demon. Under such circumstances, no course remains for me but to inflict upon you the chastisement appropriate to your character. You must be taught by stripes to know yourself, and to enable your brother officers to estimate you according to your merits, and to know how unworthy you are of the military uniform which you wear only to disgrace. This lesson will be given by me on the first occasion of meeting with you, and, as I take no secret advantage of any man, you are now apprized of my intentions, that you may go prepared; for be assured that meet you when or where I may, you shall receive the discipline of my cane or horsewhip. Should your caution enable you to elude the promised chastisement, I will then, before my departure from Mexico, expose you to this community. You shall be held up to the public gaze an object of scorn and contempt, and show how completely the fable of the ass in the lion's skin is realized in the person of him who, by official courtesy, is saluted as ''his excellency General Tornel.''[23]

Monasterio immediately sent a sharp reprimand to Butler. He said that his conduct was insulting and menacing to Tornel, that he had attempted to provoke a challenge, and that duelling was a crime in Mexico. He ordered Butler to depart within eight days and to advise the government as to the route he desired to take.[24] Monasterio also wrote to Ellis, stating that Butler's insults and threats ought to be considered as injuries to the

---

[23] *House Ex. Docs.*, 25 Cong., 2 Sess., Doc. 351, p. 600. The letter is undated, but was sent early in August.

[24] Monasterio to Butler, August 8, 1836, *ibid.*, 599.

supreme government, and he therefore asked due satisfaction from the United States.[25]

Butler refused to leave until his private affairs were arranged. Monasterio accordingly had an interview with Ellis. He said that no unfriendly feeling existed toward the United States, but Butler's conduct had been so irregular and offensive toward a member of the government, that he could not permit him to remain. Ellis replied that he regretted that a personal disagreement had occurred, but suggested that Butler was entitled to respect and protection as long as he remained in the country. He said that the publication complained of was of such a nature as to demand the interposition of the Mexican authorities. Monasterio answered that this would have been conceded, but Butler had given the government no opportunity to act. Ellis finally concluded that he was unwilling to act in such a matter until he heard from Washington.[26]

The Mexican government waited for some time without attempting to force Butler to leave, but as he did not depart, on September 7 Monasterio addressed him, saying that he had not even replied to the note requesting his withdrawal, and that the President hoped that he would leave the capital within eight days, and get out of the country within the shortest possible time.[27] Butler's answer was such as would provoke the wrath of the official still more. He said that he was justified in his course, as the original order to leave appeared to be unofficial, and, in consequence, he had been uncertain as to what course to pursue, and he had not replied, as he did not know whether to address Monasterio in a public or private capacity. He said that he was innocent of crime and that the government had taken up a private quarrel. He pointed out that Monasterio had the power, but not the right, to expel a foreign agent. He then

[25] Monasterio to Ellis, August 10, 1836, *House Ex. Docs.*, 25 Cong., 2 Sess., Doc. 351, pp. 598–599.

[26] Ellis to Forsyth, August 22, 1836, *ibid.*, 597–598.

[27] Monasterio to Butler, September 7, 1836, *ibid.*, 606.

warned the minister against Tornel, and said that he would depart as soon as he could wind up his affairs.[28]

In the latter part of September he informed Monasterio that he was ready to start and intended to return to the United States by way of Matamoras. He asked for a passport, a letter of security, a letter to the commandant at Matamoros and an escort of not to exceed twelve men.[29] Monasterio promptly refused to allow him to go by way of Matamoros because of the rebellion in Texas, and asked what other route he would take, promising that a passport would be granted.[30]

Butler answered that he had a right to go as he pleased and the United States would see that justice was done. As he did not wish to take chances on the climate of Vera Cruz and New Orleans, he said that there was no alternative but to go by Tampico. He complained that he might never arrive there, as he was aware of a plot to assassinate him on the way. As to a passport, the Mexican government might do as it saw fit; if one were not issued, he would go in spite of it.[31]

Monasterio replied that Butler's declaration concerning a passport was surprising, as no one was allowed to embark without one. He stated that he would send him one to journey where he pleased except through Texas. He asked for details concerning the alleged conspiracy in order that the government might proceed against the guilty, and offered an escort. If Butler departed without one, the government refused to assume any responsibility for his safety.[32]

A passport was issued, but Butler returned it, on the grounds that it was degrading to accept one which restricted his route. He said that he had intended to go by Tampico, but now withdrew this and would use his own discretion. He refused to

---

[28] Butler to Monasterio, September 9, 1836, *House Ex. Docs.*, 25 Cong., 2 Sess., Doc. 351, pp. 606–610.

[29] Butler to Monasterio, n. d., *ibid.*, 611–612.

[30] Monasterio to Butler, September 24, 1836, *ibid.*, 612.

[31] Butler to Monasterio, September 26, 1836, *ibid.*, 613–614.

[32] Monasterio to Butler, October 6, 1836, *ibid.*, 614–615.

present a complaint about a conspiracy, saying that he had learned about it from a French doctor named Du Perc but he treated the rumor with contempt.[33] The Mexican government at once began an investigation of the alleged conspiracy,[34] but found nothing definite concerning it.[35]

On October 11 Butler left the capital without a passport, taking the northern route, which went through Texas. Acting President Corro called a cabinet meeting to which Ellis was invited. The object of the meeting was to express surprise and regret at Butler's action. The President stated that he had a right to interdict all communication with Texas and especially to one whom he had every reason to believe was attached to the Texan cause. He was willing to refer the whole matter to Ellis, but the American minister insisted that he had no power to control Butler.[36]

The government at Washington disapproved entirely of the actions of Butler. Instructions were sent to Ellis so to inform the Mexican government, but they did not reach him before his departure, and that government was left, unfortunately, in ignorance of the fact for several months, at a period when conditions were most critical. On March 1, 1837, a communication of the views of the United States government was made to Castillo at Washington,[37] but coming thus tardily and almost simultaneously with the recognition of Texan independence, the information could hardly be looked upon by Mexico other than as hypocrisy.

---

[33] Butler to Monasterio, October 6, 1836, *House Ex. Docs.*, 25 Cong., 2 Sess., Doc. 351, pp. 616–617.

[34] Monasterio to Ellis, October 18, 1836, *ibid.*, 605.

[35] Monasterio to Ellis, October 21, 1836, *ibid.*, 617.

[36] Ellis to Forsyth, November 5, 1836, *ibid.*, 604–605.

[37] Forsyth to Castillo, March 1, 1837, *ibid.*, 750.

CHAPTER VII

THE INDIANS OF TEXAS AND THE POLICY OF THE REVOLUTIONARY GOVERNMENT

In January, 1836, General Edmund P. Gaines was ordered to the southwestern frontier, the reasons assigned being the preservation of neutrality, the prevention of a violation of American soil, and the holding of the border Indians in check. Before an intelligent exposition of the incident can be given, it is necessary to examine the Indian situation in Texas. As there is no monograph on the subject, and the material is widely scattered, the writer feels justified in giving a fuller statement regarding the location of tribes and the policy of the Texan revolutionary government toward them, than the subject would otherwise warrant.[1]

The Indians of Texas should properly be divided into two groups, those which, so far as known, were indigenous, and those which were immigrants. In turn the immigrant Indians were in two groups, those impelled by hostile northern tribes, a movement which occurred mainly in the eighteenth century, and the immigration which was the result of the advance of the white man's frontier, a movement occurring in the first three decades of the nineteenth century. For the purposes of this study, the discussion will be confined to the Indians of northern, eastern, and central Texas, as the tribes of the upper and middle Rio Grande and Pecos River region in no way immediately affect our story.

---

[1] Since the above was written Professor Bolton's work on De Mézières has appeared, in which will be found a more complete account of the Texan tribes and an excellent map showing their location.

Of the indigenous tribes, the most northern were the Caddo, most of whom lived from time immemorial in the Red River valley above the site of the modern town of Natchitoches. The term Caddo is here used in the restricted sense, meaning the compact group of tribes which dwelt in that region, and does not include the Eyeish, Hasinai, and others of the Caddoan linguistic group. The villages of the Caddo were located from a few miles above Natchitoches to, and above, the great bend of Red River in southwestern Arkansas; these were known as the Grand Caddo. The principal tribes were the Cadodachos or Caddo proper, the Natchitoches, Adaes, Yatassí, Nassonites, and Natsoos. In the Sodo Creek region, near Caddo Lake to the south of Red River, lived a less numerous branch known as the Petit Caddo. In 1800 a portion of the Red River group moved over to the Sodo Creek lands and they were still there in 1829. The advance of the whites who desired the Red River lands caused the United States in 1835 to enter into a treaty with the Caddo of that region, by which they ceded their holdings and agreed to move beyond the boundaries of the United States, the result being an influx of Caddo among those who had previously removed to Sulphur Creek, although a portion of them remained in their former haunts.[2]

The Eyeish or Ais lived about Ayish Bayou between the Arroyo Attoyac and the Sabine. The tribe was small, being decimated by war and disease. In 1779 there were only twenty families, and in 1805 Sibley claimed, although probably erroneously, that there were but twenty members left; they appear to have removed subsequently to lands between the Brazos and

---

2 Hodge, *Handbook of American Indians,* I, 179–181; Sibley, in *Annals of Congress,* 9 Cong., 2 Sess., App., 1076–1077; *Mapa original de Texas, por el ciudadano Estevan F. Austin, presentado al Exmo. Sor. Presidente, por su autor 1829,* referred to henceforth as Austin's map; Bureau of Am. Ethnology, *18th Ann. Rpt.,* Pt. 2, pp. 754–755, also Plate 5; Bolton, *Native Tribes of Texas and Western Louisiana in the Eighteenth Century,* MS., referred to hereafter as Bolton MS; Riley to Gaines, August 24, 1836, *House Ex. Docs.,* 25 Cong., 2 Sess., XII, Doc. 351, pp. 815–818; *Tex. Dipl. Corr.,* I, 25–49, calendar citation of numerous documents.

Colorado rivers, and in 1828 there were said to be one hundred and sixty families.[3]

The Hasinai or Texas group was an important confederation occupying the upper Neches and Angelina valleys. While of Caddoan stock, as were the Eyeish, they appear to have been entirely separated from the Red River Caddo. This confederation was the Great Kingdom of the Texas which played such an important part in the early Spanish missionary efforts in eastern Texas. The exact number of their villages cannot now be determined, but at least eleven have been located with reasonable certainty. In the early part of the eighteenth century they numbered about four thousand, but epidemics, poor food. and war rapidly decimated them.[4]

Between the Hasinai and the coast were three small tribes, the Bidai, Arkokisa or Orcoquisa, and the Attacapa. The Bidai were located between the Trinity and the Brazos just below the San Antonio road; in 1800 their number was estimated at about one hundred. The Arkokisa were on the lower Trinity. The Attacapa had originally occupied a large domain extending from the Calcasieu River in Louisiana along the coast to the Neches, but they, like the Bidai and Arkokisa, were greatly reduced in numbers by the early part of the nineteenth century.[5]

Following the coast, the shores and islands of Matagorda Bay were inhabited by the Karankawa. The principal tribes of this group were the Cujane, Carancaguas, Guapite, Coco, and Copane. Bolton, to whose research is due the greater part of what is known of them, says: "The Carancaguases dwelt most commonly on the narrow fringe of islands extending along the coast to the

---

[3] Bolton, in Texas State Historical Association, *The Quarterly*, XI, 255; Sibley, in *Annals of Cong.*, 9 Cong., 2 Sess., App., 1078; Hodge, *Handbook of American Indians*, I, 448–449.

[4] Bolton, in Texas State Historical Association, *The Quarterly*, XI, 249–276, XII, 147–157; Clark, *Beginnings of Texas;* Buckley, in Texas State Historical Association, *The Quarterly*, XV, 1–65.

[5] Hodge, *Handbook of American Indians*, I, 87–88, 114, 145; Austin's map; Bolton MS.

east and west of Matagorda Bay; the Cocos on the mainland east of Matagorda Bay about the lower Colorado River; the Cujanes and Guapites on either side of the bay, particularly to the west of it; and the Copanes west of the mouth of the San Antonio River about Copano Bay, to which the tribe has given its name.'' The Karankawan group contained four or five hundred warriors in the eighteenth century, but as they were the first to bear the brunt of the fight against the *empresarios* and their settlers, the tribes were soon greatly reduced.[6]

To the southwest of the Karankawa were numerous tribes of which little is as yet known. They have been grouped arbitrarily by ethnologists under the geographic name of Coahuiltican. According to Bolton they were once very numerous. Ravages of Apaches greatly decreased them and confined them to the coast regions.[7]

Inland above the Karankawa lived the Tonkawan group, acting as a buffer between the plains Indians on the one hand and the Karankawa and Hasinai on the other. The most important tribes were the Tonkawa, from whom the group was named, the Ervipiame, Yojaune, and Mayeye, the two latter being in part absorbed by the Tonkawa in the latter part of the eighteenth century. On their southern border were several other tribes, the Sana, Emet, Cavas, Toho, and Tohaha, which were probably of the same linguistic stock. They, the Tonkawa and their neighbors, lived in no fixed habitations, but their most usual range was between the middle and upper Trinity on the northeast, the San Gabriel and Colorado on the southwest, and above the San Antonio road. Various estimates have been made of their numbers. In 1778 they were estimated as having three hundred warriors; in 1805 Sibley says there were two hundred men; Davenport in 1809 placed them at two hundred and fifty

---

[6] Bolton, in Texas State Historical Association, *The Quarterly*, X, 113–119; Yoakum, *History of Texas*, I, 221–226.

[7] Hodge, *Handbook of American Indians*, I, 314–315.

families; and later reports at even less.[8] The Aranama, a small
tribe dwelling near the modern town of Goliad, were usually
allied with them after 1760. In 1822 about one hundred and
twenty-five of these were living along the San Antonio River.[9]

The central plains of Texas were the pastures of the buffalo,
a common hunting-ground where no tribe could dwell in security.
From northern Texas, impelled by other tribes, into this open
space came the eastern Apache. Recent investigations made
by W. E. Dunn have made known something of the early movements of these peoples.

The principal divisions of the Apache of Texas were the
Ypande or Lipan, the Natagés, the Mescalero, and Jumano.
Many other tribal names appear in the Spanish documents, such
as Yxandi, Chenti, Melenudo, Salinero, and Pelon. The tribe,
however, which most affected the history of eastern Texas was
the Lipan. When first known to the Spanish in the early eighteenth century, they lived to the northwest of San Antonio on
the upper courses of the Red, Brazos, and Colorado rivers.
Pushed southward by the Comanche, they gradually advanced.
until by 1750 many of them were located on the Medina and
others on the Rio Grande. The Natagés and Mescalero dwelt far
to the southwestward along the Pecos and Rio Grande, although
there were a few Natagés on the Medina in 1750. They were
never very numerous, but their mobility and aggressiveness led
to greatly exaggerated reports of their numbers. Usually the
other tribes looked upon them as a common enemy. They were
still occupying southern Texas when the *empresarios* came.[10]

The second great division of tribes found in Texas were those
which were forced down from the north. The details are obscure
and the causes of the movement somewhat problematical. The

[8] Hodge, *Handbook of American Indians*, II, 778–783.

[9] *Ibid.*, I, 72.

[10] Dunn, in Texas State Historical Association, *The Quarterly*, XIV,
198–274. A study of the Jumano was recently published by Bolton, in
Texas State Historical Association, *The Quarterly*, XV, 66–84.

tribes involved were the eastern Apache, Comanche, Wichita, Kiowa, Kiowa Apache, and a portion of the Pawnee. The movement appears to have originated through a shifting of the Sioux and other tribes, which occupied a large part of the Missouri River region. In regard to the movement Hodge says:

According to tradition the Mandan and Hidatsa reached the upper Missouri from the n[orth]e[ast], and, impelled by the Dakota, moved slowly upstream to their present location. Some time after the Hidatsa reached the Missouri internal troubles broke out, and part, now called the Crows, separated and moved westward to the neighborhood of the Yellowstone r[iver]. The Dakota formerly inhabited the forest region of s[outhern] Minnesota, and do not seem to have gone out upon the plains until hard pressed by the Chippewa, who had been supplied with guns by the French. According to all the evidence available, traditional and otherwise, the . . . Iowa, Oto, and Missouri, separated from the Winnebago or else moved westward to the Missouri from the same region. The five remaining tribes of this group—Omaha, Ponca, Osage, Kansa, and Quapaw . . . undoubtedly lived together as one tribe at some former time and were probably located on the Mississippi. Part moving farther down became known as "downstream people," Quapaw, while those who went up were the "upstream people," Omaha. These latter moved n[orth]w[est] along the river and divided into the Osage, Kansa, Ponca, and Omaha proper.[11]

Here then, it appears to the writer, was the *motif* for the migration of the tribes, the vanguard of which appeared in Texas, probably in the last half of the seventeenth century.

The Comanche were a Shoshonean tribe which originally lived in Wyoming. Attacked by the Sioux and other tribes, they were forced southward. By 1700 they had reached the Panhandle and gradually occupied the buffalo plains on the headwaters of the Arkansas, Red, Trinity, and Brazos rivers, although their war and hunting parties traversed a much wider space, being encountered from the plains of the Platte to the mountain fastnesses of Chihuahua. They were called horse Indians and were the finest horsemen of the plains. They were divided into twelve

---

[11] Hodge, *Handbook of American Indians*, II, 577–579.

bands, but were usually spoken of simply as Comanche. Their numbers have been greatly exaggerated, but no doubt there were several thousand of them.[12]

To the east of the Comanche were the Wichita, pushed southward apparently by the same forces as their neighbors. They took up their residence lower down on the same watercourses. The principal tribes were the Tawokani, Taovayas, Kichai, and Yscanis. The Waco were a branch of the Tawokani; the Wichita proper, from which the group derives its name, were of little importance and were probably incorporated with the Taovayas. About 1777 or 1778, the Taovayas were joined by the Pani-maha, a Pawnee tribe variously known as the Ouvaes, Aguajes, or Aguichi, who appear to have remained permanently near them. In the eighteenth century the probable number of the Wichita group was about four thousand; in 1824 there were about twenty-eight hundred, and their numbers continued to decrease because of wars with the whites and Osage.[13]

To the west of the Comanche and closely allied with them were the Kiowa, who migrated across the Arkansas early in the nineteenth century. They usually ranged along the upper waters of the Arkansas and Canadian rivers. With the Comanche they continually harried the frontiers of Mexico and Texas, appearing as far south as Durango. Another tribe always closely associated with the Comanche and Kiowa were the Kiowa Apache, their chief range being between the Platte and the frontier of New Mexico, although occasionally joining in depredations on the eastern settlements.[14]

The third great class of Indians was made up of those who moved into Texas directly from the United States. The great migration occurred between 1819 and 1830, and was indirectly or directly due to three causes, the cession of the lands east of the Mississippi in 1763, and to the two waves of emigration to

---

[12] Hodge, *Handbook of American Indians*, I, 327–329.
[13] *Ibid.*, II, 701–704, 705–707, 947–949; Bolton MS.
[14] Hodge, *Handbook of American Indians*, I, 699–703.

the west, the first of which followed the Revolutionary War and the other the War of 1812.[15]   Eastern Texas was an inviting ground for the hard-pressed Indians, for the revolutionary, filibustering, and piratical operations after 1810, as far as the white man was concerned, had practically depopulated the country between the Colorado and the Sabine.   The tribes which sought new lands in Texas were the Alabama, Coshatto, Cherokee, Kickapoo, Choctaw, Delaware, Shawnee, Biloxi, and Creek.[16]

After the French cessions of 1763, about one hundred and twenty of the Alibamu, familiarly called Alabama, left their former haunts on the Alabama River and established themselves about sixty miles above New Orleans.   Later they moved to western Louisiana, and sometime before 1819 settled in Texas between the Sabine and Trinity rivers above the Opelousas road.[17]

About the same time the Coshatoo, a small Florida tribe, migrated to Texas, settling in the Caddo country.   In 1829, Austin located them near the Alabama on the east bank of the Trinity River south of the Bidai.[18]

A far more important migration occurred, probably in the winter of 1819–20, namely, that of the Cherokee.   As they are more intimately connected with the Gaines incident than any of the other tribes, a history of their sojourn in Texas will be reserved until later in the chapter, only such information being here inserted as will fix their place.

At the close of the Revolutionary War, the so-called hunter class of Cherokee abandoned their villages in the Appalachian Mountains, emigrating to the White River in Arkansas and Louisiana.   Others followed, until about six thousand lived west

---

[15] U. S. Census, 1900, *Statistical Atlas*, Plates II–V, show the movement of white population.

[16] Winkler, in Texas State Historical Association, *The Quarterly*, VII, 97.   For filibusters and pirates, see Garrison, *Texas*, 110–124.

[17] Hodge, *Handbook of American Indians*, I, 43–44; Austin's map; Padilla, *Report on Texas Tribes*, 7.

[18] Morse, *Report to the Secretary of War on Indian Affairs*, Appendix, 257; Austin's map.

of the Mississippi. Troubles ensuing with the native tribes, the United States government interfered. Sixty warriors under their chief, Richard Fields, crossed into Texas, and being friendly with the Caddo, settled south of Red River in the region disputed by the Caddo and prairie tribes. Receiving frequent acquisitions, they gradually occupied the lands between the Sabine and Trinity rivers as far down as the San Antonio road, in which neighborhood they remained until expelled in 1839[19]

As early as 1763, and perhaps earlier, some of the Choctaw left their homes in Mississippi and Georgia, and migrated west of the Mississippi where they evidently encroached upon the Caddo, for in 1780 some of them were at war with that nation. About 1809 a Choctaw village was known to exist on Wichita River and another on Bayou Chicot in Louisiana. By 1820, according to Morse, more than a thousand had located on the Sabine and Neches rivers southeast of the Cherokee, and about one hundred and forty near Pecan Point on Red River.[20]

In 1789 a band of Delaware received permission from the Spanish government to take up lands in Missouri near Cape Girardeau, where, in 1793, they were joined by some Shawnee. The extensive white emigration into Missouri from the United States, which began to be considerable after the Louisiana Purchase, caused them to abandon their lands in 1815, most of them moving to southwestern Missouri. Between 1820 and 1822 several hundred of these discontented people moved over into Texas. By 1820 about seven hundred Delaware had located near the Caddo south of Red River near Pecan Point, thus being neighbors of the Choctaw. A large party of Shawnee settled in the same region in 1822.[21]

---

[19] Winkler, in Texas State Historical Association, *The Quarterly*, VII, 95–100, 108–112; Garrison, *Texas*, 234.

[20] Hodge, *Handbook of American Indians*, I, 288–289; Austin's map.

[21] Winkler, in Texas State Historical Association, *The Quarterly*. VII, 129–131; Hodge, *Handbook of American Indians*, I, 385–387, II, 535–537; Am. Bureau of Ethnology, *18th Ann. Rpt.*, II, 692–693, 724–725; Spencer, in *Missouri Historical Review*, III, 291–292.

Another tribe which found its way into Texas was the Kickapoo. From the authorities at hand it is impossible to determine as to the exact time of their arrival, but in 1826 they were there in force and were especially hostile to the whites. Austin located them on the upper Trinity and Sabine rivers.[22]

The Biloxi, a small tribe from the Mobile Bay region, moved into Louisiana as early as 1763, and eventually settled about forty miles below Natchitoches. A part of them moved into Texas. for in 1828 twenty families resided on the east side of the Neches. About the same number also resided among the Caddo on Red River. Others may have found their way as far as Little River, a branch of the Brazos.[23]

The Quapaw or Arkensa in the eighteenth century were living on the Arkansas and White rivers. In 1805 three of their villages were located on the south side of the Arkansas, twelve miles above Arkansas Post. Like the coming of the Kickapoo and Biloxi, the exact date of their entrance into Texas is obscure, but in 1828 one hundred and fifty families had found a home on Sulphur Creek, a southern tributary of Red River.[24]

In 1834 the Creeks attempted to obtain lands near Nacogdoches, but both Cherokee and American settlers objected so strenuously that the attempt was abandoned.[25]

This, so far as ascertained, completes the enumeration of immigrant tribes. It is noticeable that all of them congregated in northeastern Texas in the country most readily accessible from the United States. There, under the leadership of Fields, the Cherokee chieftain, and his successor, Bowles, with the contiguous native tribes, they became known as the "associated bands." This powerful confederation, welded together by a common hatred for the American settlers who had deprived them

[22] Winkler, in Texas State Historical Association, *The Quarterly,* VII, 145; Austin's map.

[23] Hodge, *Handbook of American Indians,* I, 147.

[24] *Ibid.,* II, 333–337; Sibley, in *Annals of Cong.,* 9 Cong., 2 Sess., App., 108,–1088.

[25] Yoakum, *History of Texas,* I, 328.

of their ancient hunting-grounds, became a menace to the Texan immigrants, and proved to be a strong factor in moulding the southwestern frontier policy of the United States.

In 1822 Richard Fields, the Cherokee chief, led a deputation to Mexico for the purpose of obtaining a land grant from the government. They were allowed to remain in Texas, but were not given a legal title to their lands. In 1824 Fields held a great council of the Indians of northeastern Texas at the *rancheria* of the Cherokee, twelve miles west of the Sabine River, at which he claimed that all were present except the Comanche and Tonkawa.

At this time Fields claimed that all lands north of the San Antonio road between the Trinity and Sabine had been granted to his tribe, a claim, however, which was denied by the Mexican government. On August 18, 1824, the general colonization law was passed and in 1825 a large American immigration began. Grants were made to Leftwich, Thorn, and Edwards on which they were to settle two thousand families. A portion of these grants conflicted with the Cherokee claim. Rumors were heard of a combination of Comanche, Tawakana, and other tribes to attack San Antonio and the new settlements, but various settlers, especially John D. Hunter, succeeded in getting Fields to desist.

When difficulties occurred between Edwards and the Mexican government, Fields threw his influence on the side of the *empresario,* an action which he took at the advice of Hunter. Bowles led the opposition party of the Cherokee, who turned against their former chief, and in 1827 they killed both Fields and Hunter.

General Terán had been sent to make an inspection of the boundary. He conferred upon Bowles the title of lieutenant-colonel and after a careful survey of the situation decided to curb the American immigration by firmly establishing the Indians. In 1830 Terán was made commandant-general of the Eastern Interior Provinces. Before he could carry out his policy, however, he committed suicide. Letona, the governor of Coahuila and Texas, who was also unfriendly to Americans, died about the same time, and once more the Cherokee were deprived of a definite settlement.

The Leftwich and Edwards grants had passed into the hands of David G. Burnet and General Filisola, and comprised practically all of the Cherokee lands. In 1833 Bowles, with several headmen of his tribe, went to San Antonio and afterward to Monclova to try to obtain a settlement of the conflicting claims. Bowles pointed out that his tribe had occupied those lands for nine years and their occupancy antedated the *empresario* grants. The state government concluded that it was a matter for the supreme government to decide, but promised that in the meantime the Indians were not to be disturbed. Nothing, however, could be legally done until the expiration of Burnet's grant, which would end on December 21, 1835.

On May 12 of that year the legislature of Coahuila and Texas passed a measure to settle the Cherokee and other "peaceful and civilized Indians" on vacant lands of Texas in a place where they would be a "line of defense along the frontier to secure the state against the incursions of the barbarous tribes." Before the policy could be carried out, the Texan revolution was in full swing.[26]

During 1835 the Indians were in a state of unrest; the advance of settlement, the presence of surveyors, and the uncertain tenure of the Indian land-holdings, caused several hostile outbreaks, which in turn kept the settlers in a continual state of fear. The depredations of the Kichai from the Navasota were especially aggravating, and in the summer of 1835 an expedition was sent against them and they were driven to the headwaters of the Trinity.[27]

---

[26] Winkler, in Texas State Historical Association, *The Quarterly*, VII, 95–165. The statement on page 151 that Terán was sent to fix the boundary is an error, his duty being to examine the region.

[27] Wood, in Texas State Historical Association, *The Quarterly*, IV, 205.

The Indian situation and the rumors of an invasion by Mexican troops placed the country in a ferment. Committees of safety were formed. The Columbia committee wrote to J. B. Miller, the political chief of the Department of Brazos, recommending that each municipality be required to furnish immediately at least twenty-five men for an Indian campaign and advised that they rendezvous at Mina on or before the end of the month of July.[28] Miller replied that he had taken steps to organize the militia and defend the frontier,[29] and so he informed General Cos.[30]

Miller's statement was no doubt true, for the same month Captain Coleman led twenty-five men from the Colorado and Brazos river settlements against the Tonkawa. A fight occurred, in which the Texans were forced to fall back to Parker's fort on the Navasota. Reinforcements were sent and the Indians were pursued to the headwaters of the Trinity and down the Brazos. The same summer the Caddo made an attack on Kitchen's fort, in the present county of Fannin, and even raided to the falls of the Brazos.[31]

A letter from Benjamin Milam, stating that Mexico intended to occupy the country with a large military force, make friends with the Indians and stir up a slave revolt, caused further, though probably groundless, excitement. "These plans of barbarity and injustice," Milam wrote, "will make a wilderness of Texas and beggars of its inhabitants, if they do not unite and act with promptness and decision."[32]

As the danger from Mexico increased, it became evident that the associated bands must be placated. The committee of safety of San Felipe, òn September 13, issued a circular which stated

---

[28] Committee of Columbia to Miller, n.d., in Southern Historical Association, *Publications*, VII, 89.

[29] Miller to Committee of Columbia, July 3, 1835, *ibid.*, VII, 90.

[30] Miller to Cos, July 2, 1835, *ibid.*, VII, 91.

[31] Wooten, *A Comprehensive History of Texas*, I, 747–748.

[32] Milam to Johnson, July 5, 1835, in Southern Historical Association, *Publications*, VIII, 104–106.

that the committee deemed it important that the just and legal rights of the civilized Indians should be protected.[33] The committee of San Augustine and Nacogdoches sent a joint deputation to the Indians, of which Sam Houston and T. J. Rusk were members. Promises were made that the surveyors should stay away from their lands and that white men should not interfere with them.[34] Houston informed the Cherokee that they should have their lands above the San Antonio Road and between the Neches and Angelina rivers.[35]

The Permanent Council, which was the governing body of Texas, October 11–27, 1835, also took action. Three commissioners, Peter J. Menard, Jacob Garrett, and Joseph L. Hood, were appointed to proceed to the Indian villages, ascertain their grievances, and give them full assurance that their case would receive prompt attention.[36] In the address to the people which was circulated by the Permanent Council, this significant statement occurred: "Already have we said we will respect the rights of the No[r]thern Indians amongst us, so as not to compromise the interests of Texas."[37] Austin also wrote that he would agree with any action taken by the council.[38]

The council, however, was not unmindful of the fact that the Indians needed watching. To overawe the plains Indians and keep an eye on the associated bands, the ranger service was extended, so that the frontier might be patrolled from east of the Trinity to beyond the Colorado, but the rangers were instructed not to interfere in any way with the friendly tribes.[39]

---

[33] Southern Historical Association, *Publications*, VIII, 20.

[34] Yoakum, *History of Texas*, I. 358.

[35] *Ibid.*, I, 378.

[36] *Proceedings of the Permanent Council*, in Texas State Historical Association, *The Quarterly*, IX, 287–288.

[37] *Journal of the Permanent Council* (Eugene C. Barker, ed.), *ibid.*, VII, 264.

[38] Yoakum, *History of Texas*, I, 378. Yoakum also says that arrangements had been made for the Indians to have a representative before the Consultation.

[39] *Journal of the Permanent Council*, in Texas State Historical Association, *The Quarterly*, VII, 260–262, 271, Yoakum, *History of Texas*, I, 378.

The Consultation took the place of the Permanent Council. The new body organized November 3 and on the fourteenth was superseded by the Provisional Government. Branch T. Archer was elected president of the Consultation. In his opening address he showed that he approved of the course of the Permanent Council, for he said, "We are surrounded by powerful and warlike tribes of Indians, some of whose chiefs are expected here in a few days, and I deem it expedient that we purchase their friendship at whatever it may cost."[40] The day before its adjournment the Consultation followed his advice by adopting the "Solemn Declaration" which read:

We solemnly declare that the boundaries of the claims of the said Indians are as follows, to wit, being north of the San Antonio road and the Neches, and west of the Angelina and Sabine rivers. We solemnly declare that the Governor and General Council immediately on its organization shall appoint commissioners to treat with the said Indians to establish the definite boundaries of their territory and secure their confidence and friendship. We solemnly declare that we will guarantee to them the peaceable enjoyment of their rights and their lands as we do our own. We solemnly declare that all grants, surveys, and locations within the bounds hereinbefore maintained, made after the settlement of the said Indians, are and of right ought to be utterly null and void, and the commissioners issuing the same be and are hereby ordered immediately to recall and cancel the same, as having been made upon lands already appropriated by the Mexican government. We solemnly declare that it is our sincere desire that the Cherokee Indians and their associate bands should remain our friends in peace and war, and if they do so we pledge the public faith to the support of the foregoing declaration. We solemnly declare that they are entitled to our commiseration and protection, as the first owners of the soil, as an unfortunate race of people, that we wish to hold as friends and treat with justice.[41]

The provisional government was composed of a governor, lieutenant-governor, and council. Henry Smith was chosen governor. In his first message to the council, on November 15, he discussed the situation of the associated bands and made the

---

[40] Stiff, *The Texan Emigrant*, 286–288.

[41] Williams, *Sam Houston and the War of Independence in Texas*, 134–135.

recommendation "that you second the measure of the late convention in this matter and never desist until the objects contemplated by that body be carried into effect."[42]

No action was taken at once, and on December 18 Smith called the attention of the Council to the matter. He said, in part:

I further have to suggest to you the propriety of appointing commissioners on the part of this government to carry into effect the Indian treaty, as contemplated by the convention. . . . I would . . . suggest the propriety of appointing Gen. Sam Houston, of the army, and Col. John Forbes, of Nacogdoches. . . . These agents, going under proper instructions, would be enabled to do right, but not permitted to do wrong, as their negotiation would be subject to investigation and ratification by the government, before it would become a law.[43]

On the twenty-second the Council passed an ordinance empowering Governor Smith to appoint a commission. General Houston, John Forbes of Nacogdoches, and Dr. John Cameron were appointed.[44]

Houston and Forbes went to Bowles' village, where a great council was held and on February 23 a treaty was entered into. Kennedy says:

By this treaty, the Cherokees and their associate bands were to receive a fee-simple title to all the land lying west of the San Antonio road, and beginning on the west at the point where the said road crosses the river Angelina, and running up said river until it reaches the mouth of the first large creek below the great Shawnee village, emptying into said river from the north-east. Thence running with said creek to its main source, and from thence a due north line to the Sabine, and with said river west; then, starting where the San Antonio road crosses the Angelina, and with said road to where it crosses the Neches, and thence running up the east side of the river, in a northwesterly direction.[45]

The Council called for a convention to meet at Washington on the Brazos on March 1, 1836. Its chief purposes were to de-

---

[42] Brown, *Life of Henry Smith*, 111.

[43] *Ibid.*, 158–159.

[44] *Ibid.*, 187; Kennedy, *Texas*, II, 159; *Ordinances and Decrees of the Consultation, Provisional Government of Texas and the Convention*, 97–98.

[45] Kennedy, *Texas*, II, 313.

clare independence, formulate a constitution and provide for a government until the constitution might be adopted. It remained in session only seventeen days and provided for a provisional government consisting of a president, vice-president, attorney-general, and secretaries of state, war, navy, and treasury. The provisional officers were given executive powers and were to remain in office until the regular government could be installed after the constitution had been submitted to the people.[46]

The convention refused to accept the Indian treaty, thus undoing all the work of pacification that had been so wisely begun.[47] It completed its work by electing provisional officers, David G. Burnet being made president.[48] This selection, following the action of the convention in rejecting the treaty, could not but aggravate the Indian situation, for it must be remembered that Burnet was one of the *empresarios* whose title conflicted with that of the Cherokee; furthermore his grant had expired in the previous December, a fact which might seem sinister to the crafty Bowles.

It thus appears that there was an Indian situation in eastern Texas which bade fair to break out into actual warfare. This must be borne in mind in a consideration of the early operations of General Gaines, as protection of the border against Indian hostility was one of the motives for sending that general to the frontier. If the government at Washington had ulterior designs, it at least could cloak them under a reasonable excuse.

---

[46] Garrison, *Texas*, 210–219.

[47] Kennedy, *Texas*, II, 313.

[48] Brown, *History of Texas from 1685 to 1892*, I, 594–596.

CHAPTER VIII

GAINES' OPERATIONS ON THE FRONTIER UNTIL THE BATTLE OF SAN JACINTO

The progress of the Texan revolution was watched with the keenest interest throughout the United States, but more intense was the interest south of the Mason and Dixon line, and in New York and Pennsylvania. This was due to two main causes: a large proportion of the Texan settlers came from the South and much of the financial backing for the various colonization projects came from New York and Pennsylvania. Money and arms were readily supplied, and hundreds of men, either individually or in companies, joined the Texans in their war for independence.

The sympathies of the government were naturally with the Texans. Jackson's persistent attempts to obtain the territory, his personal friendship for Houston, and the natural fire of the military hero, combined to draw him into the struggle. But Jackson had been chastened by years of experience; the energy which had carried him to victory at New Orleans, the audacity which had impelled him to invade Florida, the wrath which led him into the struggle with the nullifiers and the bank, had given way to craft and prudence.

The foreign policy of the United States, peculiarly a sphere belonging to the president, had been based upon principles of neutrality originally set forth in a proclamation by Washington, and incorporated into a statute by an act of June 5, 1794. From time to time new enactments were made to meet suggestions made in presidential messages. All prior legislation on the subject was finally repealed and superseded by an act passed on April 20, 1818. This act was still in force in 1836.[1]

---

[1] Moore, *Digest of International Law*, VII, 1010–1014.

The act held it to be a high misdemeanor, punishable by fine and imprisonment, for a United States citizen to accept or exercise a commission from, or enlist in the service of a foreign state, colony, or district, to serve against a state with whom the United States was at peace, to fit out vessels, or to set on foot, or provide means for, military expeditions against the territory or possessions of a foreign state with which the United States was at peace.[2]

Jackson, in no uncertain terms, announced the course which he intended to follow toward the Texan revolution. On December 7, 1835, in a message to Congress, he said:

Recent events in that country [Texas] have awakened the liveliest solicitude in the United States. Aware of the strong temptations existing, and powerful inducements held out to the citizens of the United States to mingle in the dissensions of our immediate neighbors, instructions have been given to the District Attorneys of the United States, where indications warranted it, to prosecute, without respect to persons, all who might attempt to violate the obligations of our neutrality: while at the same time it has been thought necessary to apprize the Government of Mexico that we should require the integrity of our territory to be scrupulously respected by both parties.[3]

The question of integrity of territory had been settled between the United States and Mexico in the treaty of 1831. The thirty-third article provided that each nation should do all in its power to maintain peace among its border Indians, and both bound themselves to restrain by force all hostilities and incursions on the part of tribes living within their respective boundaries.[4] Unfortunately the boundary had not been definitely determined. As we have seen, a treaty had been entered into in 1828, which renewed the line of 1819,[5] but from various causes it had not been put into effect by running the line. Since 1829 the govern-

---

[2] *Revised Statutes of the United States*, secs. 5281–5291.

[3] Richardson, *Messages and Papers of the Presidents*, III, 151.

[4] *Treaties, Conventions*, (Malloy, ed.) I, 1095–1096.

[5] *Ibid.*, I, 1082–1084.

ment at Washington had proceeded upon the erroneous assumption set up by Van Buren that the Sabine River of the treaty of 1819 was in reality the Neches River.[6]

Keenly alert to the possibilities that were opened up by the revolutionary movement in Texas, aware of the complications which might arise if a Mexican army entered the disputed zone between the Neches and the Sabine, and at the same time desirous of keeping the Indians within bounds, the government determined to mobilize a considerable force along the frontier. Lewis Cass, the secretary of war, on January 23, 1836, sent instructions to Major-General Edmund P. Gaines, commander of the western department of the army, ordering him to repair to some position near the western frontier of Louisiana and there assume personal command of all troops near the Mexican boundary.

In part the instructions read:

It is not the object of this order to change at all the relations between yourself and the military departments under your command, but to require your personal presence at a point where public considerations demand the exercise of great discretion and experience. An order will be issued, without delay, to the sixth regiment to proceed to Fort Jesup, and this force, together with all the troops in the western part of Louisiana, and in the country west of the Mississippi, and south of the Missouri rivers, will be employed, as occasion may require, in carrying into effect the instructions herein communicated to you.

The state of affairs in Texas calls for immediate measures on the part of the Government. It is the duty of the United States to remain entirely neutral, and to cause their neutrality to be respected. It is possible that the course of operations may induce one or other of the contending parties to approach the boundary line, with a view to cross it in arms. Should you find that the case, you will give notice to the persons having the direction, that they will not be permitted to cross into the territory of the United States: and if they attempt to do so by force, you will resist them with the means at your disposal.

The thirty-third article of the treaty of 1831 was stated and Gaines was instructed to use force, if necessary, to prevent an

[6] Van Buren to Poinsett, August 25, 1829, *Congressional Debates*, XIV, Pt. 2, App., 127–130.

uprising among the Indians. He was also to assist the civil authorities in preserving neutrality, if they found it necessary to call upon him, and he was to communicate freely with the district attorneys of Louisiana on points of law.[7]

These instructions, on the face, appear to be simple and straightforward, but future events throw them under suspicion. It must be remembered that the boundary was indefinite, a fact which would give a basis for an advance across the Sabine. Gaines was to assist the civil authorities to preserve neutrality, if they called upon him, but the civil authorities were in sympathy with the Texans and hence would not call upon him. The district attorneys were also imbued with the same spirit, and would give an interpretation of the law which would fit the exigencies of the case.[8]

The instructions from Cass were destined not to reach Gaines for some time, for early in January he had left Memphis, going south on a tour of inspection of the southern and eastern part of his command.[9] He arrived in New Orleans on January 14, 1836, where he heard of the massacre of Major Dade's command by Seminoles in Florida.[10] He immediately asked Governor E. D. White of Louisiana for volunteers to reinforce the regulars,[11] then passed on to Mobile and Pensacola,[12] returning later to New Orleans to take charge personally of the Louisiana volunteers.[13]

At Pensacola Gaines received a letter from Adjutant-General Jones, which gave him the first inkling of the plans of the United States regarding the southwestern frontier. The letter, written the day before Cass' formal instructions, approved the tour of

[7] Cass to Gaines, January 23, 1836, *House Ex. Docs.*, 24 Cong., 1 Sess., VI, Doc. 256, pp. 40–41.

[8] This will be fully discussed in Chapter X.

[9] Jones to Gaines, January 22, 1836, *House Ex. Docs.*, 25 Cong., 2 Sess., III, Doc. 78, p. 740.

[10] Gaines to Jones, January 15, 1836, *ibid.*, 731–732.

[11] Gaines to White, January 15, 1836, *ibid.*, 735.

[12] *Ibid.*, 736–738.

[13] Gaines to Clinch, February 2, 1836, *ibid.*, 738–739.

Gaines, but stated that affairs west of the Mississippi might require attention and that he was to await orders at New Orleans. It also stated that General Winfield Scott had been ordered to Florida.[14]

Gaines refused to leave that portion of his command until the state of affairs in Florida was known at Washington. He said that he had given his personal pledge to the governor of Louisiana that the volunteer corps would not be required to go further than he himself would go, and to leave would be breaking his pledge.[15] The appointment of Scott to take command in Florida also piqued him.[16] He went steadily ahead with preparations for a Florida campaign and began active operations against the Seminoles.[17]

On February 22, Jones, who was now fully informed of conditions in Florida, again instructed Gaines to proceed without delay to the western frontier to take the personal command.[18] Instructions were also sent to Brigadier-General Arbuckle at Fort Gibson, Arkansas, to take command until Gaines' arrival.[19]

---

14 Jones to Gaines, January 22, 1836, *House Ex. Docs.*, 25 Cong., 2 Sess., III, Doc. 78, p. 740.

15 Gaines to Jones, February 6, 1836, *ibid.*, 741–742.

16 Gaines to Jones, July 4, 1836, *ibid.*, 753–765. There was a long-standing quarrel between Scott, Macomb, and Gaines. Scott and Gaines had been aspirants for the office of Major-General in Adams' administration. Charges and counter-charges, letters and pamphlets, had been spread broadcast, to the annoyance of the President. Both were rejected and Macomb was appointed, a fact which tended to increase the unfriendly feelings of all concerned. This must be taken into consideration in the interpretation of the documents. Macomb naturally wished to belittle Gaines. Gaines in turn was jealous of Scott and Macomb. When Scott was placed in command in a locality where hostilities were actually in progress, and Gaines was sent to the western frontier, Gaines naturally felt that his rival was being favored. The desire to outdo Scott was probably a strong factor in the operations along the frontier. For the controversy over rank, see Adams, *Memoirs*, VI, 547–548, VII, 23, 205, 225–226, 251–254, 391–392, 447–449, 455–456, 505–508, VIII, 11–15, 19–20, 22, 41–44, 74–75.

17 Gaines to Jones, February 22, 1836, *House Ex. Docs.*, 25 Cong., 2 Sess., III, Doc. 78, p. 744; Gaines to Clinch, February 28, 1836, *ibid.*, 748–749; Hitchcock to Lyon, March 11, 1836, *ibid.*, 803–808.

18 Jones to Gaines, February 22, 1836, *ibid.*, 742.

19 Jones to Arbuckle, March 10, 1836, *House Ex. Docs.*, 24 Cong., 1 Sess., VI, Doc. 256, p. 58.

Cass' instructions to Gaines finally reached him in March and he proceeded at once to take up his duties on the western border.[20]

Gaines left New Orleans on the steamboat ''Levant'' on March 28 and stopped at Baton Rouge to see if sufficient ordnance stores could be provided, and then hastened on to Natchitoches. While on board the ''Levant,'' he addressed a lengthy letter to the War Department; as this letter shows the plans which were already formulating and throws much light on his future operations, a rather lengthy quotation seems necessary. He spoke of the importance of making certain that supplies were sufficient and of the necessity of inspecting the Baton Rouge arsenal—

duties which derive great importance from the recent accounts of the sanguinary manner in which the Mexican forces seem disposed to carry on the war against our Texian [neighbors]. . . . Upon this point I take leave to suggest whether it may or may not become necessary, in *our own* defence, to speak to the contending belligerants in a language not to be misunderstood—a language requiring *force* and military supplies that shall be sufficient, if necessary, for the protection of our frontier, to check the savage operations of each of the contending parties who may forget to respect the laws of war and our neutral rights, until Mexico and the United States shall by an adjustment of existing difficulties, put an end to scenes of barbarism which cannot but endanger the peace and other vital interests of all the parties concerned—scenes of barbarism disgrace-ful to all who enact or tolerate them.

Should I find any disposition on the part of the Mexicans or their red allies to menace our frontier, I cannot but deem it to be my duty not only to hold the troops of my command in readiness for action in defence of our slender frontier, but to anticipate their lawless movements, by crossing our supposed or imaginary national boundary, and meeting the savage marauders wherever to be found in their approach towards our frontier.

Should I err in this view of the subject, in which, however, I am convinced the laws of war and of nations will bear me out, I shall be gratified to receive the views of the President, to which I shall scrupu-lously adhere. But if it be otherwise, if my own views are approved, I shall, in that event, have occasion for some mounted volunteers, with

20 Gaines to Jones, July 4, 1836, *House Ex. Docs.*, 25 Cong., 2 Sess., III, Doc. 78, pp. 753–765; *ibid.*, 811–820.

other forces, sufficient to make my numerical strength equal of the
estimated strength of the contending parties, which is now estimated
at eight to twelve thousand men. . . . With a view to this possible con-
tingency, I have already desired the fine legionary brigade commanded
by General Planche, of the city of New Orleans, *to calculate on the possibility of my having occasion to invite the legion to join me.* To this
suggestion the officers of the legion, with the gallant general at their
head, cordially responded that they would, whenever it might be deemed
necessary, promptly repair to the frontier, delighted with the opportunity
of carrying into effect the wishes of the President, under whose immediate command many of the officers had distinguished themselves in
the defence of their city and State in the memorable triumphs of December, 1814, and January 1815.[21]

It is evident from this letter that before leaving New Orleans,
and while still ignorant of the exact state of affairs on the border,
Gaines had determined on his course of action unless stopped by
Jackson. The looseness of his instructions had evidently been
interpreted to mean that the government wished him to occupy
the disputed territory. He had also determined to collect a force
large enough to meet the combined strength of the Mexican and
Indian forces. Two distinct motives appear to have influenced
him; first, the desire to defeat the Mexicans for the double purpose of helping the Texans and occupying the disputed territory,
and secondly, to protect the frontier against an Indian war. It
must be borne in mind that Gaines had just returned from the
scene of hostilities in a country where Jackson had once shown
no scruples in the violation of foreign territory. Furthermore,
Gaines had served under Jackson in Florida and both were from
Tennessee. He had been deprived of his command where there
was opportunity of gaining military laurels, and it was but
natural that he should wish to overshadow his rival, Scott, by a
greater military exploit.[22]

---

[21] Gaines to Cass, March 29, 1836, *House Ex. Docs.*, 25 Cong., 2 Sess.,
XII, Doc. 351, pp. 768–769.
[22] *The National Cyclopædia of American Biography*, IX, 372.

Gaines arrived at Natchitoches on April 4, where he at once began an investigation of border conditions. The Alamo had fallen, the Texan forces under Grant and Fannin had been captured, and all of southern Texas was in the power of Santa Anna. The Mexican victories, furthermore, had been accompanied by acts of extreme cruelty and barbarity.[23] Houston, who was in command of the main Texan force, was in full retreat toward the eastward.[24] The entire Anglo-American population was in a state of panic. Homes were abandoned and a wild scramble to reach the border ensued. Thousands of women, children, and slaves joined in the rout, every river-crossing being deluged with people frantically attempting to get to the Sabine.[25]

Many of them crossed into western Louisiana and remained there, in extreme misery, until after the battle of San Jacinto. An eye-witness thus described the conditions:

> We encamped near the Sabine. Hundreds of families were returning from Texas, and there was more misery among them than could well be imagined. All throughout the woods, were living under sheds, those going to Texas, who had been stopped by the accounts they had heard, and others who were returning to their old homes. Under the same sheds were to be seen blacks and whites, who had sickened with the measles, some of whom were constantly dying, and the whole destitute of the means of relief. It made one's heart sick to witness these spectacles.[26]

The Indian situation on both sides of the border caused the deepest apprehension. As previously shown, the Cherokees and their associated bands of eastern Texas were extremely restless; they had long been the legal contestants of the whites for lands, and the convention, which had begun its work on March 1, had refused to accept the treaty which Houston and Forbes had

---

[23] Yoakum, *History of Texas*, II, 45–101.

[24] Barker, in Texas State Historical Association, *The Quarterly*, IV, 237–343.

[25] Harris, *ibid.*, IV, 160–167; Kennedy, *Texas*, II, 229.

[26] Extract from the *Journal of a Military Journey to the Sabine*, in *Niles' Register*, L, 385–386.

made with them.[27]   Mexican emissaries had been among the
Indians, and General Gaona, with one division of the Mexican
army, was advancing along the frontier toward Nacogdoches, his
route being eastward toward the upper crossing of the Trinity.[28]

The greatest alarm prevailed at Nacogdoches and San
Augustine, the flight of the settlers, rumors of the advance of
Gaona and of a Cherokee uprising, combining to affright the
authorities and citizens.   A fear that the Caddo and other tribes
from north of Red River would join with the Texan Indians was
an added terror, it being known that Manuel Flores, a Mexican
resident of Spanish Town near Natchitoches, had been among the
Red River Indians to incite them to attack the settlements.[29]

The committees of vigilance and safety were active at both
Nacogdoches and San Augustine.   On March 19 Henry Raguet,
chairman of the Nacogdoches committee, wrote to A. Hotchkiss,
chairman at San Augustine, that they believed themselves to be
in imminent danger of a combined attack of Cherokee and
Indians arriving daily from the United States, and that a report
had came that a thousand Sacs and Foxes would be in the country
as soon as the grass grew enough to feed their horses.   He asked
that this information be forwarded to the commanding officer at
Fort Jesup with a request that he get the United States to stop
the Indians from crossing into Texas.[30]

In response, the San Augustine committee reported to the
citizens that large bodies of Caddo, Shawnee, Delaware, Kickapoo, Cherokee, Creek, and other tribes were assembling at the
three forks of the Trinity to make war on the inhabitants of the
frontier.   They appointed Dr. G. Rowe and Colonel P. H.

---

[27] Kennedy, *Texas*, II, 313; Brown, *History of Texas from 1685 to 1892*,
I, 594–596.

[28] Yoakum, *History of Texas*, II, 126.

[29] Green to Jackson, March 11, 1836, *House Ex. Docs.*, 24 Cong., 1 Sess.,
VI, Doc. 256, p. 59.

[30] Raguet to Hotchkiss, March 19, 1836, *House Ex. Docs.*, 25 Cong., 2
Sess., XII, Doc. 351, pp. 777–778.

Sublette to proceed to Fort Jesup to enter into correspondence with Gaines in regard to the condition of affairs.[31]

John T. Mason of Nacogdoches, on March 20, also wrote in similar vein to Major Nelson, the commander at Fort Jesup, asking that a messenger be sent to the Caddo to keep them quiet.[32] On April 1 he wrote directly to Gaines that the settlers had no protection except the troops of the United States. He said that the discontented tribes of the Missouri and Arkansas frontier and the immigrant Indians of Texas, all of whom had been deprived of their lands, would be glad to enter into a war against the whites. He accordingly asked that troops be sent to Nacogdoches. He continued, ''I confess this is a question of great delicacy, and I presume can only be solved by reference to a higher authority. But that in the case presented this authority has spoken I am induced to believe, and that your powers are adequate I have every confidence.''[33]

The committee at Nacogdoches also despatched agents to the tribes, C. H. Sims and William Sims being sent among the Cherokee, and M. B. Menard to visit the Shawnee, Delaware, and Kickapoo tribes seventy-five miles north of Nacogdoches.[34]

Such was the condition of affairs when Gaines arrived at Natchitoches. He realized that a serious condition existed and at once determined upon his line of action. Four days after his arrival he sent letters to the governors of Louisiana, Mississippi, Alabama, and Tennessee, informing them of the nature of Cass' instructions of January 23. He quoted a portion of the thirty-third article of the treaty of 1831, regarding the restraint of Indians, and stated that he had informed the tribes on the Red and Arkansas rivers not to make hostile incursions into Texas,

---

[31] Report of A. Hotchkiss, March 21, 1836, *House Ex. Docs.*, 25 Cong., 2 Sess., XII, Doc. 351, p. 777.

[32] Mason to Nelson, March 20, 1836, *ibid.*, 773–774.

[33] Mason to Gaines, April 1, 1836, *ibid.*, 778–789.

[34] Depositions of agents before the Nacogdoches committee, April 11, 1836, *ibid.*, 776. Barker believes that the reports of danger from the Indians were either manufactured evidence or were greatly exaggerated. See *The Mississippi Valley Historical Review*, I, 18–19, 24–26.

and that if any attempts were made, force would be used. He also told of Manuel Flores and stated that some of the Caddo had crossed the line. He then continued:

These facts and circumstances present to me the important question, whether I am to sit still and suffer these movements to be so far matured as to place the white settlements on both sides of the line wholly within the power of these savages, or whether I ought not instantly to prepare the means for protecting the frontier settlements, and, if necessary, compelling the Indians to return to their own homes and hunting grounds? I cannot but decide in favor of the last alternative which the question presents; for nothing can be more evident than that an Indian war, commencing on either side of the line, will as surely extend to both sides as that a lighted quick-match thrust into one side of a powder magazine will extend the explosion to both sides.

He then asked each of the governors of Alabama, Mississippi, and Tennessee to furnish him with a brigade of volunteers, and from the governor of Louisiana he asked for a batallion, urging that they be mounted men.[35]

The same day he wrote to Cass stating that he had learned that many Indians had gone from the United States into Texas. Because of this, with the added fact that Santa Anna was rapidly advancing in his war of extermination, and that as soon as he reached the Trinity the Indians would turn loose upon the settlements and that only an efficient military force could restrain them, he deemed it his duty to prepare for action and had asked the governors for volunteers.

"This force," he continued, meaning the combined regulars and volunteers, "though not equal in number to that which it may be my duty to meet in battle, will enable me at least to secure the confidence of the frontier settlements, and keep them at home to plant their crops; and, moreover, to enable me to inflict summary punishment on such of the enemy by whom they are now

---

[35] Gaines to the governors, April 8, 1836, *Congressional Debates*, XII, Pt. 3, pp. 3516–3517; H. H. Bancroft, *North Mexican States and Texas*, II, 286.

menaced as may teach them to respect us, and in future to pay
more regard than they seem now disposed to pay to our rights
and treaties.''[36]

In the meantime the excitement at Nacogdoches continued;
every rumor was accepted. Gaona had been ordered to change
his route and head for San Felipe instead of Nacogdoches, but
of course this was unknown to the inhabitants of the latter place.
There was fear that the Mexican inhabitants would join the
enemy and on the ninth, Hoffman, the *alcalde,* ordered every
able-bodied Mexican within the municipality to take up the
line of march to join the advancing army or to cross the Sabine.
The Mexican citizens were misjudged, as the committee learned
a few days later, and the order was not enforced.[37]

The return of C. H. and William Sims and Menard occurred
on the eleventh and they immediately appeared before the committee. C. H. Sims stated that he had visited the Cherokee thirty
miles west of Nacogdoches and found them hostile and prepared
for war, that they had murdered Brooks Williams, an American
trader, and further informed Sims that a large body of Caddo,
Kechies, Inies. Towakanas, Waco, and Comanche were to attack
the settlements. He stated that there was every indication that
the Cherokee intended to join them and that about seventeen
hundred warriors were gathered on the Trinity. Chief Bowles
advised Sims to leave the country, as there was great danger.
The testimony of William Sims was similar, adding that there
were large bodies of Mexicans and Indians crossing the Trinity
about one hundred miles west by north of Nacogdoches. Word
also came from James and Ralph Chesher, who were in command of a military company, that they believed that Nacogdoches
was in danger. They stated that they had a piece of artillery
mounted and asked that aid be sent them. According to their
account, the Mexican and Indian force had already crossed the

[36] Gaines to Cass, April 8, 1836, *Congressional Debates,* XII, Pt. 3, pp.
3515–3516.

[37] Yoakum, *History of Texas,* II, 126–129.

Trinity and was being conducted by Caddo. M. B. Menard also returned from his mission, reporting that he had visited the Shawnee, Delaware, and Kickapoo to the northward and found them friendly. The chiefs reported that Bowles had visited them, but that they had refused to comply with his request to assist in attacking the whites.[38]

When the reports were heard, the committee decided that the civil authority be suspended and appealed to John T. Mason to place himself at the head of affairs. They pointed out that there were five hundred defenceless families between Nacogdoches and the Trinity, and unless relieved at once, they would be slaughtered. They asked him to make a personal appeal to the American commander at Fort Jesup.[39] News of this proceeding reached Mason at Thompson's Tavern on the night of the twelfth and he at once despatched a messenger to the fort with the statement of the committee, directing that it be placed in the hands of Gaines, and that, if he were absent, it be forwarded to him at once.[40]

The day after the appointment of Mason, R. A. Irion, who had been appointed acting commandant of Nacogdoches, sent a second despatch to Mason stating that the news of the movements of the Indians had been confirmed, and that on April 10 a large force, led by Caddo, had encamped at the Sabine sixty miles north of Nacogdoches. He reported that the inhabitants were abandoning the town and would concentrate at Attagas or San Augustine.[41]

Mason arrived at Fort Jesup on the night of April 13, but Gaines was at Natchitoches. He at once sent a despatch to him

---

[38] Depositions of C. H. and William Sims, Menard, and letter of James and Ralph Chesher to the committee of vigilance and safety of Nacogdoches, all of April 11, 1836, *House Ex. Docs.*, 25 Cong., 2 Sess., XII, Doc 351, pp. 775–776.

[39] Committee to Mason, April 11, 1836, *ibid.*, 779–780.

[40] Mason to Gaines, April 12, 1836, *ibid.*, 779.

[41] Irion to Mason, April 12, 1836, *ibid.*, 781. In the printed document the name is spelled Irvin.

stating that it was probable that by this time Nacogdoches was occupied by Indians and Mexicans. He said that he had ordered the two hundred men of Nacogdoches to form a barrier to fight in the woods until the women and children might escape, but he had learned since his departure that one hundred had fled and that Judge Quitman from Natchez was trying to form a rear guard. Unless five hundred men marched on the following day, there would be no protection as far as the Sabine and the stream was so flooded that hundreds would be unable to cross and would be sacrificed. He stated that the road from Nacogdoches to the Sabine was an unbroken line of women and children on foot, with nothing but their clothing on their backs.[42]

While these conditions prevailed at Nacogdoches, Gaines was making an effort to find out the true state of affairs among the Indians. J. Bonnell, a lieutenant in the Third Infantry, was sent to the Caddo villages but did not return until April 20,[43] and in consequence his report could have no influence upon the action of Gaines on the receipt of Mason's letter. But on April 12 Miguel de Cortínez was brought before Gaines and testified that, in the previous February, he had heard that his brother, Eusebio, was among the Cherokee. He repaired to their village, where he found him. Eusebio had informed him that he held a commission from the Mexican General Cos to raise the Indians against the Texans, that he intended to attack and set fire to Nacogdoches. Bowles verified the statement concerning the commission from Cos and also showed Cortínez a commission from

---

[42] Mason to Gaines, April 13, 1836, *House Ex. Docs.*, 25 Cong., 2 Sess., XII, Doc. 351, pp. 780–781. The statement of what was done to protect Nacogdoches is mainly confirmed by Yoakum, who adds that three military companies were detailed. He makes no mention, however, of the flight of the hundred men. See Yoakum, *History of Texas*, II, 127. A letter by Colonel Darlington, a former United States army officer, who was in that region during the excitement, says, "On the 14th April, Nacogdoches was safe but deserted." He knew nothing of any gathering of Indians at the Sabine and thought there was no reason for the abandonment of Nacogdoches. *House Ex. Docs.*, 24 Cong., 1 Sess., VI, Doc. 256, pp. 56–57.

[43] Report of Bonnell, April 20, 1836, *House Ex. Docs.*, 25 Cong., 2 Sess., XII, Doc. 351, pp. 774–775.

the Mexican government making him a lieutenant-colonel, his pay to commence as soon as the Cherokee took up arms against the Texans, and he declared that he would fight as long as a man of his tribe remained.[44]

The testimony of Cortínez, the letter of Mason, the scenes of wild disorder above described, and the numerous rumors which were current, determined Gaines on his line of action. He accordingly ordered eight companies of the Sixth and five companies of the Third Infantry to advance at once to the Sabine River, where they went into encampment on the site of Wilkinson's former camp, the place to be designated henceforth as Camp Sabine. On the road Gaines observed several hundred women and children and a few men retiring in panic from eastern Texas. But on arrival at the river, as he received no other confirmations of general hostility, he determined to halt, and to send word to Bowles and other chiefs that they would be punished if they attacked "the inhabitants of that or this border of our unmarked boundary," information which must have been somewhat enigmatical to the sachems.[45]

Bonnell reported at Camp Sabine on April 20. He said that he was at the Caddo villages on April 14 and found that Manuel Flores had been there about two months before, promising free plunder if they would help to destroy the Texans, whom he represented as Americans who had deserted. At the first village Bonnell found only two or three squaws and a few children; the absence of the warriors was accounted for by saying that the warriors had gone to the prairies because Flores had told them that the Americans were going to kill them. A few warriors were found to be in the neighborhood, and Bonnell sent for them and assured them that the Americans were friendly. The Indians

---

[44] Testimony of Cortínez, interpreted by Nathaniel Amory, given before Gaines, April 12, 1836, *House Ex. Docs.*, 25 Cong., 2 Sess., XII, Doc. 351, pp. 781–782.

[45] Gaines to Cass, April 20, 1836, *ibid.*, 771–773; *Texan Dipl. Corr.*, I, 83–84.

declared that Flores had made no impression on their loyalty and that they were glad to know the truth.

At the second village twelve miles farther Bonnell found Chief Cortés, who said that when the head chief led the men to the prairie to hunt, he (Cortés) had told them to be quiet and not trouble the whites. He promised to send word to the Indians on the prairies and asked that Gaines be informed that the Caddo would not take part in any way.

Upon his return to the first village, Bonnell learned that Flores had been accompanied by "a thick, short man, about middle-aged, who had formerly lived at Nacogdoches," and that there were three Mexicans then with the Indians on the prairies. An Indian said that if it had not been for the lies that Flores had told them, the Caddo would long since have returned and planted their corn. He also insisted that the tribe would not join in a war against the whites. He admitted that Flores was then with the Indians on the prairies, a fact which he accounted for by saying that, as Flores had not been able to prevail upon the Indians to go with him, he had decided to go with them.[46] Bonnell also ascertained that the "thick, short" man was Cortínez.[47]

Three of the circumstances brought out in Bonnell's report tend to confirm the opinion that the Caddo were in league with the Cherokee in spite of all their friendly protestations; the first striking fact is the absence of the warriors; the second, that the Indians had done nothing toward their corn planting, an operation which the squaws usually performed; and third, the fact that the Mexican emissaries were admitted to be with the warriors.

Gaines informed Cass of his advance to the Sabine and of Bonnell's report. He observed that it might appear on the sur-

---

[46] Report of Bonnell, April 20, 1836, *House Ex. Docs.*, 25 Cong., 2 Sess., XII, Doc. 351, pp. 774–775.

[47] Bonnell to Gaines, April 20, 1836, *ibid.*, 784–786.

face that there was no need of additional troops, but as long as Flores was among the Caddo they might still unite with Bowles. He thought that mounted men should be at Camp Sabine as soon as possible after May 1, in order to be prepared to meet mounted Comanche or other tribes which might be hostile.[48]

Let us now turn our attention to Washington to see what action would be taken by the President and the secretary of war. On April 25 Cass replied to Gaines' letter of March 29, which was written while on the ''Levant.'' He enclosed a memorandum of a conference which had taken place on the twentieth between Forsyth, the secretary of state, and the Mexican minister, Gorostiza. The document read as follows:

> Mr. Forsyth stated to Mr. Gorostiza that, in consequence of the contest in Texas, the movements of some citizens of the United States on the Red river, and apprehended hostile intentions of the Indians in Mexico against the United States, and of the Indians within the United States against Mexico, orders would be given to General Gaines to take such a position with the troops of the United States as would enable him to preserve the territory of the United States and of Mexico from Indian outrage, and the territory of the United States from any violation by Mexicans, Texians or Indians, during the disturbances unfortunately existing in that quarter, and that the troops of the United States would be ordered to protect the commissioners and surveyors of the two Governments, whenever they should meet to execute the instructions to be prepared under the treaty of limits between the United States and the United Mexican States. Should the troops, in the performance of their duty, be advanced beyond the point Mexico might suppose was within the territory of the United States, the occupation of the position was not to be taken as an indication of any hostile feeling, or of a desire to establish a possession or claim not justified by the treaty of limits. The occupation would be precautionary and provisional, and would be abandoned whenever (the line being run and the true limits marked) the disturbances in that region should cease, they being the only motive for it.[49]

As the memorandum was made before Gaines' first letter arrived and before he had any opportunity of investigating con-

---

[48] Gaines to Cass, April 20, 1836, *House Ex. Docs.*, 25 Cong., 2 Sess., XII, Doc. 351, pp. 771–773. •

[49] *House Ex. Docs.*, 24 Cong., 1 Sess., VI, Doc. 256, p. 45.

ditions, it is evident that the idea of occupying the disputed territory originated at Washington, and that Gaines' apparent suggestion to that effect was merely due to the fact that he had correctly interpreted the implications of Cass' original instructions. Furthermore Gaines, in spite of the conditions west of the Sabine, had decided to halt at that river. It would appear from this action that he wished to be assured from the war department in more explicit terms, before invading Mexican territory.

Cass' letter, commenting upon the memorandum, stated that Gaines was to consider what Forsyth had said as a part of his instructions and act accordingly. He said that it was not the wish of the President to take advantage of present circumstances and thereby obtain possession of any portion of Mexican territory, but neutrality must be preserved. He commented on the conditions in Texas and the Indian situation on the border and stated that, from information recently received, he had reason to believe that efforts were being made to induce the savages to join the Mexicans. He then continued, throwing the responsibility upon Gaines:

> It may, therefore, well be, as you anticipate, that these various contending parties may approach our frontiers, and that the lives and property of our citizens may be placed in jeopardy. Should this be the case, the President approves the suggestion you make and you are authorized to take such position, on either side of the imaginary boundary line, as may be best for your defensive operations. You will, however, under no circumstances, advance farther than old Fort Nacogdoches, which is within the limits of the United States, as claimed by this Government. But you will please to observe, that this permission will not be exercised, unless you find such an advanced position necessary, to afford due security to the frontier, in consequence of the unsettled state of things beyond you.

Cass approved the call for state troops, stating that he had that day, with Jackson's approval, called upon the governors of Louisiana and Mississippi for any force Gaines might find necessary, their term of service to be for six months or less. He also told Gaines to explain the instructions to any armed forces marching toward the border, and if they continued, he was to attack and repel them. After this bold statement, the closing instruction seems inconsistent:

> I need hardly say, that the duty committed to you is one of great importance, as well as of great delicacy; and I do not doubt it will be so executed as to preserve, on the one hand, the proper safety of the frontier, while, on the other hand, as little cause of offence as possible will be given to any foreign authority.[50]

The following day orders were sent to Captain M. Duncan at Fort Leavenworth and to Captain E. Trenor at Fort Gibson to keep the dragoons close to the forts so that they might be sent to Gaines if necessary,[51] and Gaines was immediately informed of what had been done.[52]

The activities of Cass were not devoted alone to ordering of troops. On April 18, before he had received Gaines' letter, he addressed a communication to R. M. Johnson, the chairman of the House Committee on Military Affairs, in which he advised that legislation be enacted allowing the period for volunteer service to be extended from three months to a year.[53] A bill was

---

[50] Cass to Gaines, April 25, 1836, *House Ex. Docs.*, 24 Cong., 1 Sess., VI, Doc. 256, pp. 43–44. The information which Cass had received in regard to the Mexicans inciting Indians was derived from a letter of T. J. Green to Colonel J. B. Many at Fort Jesup written on March 11, and which had been forwarded to Adjutant-General Jones. Jackson's endorsement on the back was as follows: ''Referred to the Secretary of War, that he cause orders to be forthwith given to the commanding officer at Fort Jesup, to arrest all individuals who under the orders of General Santa Anna, are engaged in exciting the Indians to war, and to notify all concerned that all his military force will be employed to put down or support our neutrality. A. J.'''' See *House Ex. Docs.*, 24 Cong., 1 Sess., VI, Doc. 256, pp. 58–59. The instructions of Cass to Governor E. D. White of Louisiana and to Governor Charles Lynch of Mississippi will be found in *ibid.*, 45–46.

[51] Jones to Duncan and Trenor, April 26, 1836, *House Ex. Docs.*, 24 Cong., 1 Sess., VI, Doc. 256, p. 60.

[52] Jones to Gaines, April 27, 1836, *ibid.*, 61.

[53] Cass to Johnson, April 18, 1836, *Congressional Debates*, XII, Pt. 3, p. 3322.

immediately prepared and was considered in the House on April
21.[54] On the following day it was debated and several of the
speeches disclosed the fact that there was great fear of the possible results of the Mexican advance.[55] It was debated again on
the twenty-sixth and passed the House on the following day. On
May 4 Benton presented the bill in the Senate and the debate
brought out a decided anti-Mexican feeling.[56] On May 10 the
bill was amended in several minor particulars[57] and was finally
passed by the Senate on May 18.[58] The House refused to accept
the amendments, and the Senate at once appointed a conference
committee,[59] which, however, failed to come to an agreement
and another committee was appointed.[60] This and the House
committee were able to agree, the House yielding several points,
but insisting that a clause be inserted restricting the call for
volunteers to cases of Indian hostilities or to repel invasion. The
time of service was to be for six or twelve months after troops
had arrived at the place of rendezvous, unless sooner discharged.
The act provided for a force of ten thousand volunteers and an
additional regiment of dragoons or mounted riflemen. A provision was also inserted to the effect that the act was to be in
force for two years; it became a law on May 23.[61]

In the consideration of the bill, it is interesting to note that
the Senate was far more radical and bellicose than the House.
It may also be observed that when Cass sent his instructions to
the governors asking for troops to serve for six months, his
action was illegal; he must have been aware of the temper of
Congress and exceedingly sure of his ground to dare to take

---

[54] *Congressional Debates*, XII, Pt. 3, pp. 3322–3325.

[55] *Ibid.*, 3330–3354.

[56] *Congressional Debates*, XII, Pt. 2, pp. 1385–1396.

[57] *Ibid.*, 1425–1426.

[58] *Ibid.*, 1458.

[59] *Ibid.*, 1463–1464.

[60] *Ibid.*, 1503–1512.

[61] *Acts passed at the first Session of the twenty-fourth Congress of the
United States*, 57–58.

such a stand. When we remember that the acts of the cabinet members were dominated by Jackson, the responsibility must be placed upon the President.

On May 4 another demand upon Congress came from the Secretary of War. In a letter to C. C. Cambreleng, the chairman of the ways and means committee, he set forth the conditions on the border and asked that a million dollars be immediately appropriated to meet the expense which must accrue, and on the following day he informed Cambreleng that Jackson gave his entire approval.[62]

On May 6 Cambreleng reported a bill which followed Cass' recommendation.[63] On the following day a lengthy debate occurred which showed plainly that Mexico and not the Indians was the mainspring of legislative activity. John Quincy Adams proved to be the firebrand of the debate. He took the position that they were being asked to provide funds for a war against Mexico without being properly informed. He added fuel to the fire when he stated that citizens of the United States were helping Texas, and that there was an intention to reconquer it and re-establish slavery which Mexico had abolished. If we were to acknowledge the independence of Texas and then admit her as a state, he thought the House should be informed, and he was opposed to a war for that purpose.

Waddy Thompson from South Carolina defended the idea that the preparations were defensive, and claimed that he had information to the effect that a war against the United States was the principal topic of conversation in Mexico. He criticized Adams for injecting slavery into the debate. He said that Adams had negotiated Texas away and that it was but natural that he should wish to guarantee the peaceable enjoyment of what he had conveyed. He pointed out that, at the time of the treaty,

---

62 Two letters, Cass to Cambreleng, May 4 and 5, 1836, *House Ex. Docs.*, 24 Cong., 1 Sess., VI, Doc. 249, pp. 1–2.

63 *Congressional Debates*, XII, Pt. 3, pp. 3493–3495.

the enemies of Adams had declared that his motive in giving up
Texas in 1819 was to prevent an addition to the slave-holding
interest. Thompson said that he had not joined in those charges
but regretted that Adams had furnished such strong evidence of
such feelings.

Harmony was restored by the avowal of Adams that he was
not against the appropriation but was asking for more information. He stated that when he negotiated the treaty of 1819, he
acted under the instructions of Monroe, and that he was the last
member of the cabinet to assent to the Sabine boundary. He said
that by Monroe's direction he had taken the treaty to Jackson,
who had approved it.

The question of the Sabine or the Neches boundary was also
presented, both views being defended, Ripley and Garland of
Louisiana taking opposite sides. Williams of Kentucky made an
incendiary speech in which he said that if Santa Anna gave a
justifiable cause for war, he was in favor of hostilities. A portion
of his remarks were as follows: "If he shall only cross our line,
only put one foot over on our territory for purposes of war; or
if he shall only ·menacingly shake his fist at us, or grit his teeth,
or excite and encourage the Indians upon our frontier to deeds
of massacre and outrage, I am for severing his head from his
body." He said that Santa Anna was a bloody tyrant, that the
people of Texas had no legal right of protection, but they de-
served our sympathies, anxieties, and wishes for success.

After this outburst the debate became more tempered, but
considerable sectional feeling, and emotion rather than reason,
continually appeared to cloud the real issue. When it came to
a vote, the bill was carried by an almost unanimous vote, Adams
being among those voting in the affirmative.[64] The bill, however, does not appear to have been passed by the Senate.

---

[64] *Congressional Debates*, XII, Pt. 3, pp. 3510–3548. The statement that
Jackson approved the treaty of 1819 was denied by him, and Adams re-
iterated his statement on the floor of the House. See *ibid.*, XII, Pt. 3,
pp. 3579–3580.

On May 6 Jackson sent a message to Congress requesting that legislation be passed to carry out the stipulations of the treaty of 1832.[65] Coming at such a time and it having been made apparent that the administration for four years had grasped every opportunity to delay the fulfillment of the treaty, this message can be looked upon only as a piece of hypocrisy on the part of Jackson, which, however, would bear out the claims of his supporters that he was consistently striving to preserve neutrality.

A bill to carry out the request was introduced in the Senate on May 11.[66] The *Congressional Debates* give no record of its passage, but it evidently met with success in that body, for it was introduced in the House on May 16. The debate was distracted by considerable discussion of the annexation of Texas, in which sectional feeling again appeared. The House adjourned without coming to a decision, and the bill never became a law.[67]

To return again to the activities of the secretary of war; on May 4 he sent a letter to Governor Cannon of Tennessee, saying that Gaines had asked for troops, and informing him that the President approved the request. A similar letter was sent to Governor Clay of Alabama. In both cases the men were to serve for three months, in this instance the request being within the law.[68] The quartermaster of the regular army was ordered to assist the governors in facilitating the movements of troops,[69] and the governors of Tennessee, Alabama, Louisiana, and Mississippi were informed of the fact.[70] A despatch was also sent to J. T. Morehead, the acting governor of Kentucky, that troops were to be furnished to Gaines if necessary.[71]

---

[65] Richardson, *Messages and Papers of the Presidents*, III, 226.

[66] *Congressional Debates*, XII, Pt. 2, p. 1427.

[67] *Congressional Debates*, XII, Pt. 3, pp. 3723–3733.

[68] Two letters, Cass to Cannon and C. C. Clay, May 4, 1836, *House Ex. Docs.*, 24 Cong., 1 Sess., VI, Doc. 256, pp. 49–50.

[69] Order of Cass of May 9, 1836, *ibid.*, 52.

[70] Two letters, Cass to C. C. Clay and Cannon, May 9, 1836, and two letters, Cass to White and Lynch, May 10, 1836, *ibid.*, 52–54.

[71] Cass to Morehead, May 6, 1836, *Niles' Register*, L, 385.

On May 4 Cass wrote to Gaines informing him that the government had ordered the governors to assist in raising troops. The letter was more temperate than might have been expected, but much was left to Gaines' discretion, and none of the previous orders were suspended. The entire spirit of the despatch was to proceed, but with caution, much stress being laid upon defence and neutrality. In part the letter read:

> The theatre of operations is so distant from the seat of Government, that much must be intrusted to your discretion. The two great objects you have to attain are, first, the protection of the frontiers; and secondly, as strict a performance of the neutral duties of the United States as the great object of self-defence will permit. You will take care and do no act which can give just cause of offense to any other Government; and, on the other hand, you will not permit the frontiers to be invaded by any forces whatever.

Cass then urged upon Gaines the necessity of being economical and of calling out no more troops than the exigencies of the case really required. He also told him to communicate with the commanding officers of any parties which might approach the frontiers, and inform them that, "while you have been ordered to that quarter with a view to the execution of the neutral obligations of the United States, you have also been instructed to defend their territory from any invasion whatever, and that this duty will be executed under any circumstances that may happen." Gaines was also instructed to remonstrate against the employment of any of the Indians, as it was against humanity, and experience had proved that they could not be restrained. The letter continued: "All this you will represent to the proper officers, and you will use your best exertions to keep such a force from marching towards our frontier; and if they do so, to repel and disperse it."[72]

---

[72] Cass to Gaines, May 4, 1836, *House Ex. Docs.*, 24 Cong., 1 Sess., VI, Doc. 256, pp. 48–49. It is interesting to note that the United States was using a large force of Indians in the Seminole and Creek wars at this time.

It will be observed that the first and last parts of this letter seem hardly consistent. Acting under the last part of the instructions, an impetuous officer could easily have produced a war with Mexico; furthermore, the instructions were of such a nature that they could be used as a defence of the government, if occasion required.

The course of the government called out the bitter denunciation of the opposition press. The *National Intelligencer* of May 9 stated that the government was taking deliberate steps which might lead to difficulties with Mexico, and pooh-poohed the idea that defense against the Indians and fear of Mexican invasion were the causes of massing troops on the border.[73] On the following day it attacked Jackson's claim that the Neches was the boundary. It said that it would be convenient to have that far, but there were only two ways to get it, with the consent of Mexico or by conquest, and the latter method was objectionable.[74] The *Richmond Enquirer* gave as its impression that if Jackson were at liberty to indulge his private feelings, he would not hesitate to speak liberty to Texas and an affiliation with the United States.[75]

A letter from Major General Alexander Macomb on April 25 had been written to Cass from New Orleans and it reached the hands of the secretary just at this time. Macomb stated that he had just heard of Gaines' requisition for state troops to check the Caddo. He said that the governor of Louisiana thought that he was not authorized by law to comply, and, from what he had learned, that it was not necessary, as the country was not invaded, and to his mind, not likely to be, and that he believed it was a scheme of interested land speculators who had made Gaines believe that the Mexican authorities were tampering with the Indians, and by false rumors stimulating belief in

---

[73] Quoted in *Niles' Register*, L, 177.
[74] *Ibid.*, L, 185–186.
[75] *Ibid.*, L, 177.

the minds of the people of New Orleans to get the United States authorities to lend aid in getting up a force composed of interested persons who should move to the Texan frontier, and afterward, under false pretenses, cross into Texas and take part in the war, thus implying sanction of the government and causing the people of Texas to believe that they could rely on the United States for protection. Gaines had a sufficient number of regulars, he thought, to carry out his instructions.[76]

The *National Intelligencer* seized upon this letter as supporting its views and published it with obvious glee in its issue of May 10. To quote: "After our paper was ready for press, last evening, we were happy to learn that a letter had just been received in this city from an officer of the army of the highest rank, at New Orleans, stating that there was not the least danger of any hostilities on the Texian frontier either from Indians or Mexican troops."[77]

The opposition in Congress also became forceful, and on May 10 a resolution was introduced in the House calling upon Cass to submit every document in the possession of the War Department which had to do with Gaines.[78]

The combination of circumstances and the possibility that the whole affair on the border would turn out to be a fiasco profoundly affected the administration. If the Macomb letter presented the true state of affairs, the opposition to Jackson would crystallize and gain unwonted strength. It was necessary to protect the executive before submitting the correspondence to Congress.

---

[76] Macomb to Cass, April 25, 1836, *House Ex. Docs.*, 24 Cong., 1 Sess., VI, Doc. 256, pp. 55–56. Macomb's letter as evidence is worthless. He was a partisan of General Scott in his controversy with Gaines and Jesup; he had not been on the border and was not fully acquainted with conditions. Furthermore, the reason for the refusal of the governor of Louisiana to send troops was an entirely different one, as will be shown later.

[77] Quoted in *House Ex. Docs.*, 25 Cong., 2 Sess., XII, Doc. 351, pp. 790–792.

[78] Cass to Jackson, May 14, 1836, *House Ex. Docs.*, 24 Cong., 1 Sess., VI, Doc. 256, p. 40.

On May 12 Cass penned an extremely cautious letter to Gaines. He said that the President was solicitous that the commander act with the greatest caution and in no wise compromise our neutral relations, the great object being to defend the frontier and keep neutrality. If the Indians were not employed immediately on the border, there was no need of advancing beyond territory heretofore actually occupied by the United States, unless armed parties approached so close to our frontier that it was evident they meant to violate our territory. He observed that the contending parties would hardly venture to do that, but it would be otherwise with Indians. To quote:

> It was principally with a view therefore to this state of things, that you were authorized to cross the line dividing the country actually in the occupation of the United States from that heretofore in the possession of Mexico, if such a measure be necessary for the defense of the frontier. But I must impress upon you the desire of the President, that you do not advance unless circumstances distinctly show this step is necessary for the protection of the district of our country adjoining the scene of operations in Texas.

If Gaines advanced, he was told to inform the parties of his object and orders, and under no circumstances was he to cooperate with any of them or allow them to join him, nor to interfere with military operations in Texas, except for self-defence. If Gaines crossed the imaginary line, he was to return as soon as the safety of the frontier would permit.[79]

Two days later the correspondence with Gaines, including the letter of the twelfth, was submitted to Congress,[80] and as the legislation above noted was passed after that date, it appears to have satisfied the legislators.

---

[79] Cass to Gaines, May 12, 1836, *House Ex. Docs.*, 24 Cong., 1 Sess., VI, Doc. 256, pp. 54–55. An added proof that this letter was merely for immediate effect is found in the fact that the troops were allowed to remain on Mexican soil long after all danger of hostilities had subsided, a state of affairs which led to Gorostiza demanding his passports. This will be discussed at length later.

[80] Cass to Jackson, May 14, 1836, *ibid.*, 40.

The governors, with the exception of White of Louisiana, complied readily. Governor Cannon of Tennessee wrote to Cass that the young men were complying with alacrity and within two weeks he would have a respectable force of mounted men to send to the front. He asked information as to the views of the war department, and in regard to transportation.[81] Governor White, however, refused to comply because of lack of funds, the legislature not being in session. He reported, however, that the force of General Planche was assembled and ready to march.[82]

It is time now to return to the operations on the Sabine where we left Gaines on April 20. On April 25 he penned letters to Santa Anna and Houston to warn them against any military operations east of Sabine Bay or any of the principal watercourses that emptied into it, or in the region to the south of Red River near Fort Towson, or across any portion of the unmarked boundary. He also warned them against the employment of Indians. Before the despatches could be sent, however, rumors reached Camp Sabine that the battle of San Jacinto had occurred. He immediately added postscripts to the letters to the effect that if any of the officers or troops had been placed by the fortunes of war in a situation requiring the humane offices of a friendly neighbor, he would take great pleasure in extending any act of kindness not incompatible with neutrality.[83]

On April 28 Gaines reported to Cass that there was no doubt of the battle of San Jacinto. He said that Santa Anna had declared himself ready and willing to acknowledge the independence of Texas, a point upon which, he presumed, the constituted authorities of Mexico would have to be consulted. The Cherokees and other Indians, he reported, were now disposed to return to their villages, and in consequence he thought it proper to com-

---

[81] Cannon to Cass, April 28, 1836, *House Ex. Docs.*, 24 Cong., 1 Sess., VI, Doc. 256, pp. 50–51.

[82] *Congressional Debates*, XII, Pt. 3, p. 3342. This, it will be observed, was quite different from Macomb's statement.

[83] Gaines to Santa Anna and Houston, April 25, 1836, *House Ex. Docs.*, 25 Cong., 2 Sess., XII, Doc. 351, pp. 782–783.

municate with the state governors, suspending the movement of volunteers.[84]

On May 2 he wrote a more detailed despatch, confirming his letter of the twenty-eighth. Gaines showed in this letter that he was in an anxious state of mind, for he could not but realize that the defeat of Santa Anna had completely changed the border conditions, depriving him of any immediate prospect of military success. The war with Mexico, in which he hoped to gain a great name, had suddenly become a remote possibility.[85]

---

[84] Gaines to Cass, April 28, 1836, *House Ex. Docs.*, 25 Cong., 2 Sess., Doc. 351, p. 783.

[85] That this idea was long an active one in the mind of Gaines is evident from an incident which occurred in May, 1837. He was then at Mobile, where he heard that some American merchant vessels had been captured by Mexicans. He immediately sent to the Adjutant-General a plan of preparation for a war against Mexico. In closing he said: "If I am permitted to make an arrangement in accordance with foregoing suggestions, I feel confident that I can thereby obtain and call to the frontier, ready for an active campaign to the city of Mexico, from 50,000 to 100,000 first-rate men for the most part mounted, before the first day of October next, the time they should reach westward from the Sabine." (Gaines to Jones, May 22, 1837, *ibid.*, 820–821.) Gaines' unauthorized action in recruiting men for the Mexican war caused Polk much embarrassment. See Polk, *Diary*, I, 450–451, 480; II, 82–83.

CHAPTER IX

THE OCCUPATION OF NACOGDOCHES

From the date of the reception of the news of San Jacinto, the border situation was changed. There was no longer danger of an immediate collision with Mexican troops, the Indians became less hostile, and the Texans were freed from impending disaster. Mexico, prostrate in defeat, could not contend against an American force which might cross her border. The United States had thus far cloaked her designs under the excuse of preservation of neutrality and protection against Indians. But with the capture of Santa Anna, the excuse disappeared.

None realized this more keenly than Gaines. Feeling the uncertainty of his position, he appealed indirectly to Jackson for support. In a letter to Cass he said:

I purposely abstain, as I have long abstained, from the ceremony which I think is not in accordance with our institutions, of expressing a hope that *the President of the United States will approve my conduct*, because I think I should do that distinguished officer great injustice to suppose that he would not, unsolicited, approve what he may deem to be right. And I should feel that I was unworthy the trust reposed in me, and unworthy the many great honors conferred upon me by the United States, and by several of the great and patriotic States separately, were I capable of cherishing a wish that any act of mine found to be *wrong*, taking into view the *circumstances of the case* at the time, *should be approved by him.*[1]

That the acquisition of Texas was uppermost in the mind of Gaines there can be no doubt, and it is also clear that he believed it to be equally potent in Jackson's policy; this is shown by his next despatch, which stated:

The affairs of this infant republic are . . . assuming an aspect not only of deepest interest to its inhabitants of the present moment, and

[1] Gaines to Cass, May 2, 1836, *House Ex. Docs.*, 25 Cong., 2 Sess., XII, Doc. 351, p. 784.

of the millions and *tens* of millions destined in the present century to enjoy its fertile soil and salubrious atmosphere, but an aspect of incalculable importance to our beloved country; to whose benign institutions the inhabitants of Texas of all classes already look as the only guide and sure basis of their present safety and future prosperity and happiness.

It is believed, by all whose opinion I have had the means of knowing, that the people of Texas are all willing, and most of them extremely anxious, as soon as possible to apply to our Government for admission into the Union . . .

Believing it to be of great importance to our country, as well as to Texas and Mexico, and indeed to the whole people of the continent of America, that our Government should be prepared to act promptly upon the anticipated application of the people of Texas for admission; and desiring, as fervently as any one of the early friends of the President can possibly desire, that this magnificent acquisition to our Union should be made within the period of his presidential term, and apprehending that unlooked for changes and embarrassing interferences by foreign Powers might result from delaying our national action upon the subject to another session of Congress, I have taken leave to order to the city of Washington Captain E. A. Hitchcock, . . . whose discriminating mind and perfect integrity and honor will enable him to communicate more fully than my present delicate health . . . will allow me to write, the facts and circumstances connected with this interesting subject, the opinions and wishes of the inhabitants of the eastern border of Texas, together with the late occurrences, and present state of my command.[2]

On the same day that Gaines wrote the above letter, Captain Dean of the Third Infantry and aide-de-camp George A. McCall, who had been inspecting the region south of Red River, reported to Lieutenant Colonel J. H. Vose, commander at Fort Towson. They said that the inhabitants of Jonesborough were much alarmed by Indian reports and the leading men had gone

---

[2] Gaines to Cass, May 10, 1836, *House Ex. Docs.*, 25 Cong., 2 Sess., XII, Doc. 351, pp. 786–787. Gaines' letter seems almost prophetic in regard to foreign interference. See Smith, *The Annexation of Texas,* 76–100; Adams, *British Interests and Activities in Texas;* Tyler, *Letters and Times of the Tylers,* II, 425, 428. Captain Hitchcock proceeded to Washington with Gaines' letter, and with two other communications, one from Houston, the other from Rusk, the Texan Secretary of War. Houston's note told of the victory at San Jacinto. When Jackson recognized the handwriting and grasped the import of the news, he took no pains to conceal his delight. Hitchcock, *Fifty Years in Camp and Field,* 108.

to Sulphur Prairies to a general assemblage of the inhabitants
of Miller County. Dean and McCall reported that they had
arrived there after the meeting had dissolved, but found that
two companies of rangers had been formed and an application
made to the governor of Arkansas for military protection. Two
companies had been sent out, one of which reported that they
had ascertained that the Indian villages were deserted and the
warriors assembled on the Sabine, with a Mexican officer among
them; that the old and helpless were secreted in the woods, and
that a council had been called for May 2. It was reported also
that Caddo were massacring Americans on the upper Brazos,
regardless of age or sex. It was learned that not a Cherokee,
Delaware, or Shawnee had been seen that season in any part of
the settlement, another indication of hostility. There were two
hundred families on the Sulphur Prairies; the remote ones had
moved into the more settled regions, and at one place twenty-five
families had built a stockade. The settlers asked if they would
be protected by the United States, to which the officers had
replied, that though there was a question regarding the right of
territory, there was none regarding their citizenship. Dean and
McCall recommended that dragoons be sent into the territory.
They estimated the number of Indians who could be mustered
at one thousand eight hundred and fifty warriors, exclusive of
Comanche and other interior tribes.[3]

Gaines also received a communication from Larkin Edwards,
formerly interpreter of the Caddo agent, that Flores was still
active among the Indians.[4] Bonnell was sent out to obtain
further information concerning Flores, and his report of June
4 confirmed what had previously been learned about him, adding
that another Mexican named José María Medrano had been
operating with Flores.[5]

---

3 *House Ex. Docs.*, 25 Cong., 2 Sess., XII, Doc. 351, pp. 788–790.

4 Edwards to Gaines, May 13, 1836, *ibid.*, 814–815.

5 Bonnell to Gaines, June 4, 1836, *ibid.*, 809–810.

These reports were probably a factor in shaping the next step in the movements of Gaines. On June 6 he wrote a letter to Governor Cannon of Tennessee, which gives the first inkling of his intended movements. He reviewed the recent state of Indian hostilities and stated that he was convinced that the advance to the Sabine had prevented a great Indian war. He stated that the report that Mexico would acknowledge the independence of Texas was not given as much credence as it had been, and that the Indians might, in consequence, be induced to renew hostilities in the disputed region. "In this apprehension," he said, "I cannot but feel some reproach, that I should so hastily have denied myself the pleasure of receiving at this place and retaining in the service of the public, until every difficulty among the Indians and their allies had been permanently settled, the brigade of Tennessee volunteers. . . . I think it is my duty to request your excellency, to authorize the brigade of Tennessee volunteers, enrolled agreeably to your proclamation, to calculate on the probability of another call to this frontier."[6]

On the following day Gaines wrote to Cass in a similar vein, and pointed out that there were but sixteen hundred troops to four hundred miles of territory, and "that the chivalry of Mexico may be expected to fly to the rescue of their President, and reinstate his red allies, and inspire them with a spirit of revenge against those recently screened from their barbarism." He informed Cass of his communication to Cannon regarding the possibility of another call for troops.[7]

On June 7 Bonnell sent further information from Fort Jesup

---

[6] Gaines to Cannon, June 6, 1836, *Niles' Register*, L, 384–385. It is stated by Bancroft, (*North Mexican States and Texas*, II, 287) that Gaines' second call for troops was due to advices received from Rusk and to Indian hostilities that occurred on the Navasota. This is literally true, but it is interesting to note that Gaines was contemplating the move before he knew of the renewed hostilities, or had heard from Rusk.

[7] Gaines to Cass, June 7, 1836, *House Ex. Docs.*, 25 Cong., 2 Sess., XII, Doc. 351, pp. 787–788.

concerning Flores and Medrano,[8] and on the sixteenth witnesses were called before Robert K. McDonald, justice of the peace at Natchitoches, to obtain further evidence. The testimony of the witnesses confirmed the previous statements concerning Flores.[9]

Opportunely for Gaines, the Indians perpetrated several atrocities about this time. On May 18 Parker's Fort, a settlement containing thirty-four people, located on the headwaters of the Navasota River, was attacked by a force of Comanche and Kiowa, variously estimated as containing from three hundred to seven hundred warriors. Five of the inhabitants were killed, three dangerously wounded, and five carried into captivity.[10]

Several depredations had also occurred in the colony of Sterling C. Robertson. James Dunn, the *regidor* of the municipality of Milam, testified that having heard of the massacre at Parker's Fort, he prepared to move to Nashville on the Brazos. with a view of "forting," and that he and two others were attacked by about fifty Indians; one was wounded, many cattle were killed and the balance driven off. Some of the Indians then attacked other settlers in the neighborhood, killing two of them. Dunn claimed that he recognized a Caddo chief named Douchey among the assailants. Montgomery B. Shackleford, who was one of the settlers who had been attacked, confirmed the statement of Dunn. Robertson sent the depositions of Dunn and Shackleford to Gaines, calling attention to the fact that the Caddo had taken part. He appealed to the sympathies of the American commander—

Already we hear from lisping infancy and weary and withered age throughout this wide-spreading republic, that you are a friend to Texas. If the facts as stated will justify your march against the Caddoes, the

[8] Bonnell to Gaines, June 7, 1836, *House Ex. Docs.*, 25 Cong., 2 Sess., XII, Doc. 351, pp. 810–811.

[9] *Ibid.*, 812–814.

[10] De Shields, *Cynthia Ann Parker: The Story of her Capture at the Massacre of the Inmates of Parker's Fort*, 13–16.

country, we trust, will shortly be relieved from Indian hostility, and the occasion will furnish other proofs of the zeal and ability (if any can be wanting) with which you are ever ready to serve your country.[11]

That this communication from Robertson determined Gaines to occupy Nacogdoches is evinced by his reply. He pointed out that it was not entirely clear that Caddo had taken part in the outrages, but he thought the evidence sufficient to justify an investigation as soon as the dragoons could arrive, which he had ordered from Fort Jesup to Camp Sabine.

In the interim, [he wrote] I have to request the favor of you to obtain and transmit *to the officer* commanding a detachment of United States troops at or near Nacogdoches whatever additional information may be in your power; and name the distances from place to place, and the persons on the road to whom you would refer . . . for information as to the topography and character of the country . . . ; and as to the latest movements, most recent position of the Indians, their probable number, how armed, and whether mounted or otherwise; and whether Bowles or any of the Cherokees, Delawares, Shawnees, Kickapoos, Saxes, or Foxes, were concerned with the Caddoes and Comanches in the late murders.

He further advised Robertson to have blockhouses enclosed with pickets at every settlement, to supply them, and make it the duty of every man and "every spirited lady" to guard them by turns.[12]

It is necessary at this point to revert to the attitude of Mexico toward Texas at this time. After his capture, Santa Anna and President Burnet entered into the treaty of Velasco, by which it was agreed that all hostilities were to cease and the Mexican army to pass beyond the Rio Grande.[13] Led by General Filisola,

---

[11] Robertson to Gaines, June 16, 1836, with enclosures of the depositions of Dunn and Shackleford of June 15, *House Ex. Docs.*, 25 Cong., 2 Sess., XII, Doc. 351, pp. 792–794.

[12] Gaines to Robertson, June 22, 1836, *ibid.*, 794–795. From the above it might be inferred that Gaines had already sent troops into Texas; being unable to locate the army orders, it is impossible to state with positiveness. The main body of troops was certainly despatched later.

[13] Copy of the Treaty in Yoakum, *History of Texas*, II, 526–528; Marshall, in Texas State Historical Association, *The Quarterly*, XIV, 281–282.

the army retreated with great hardship, arriving on May 13 at Victoria,[14] and later falling back to Matamoras.[15]

The Mexican government at first acted with extreme caution, evidently desirous of saving the life of Santa Anna; but it soon determined to prosecute the war.[16] Filisola was removed from his command, General Urrea superseding him.[17] On May 20 the Mexican Congress passed a decree to carry the war into Texas regardless of any agreement of Santa Anna,[18] a course which was strengthened on July 29 by the issuance of a manifesto calling upon the people to support the war.[19] On June 6 Urrea issued a proclamation to the troops at Matamoras that he would lead them against Texas as soon as the government gave the command.[20]

Karnes and Teal, two Texan officers, had been sent to Matamoros to carry into effect the agreement with Santa Anna, which had been assented to by Filisola; Urrea held them in surveillance at Matamoros.[21] From there Teal addressed a letter to Rusk, then the Texan commander, informing him of military preparations at Matamoros. He wrote that four thousand men would leave for La Bahia in a few days and an equal force would go from Vera Cruz by water, headed for Copano or some other point.[22]

The news alarmed everyone in Texas. Rusk wrote to Thomas J. Green on June 17 that his force at Victoria was then only three hundred and fifty men and asked that troops be collected at once,[23] and on the following day wrote to Gaines that Mexicans

[14] Filisola, *Memorias para la Historia de la Guerra de Tejas*, II, 472–493.
[15] Bancroft, *North Mexican States and Texas*, II, 720.
[16] Yoakum, *History of Texas*, II, 166–167.
[17] *Ibid.*, II, 202.
[18] *Niles' Register*, L, 336.
[19] *Manifiesto del Congreso General, July 29, 1836*, 1–20.
[20] *Niles' Register*, L, 335–336.
[21] Potter, in Texas State Historical Association, *The Quarterly*, IV, 71–84.
[22] Teal to Rusk, June 9, 1836, in *Niles' Register*, L, 350.
[23] *Niles' Register*, L, 383–384.

were advancing and that their motto was, "Extermination to the Sabine, or death." This communication determined Gaines to call again upon the governors for troops. In a letter to General Bradford of the Tennessee volunteers, he told of the contents of Rusk's letter and of the recent Indian hostilities which had caused him to call upon "your excellent governor Cannon," and the governors of Kentucky, Mississippi and Louisiana for troops. He wrote:

If you come, come quickly; and say so to all my young friends near you. I am resolved, in case the Mexicans or Texians employ the Indians against the people of either side of the imaginary line, to inflict on the offenders serious and severe punishment.[24]

In his letter to the governor of Kentucky, Gaines said that the recent Indian hostilities and the bloody character of the Santa Anna invasion indicated the nature of approaching events. To maintain neutrality, stay the work of devastation in the disputed territory, and preserve the frontier from savage war, a force equal to that of the principal belligerents was necessary. In consequence he asked him for a regiment of mounted gunmen.[25]

When Gaines called upon the governor for aid, he had already received Cass' instructions of May 12. He wrote to Cass that he greatly regretted the restricted limits to which the instructions confined him, and stated that no doubt the publication of Macomb's letter in the *National Intelligencer* was the cause. He said that if that officer had come to Camp Sabine, he could soon have convinced him of the true state of affairs. He enclosed to Cass the recent communication from Robertson's colony.[26]

From this point Gaines certainly interpreted his instructions very broadly. It is probable that he thought the situation justified him, and that he would be upheld, as he had been

---

24 Gaines to Bradford, June 28, 1836, *Niles' Register*, L, 384.

25 Gaines to the governor of Kentucky, June 28, 1836, *ibid.*, L, 385.

26 Gaines to Cass, June 22, 1836, *House Ex. Docs.*, 25 Cong., 2 Sess., XII, Doc. 351, pp. 790–792.

previously, as soon as the executive was aware of the true state of affairs.[27]

During this period Gaines was in communication with S. H. Everett of Jasper, Texas, who was destined to represent his district in the Senate in the first Congress of the Texan republic. Everett posted the American commander on the Indian situation[28] and the topography of the country.[29] On July 2 he wrote that he believed the Indians knew of the return of the Mexican army. He said that the Indians declared that the Texans had lied, as the American troops had never intended to cross the Sabine. He reported that the Biloxi had moved toward the Trinity. If the United States claimed jurisdiction over the disputed territory and wished to prevent an Indian war, he urged that Gaines march into Texas. He said that the Texan government had called on every man who was capable of bearing arms to repair to the army, and the women and children would be left unprotected.[30]

Finally, on July 10, Gaines ordered Colonel Whistler to repair to Nacogdoches, which he was to fortify with a small breastwork with two block houses at opposite angles.

Should you find any of the Indians, of our side of the supposed national boundary, manifesting a hostile spirit, you will urge them to return to their villages and be peaceable. But should they, or any other Indians, or other armed forces, be found in warlike attitude, or in the act of any decided hostility against the United States troops, or against any of the inhabitants of this frontier, or of the disputed territory of the *south* or *east* or *north* of Nacogdoches, you will in that case employ the forces of your command to avert or otherwise restrain them from such hostility, notifying the commanding officer here [Camp Sabine] of their *position*, probable *numbers* and *conduct;* to the end that the forces

----

[27] The writer ventures the opinion that Gaines had judged the situation at Washington correctly, but he could not forsee that the threatened invasion would not materialize.

[28] Everett to Gaines, June 27, 1836, *House Ex. Docs.*, 25 Cong., 2 Sess., XII, Doc. 351, p. 804.

[29] Everett to Gaines, July 1, 1836, *ibid.*, 804–805.

[30] Everett to Gaines, July 2, 1836, *ibid.*, 806.

at this place may promptly support and co-operate with you in their arrest or punishment. But you will not attack them without evidence of their hostility, demonstrated by their *conduct*, rather than by their threats, taking care to conform strictly to the precautionary measures prescribed in the instructions herewith enclosed, as well as the general regulations of the War Department.[31]

On the following day additional instructions were issued, the wording of which seems significant:

The present posture of affairs in Texas indicates the probability of Indian disturbances on the western and southwestern borders of the United States in the course of the summer and autumn. On this hypothesis must be predicated all military movements on this frontier.[32]

Six companies of infantry and three companies of dragoons were also ordered from Fort Towson.[33] Two weeks were required to make the march of two hundred miles to Nacogdoches. Much of the route had never been traversed except by men on horseback, and it was necessary to cut a road for the ox-teams carrying supplies. The forces encamped on a hill within the town. The few inhabitants proved friendly to the troops, but many were still absent through fear of the Indians.

The American force was in close touch with the Texan army, Houston and his staff visiting the town in the latter part of July. It was reported in the *Pensacola Gazette* that many of the soldiers deserted to the Texan army, which was rapidly in-

---

[31] Orders of Gaines of July 10, 1836, *House Ex. Docs.*, 25 Cong., 2 Sess., VII, Doc. 190 p. 98. Bancroft, (*North Mexican States and Texas*, II, 287), gives the date as July 11. Yoakum, (*History of Texas*, II, 181–183), makes much of the fact that Austin had written to Houston to the effect that it would be highly desirable to have Gaines occupy Nacogdoches, and that Houston communicated this to Gaines; that also on July 13 he sent a report about Indians to the American commander. Neither of these influenced Gaines in the sending of troops, as they were both received some time after the actual order of occupation had been issued. Gaines claimed that his action was to carry out Cass' instructions of May 12; it is difficult to see how such latitude could be taken under those instructions.

[32] Order of July 11, 1836, *House Ex. Docs.*, 25 Cong., 2 Sess., VII, Doc. 190, p. 99.

[33] *Niles' Register*, L, 377.

creasing; an officer was sent to reclaim them and found two
hundred wearing the American uniform. The Texan officer gave
them freedom to return, but they refused.[34]

Lieutenant Joseph Bonnell reported to Gaines from Nacogdoches on July 19, saying that the committee of safety and
vigilance had just been called together because of the report of
a Shawnee Indian named Spy Buck. The Indian declared that
his uncle had left Red River ten days before and brought word
that the Comanche, Waco, Tawaconi, Towaash, and Kichai had
made peace and again combined against the whites, and had
killed nine men on Sulphur Fork. The Americans had taken
refuge in the fort at Kiamichi, and two hundred men were in
pursuit of the murderers. He reported that Indians were watching all the river crossings and that twelve tribes had placed
all their old men, women, and children at the three forks of
the Trinity. Bonnell wrote that he did not know whether the
report was true or false, but that it was fully believed at Nacogdoches.[35]

Gaines reported at once the contents of Bonnell's despatch
to Cass. He wrote that if the report were true, a movement
should be made at once against the Indians, "and it should be
made without a word being said or written *publicly* on the subject. If it is spoken of here, the Indians will know it through
their friendly traders." He stated that he would be restricted
to defensive measures until the arrival of volunteers, which he
expected in August. He said that at Camp Sabine a blockhouse
and eight storehouses had been ordered erected, and when completed would contain nearly three thousand bushels of grain and
over a hundred and fifty thousand rations.[36]

An effort was made by Bonnell and the Texan Indian agent,
Menard, to ascertain the true Indian situation. Isadore Pan-

---

[34] *Niles' Register*, LI, 21.

[35] Bonnell to Gaines, July 19, 1836, *House Ex. Docs.*, 25 Cong., 2 Sess.,
XII, Doc. 351, pp. 796–797.

[36] Gaines to Cass, July 21, 1836, *ibid.*, 795–796.

tallion was sent out as a secret agent,[37] and Menard himself went among the Shawnee. On August 9 Menard reported to Houston at Nacogdoches, where the Texan commander had been since August 4. He stated that most of the Shawnee were friendly, but that the plains Indians were hostile and were collected at the three forks of the Trinity. He believed them to be cowardly and inclined to do little but steal cattle. The Cherokee, Biloxi, Choctaw, Alabama, and Caddo were very hostile, and he believed they would soon begin incursions against the settlements; the Cherokee he thought would concentrate seventy-five miles northwest on the Sabine, and the rest forty miles south of Nacogdoches on the Neches.[38]

Pantallion reported that he had passed among the Cherokee as a Mexican officer. Bowles had sworn to him that he would assist the Mexicans and was then making preparations. He asked why the Americans had occupied Nacogdoches, and on being told that the United States claimed as far as the Neches, he said, "Just like the Americans, always stealing piece by piece."[39]

Bonnell forwarded the reports of Menard and Pantallion to Gaines, adding the information that the reports were confirmed by a Frenchman named Michael Sacco.[40] Gaines immediately sent them to Cass, with the letters of Everett. He also informed him that he had called upon the governor of Missouri for a thousand men, one half of whom were to be mounted. These troops, he requested, should be held in readiness at forts Leavenworth and Gibson.[41]

Major B. Riley was also sent among the Caddo. He found them peaceably inclined, very much degraded, and addicted to the use of liquor; "a poor miserable people, incapable of the

---

[37] *House Ex. Docs.*, 25 Cong., 2 Sess., XII, Doc. 351, p. 800.
[38] Menard to Houston, August 9, 1836, *ibid.*, 800–802.
[39] Report of Pantallion, August 9, 1836, *ibid.*, 802–803.
[40] Bonnell to Gaines, August 9, 1836, *ibid.*, 790–800.
[41] Gaines to Cass, August 11, 1836, *ibid.*, 798.

smallest exertion, either as regards living, or anything else, except liquor.''[42]

Having considered at length the activities on the border, it is time to turn again to affairs at Washington. On July 11 Cass replied to Gaines' letter of June 7 in which that officer had stated that he was regretful that he had suspended the movements of volunteers. The Secretary of War expressed himself as fearful of the Indian situation. He now instructed Gaines that, if he considered it necessary, he might advance as far as Nacogdoches without hesitation, a view concurred in by the President. No mention was made of state troops, as Cass then had no definite information that the call had actually been made.[43]

It will be observed that the attitude of the war department was much bolder than that of two months previous. There were two probable reasons for it: first, the legislation for which Cass had asked had been passed; and secondly, he had evidently become convinced that Gaines, rather than Macomb, had given the true border conditions.

But the fair weather predicted by Cass' letter was not to continue, as Jackson decided to stop the sending of troops by the governors. On August 5 he addressed a letter to Governor Cannon, in which he stated that he wished to maintain a strict neutrality and believed that to sanction so large a mobilization would furnish the government of Mexico a reason for supposing that the United States might be induced, for inadequate causes, to overstep the lines of neutrality. That he was piqued because Gaines had acted on his own authority, is evident from the fact that he criticized the governor for considering instructions for a requisition in May to apply also to one in June. Gaines also came in for criticism:

---

[42] Riley to Gaines, August 24, 1836, *House Ex. Docs.*, 25 Cong., 2 Sess., XII, Doc. 351, pp. 815–818.

[43] Cass to Gaines, July 11, 1836, *House Ex. Docs.*, 25 Cong., 2 Sess., VII, Doc. 190, p. 97.

The Government of the United States having adopted, in regard to Mexico and Texas, the same rule of neutrality which had been observed in similar cases before, it was not to have been expected that General Gaines should have based his requisition for additional military force on reasons plainly inconsistent with the obligations of that rule. Should Mexico insult our national flag, invade our territory, or interrupt our citizens in the lawful pursuits which are guaranteed to them by the treaty, then the Government will promptly repel the insult, and take speedy reparation for the injury. But it does not seem that offences of this character have been committed by Mexico, or were believed to have been by General Gaines.

The President also stated that there was no reason to justify apprehension of extensive Indian hostilities, but if more troops were needed, they would be asked for from Ohio, Kentucky, Indiana, and Illinois. He also said that before leaving Washington, being then at the Hermitage, he had directed the Secretary of War to inform Gaines of the apportionment which had been made under the new volunteer act, and that he had given him permission to call upon Arkansas and Missouri for a thousand men from each.[44]

Jackson's position, then, was to acquiesce in the occupation of Nacogdoches, to make it possible to call for troops from Arkansas and Missouri, but to countermand Gaines' other requisitions. It is evident that the latter was a departure from the course pursued in the previous May and June. An examination of certain other events transpiring at this time may throw some light on the actions of the President.

Austin and other Texan governmental agents had been in the United States urging that their country be annexed or its independence recognized.[45] Jackson was considering the question deeply at this time. Determined to get at the true state of affairs, he despatched Henry M. Morfit to Texas to examine and make a

---

[44] Jackson to Cannon, August 5, 1836, *House Ex. Docs.*, 25 Cong., 2 Sess., VII, Doc. 190, pp. 101–102. See also *Niles' Register*, L, 412–413, and Barker, in *The Mississippi Valley Historical Review*, I, 21–22.

[45] *Texan Dipl. Corres.*, I, 76–77, 79–80, 84–86, 89–92.

report of the exact state of affairs. Morfit was then on the way and Jackson was waiting to receive his first report.[46]

To sum up the reasons of Jackson for his action in stopping the sending of troops: first, he did not consider an Indian outbreak as imminent; second, he did not wish to hamper the administration in its future course, whatever that might be, by unnecessarily irritating Mexico; and third, he wished to get definite information before taking the next step. Satisfied that, for the time being, Texas was in no immediate danger of being reoccupied by Mexico, he was willing to wait until sure of his ground without aggravating the case more than necessary.

Gaines heard of the action of the President late in August in a letter from Governor Cannon. Although the Mexican invasion did not materialize, he still insisted that there was danger of an Indian war and that the Mexicans were still tampering with the Indians.[47] The country remained in a state of alarm for some time,[48] and reports continued to come in regarding possible Indian hostilities,[49] but there was no uprising,[50] and domestic and financial troubles prevented Mexico from invading Texas.[51] The troops, however, were allowed to remain at Nacogdoches.

Early in October Cass resigned to become minister to France,[52] and B. F. Butler temporarily filled the position of secretary of war.[53] Early in October Gaines left the frontier to attend the military inquiry which had been called to meet at Fredericktown, Maryland, on November 7.[54] Before his departure, he made

---

[46] Several of Morfit's letters appear in *Congressional Debates*, XIII, Pt. 2, App., 83–96. Also in *Sen. Docs.*, 24 Cong., 2 Sess., Doc. 20, as an appendix to Jackson's message of December 21, 1836.

[47] Gaines to Cannon, August 28, 1836, *Niles' Register*, LI, 87–88.

[48] Houston to Citizens of Texas, August 29, 1836, *ibid.*, LI, 67.

[49] Report of. Juan Francisco Basques, September 7, 1836, *House Ex. Docs.*, 25 Cong., 2 Sess., XII, Doc. 351, p. 819.

[50] Yoakum, *History of Texas*, II, 191.

[51] *Ibid.*, II, 202.

[52] *Niles' Register*, LI, 82.

[53] *House Ex. Docs.*, 24 Cong., 2 Sess., I, Doc. 2, pp. 103–105.

[54] *House Ex. Docs.*, 25 Cong., 2 Sess., III, Doc. 78, pp. 123, 129.

several changes in the disposition of the troops. Five companies of the Sixth and two companies of the Third Infantry were returned to Fort Jesup. Major Riley was ordered to take three companies of the Sixth Infantry to a position on the Sabine River ninety miles north of Camp Sabine. Major Belknap, with two companies of the Third and two of the Seventh Infantry, was ordered to Camp Sabine.[55] Brigadier-General Arbuckle, stationed at Fort Gibson, was left in command during the absence of Gaines.

In his report of November 30, 1836, Macomb stated that, according to the latest advices he had received, there were four hundred and twenty-eight men at Nacogdoches. From the reports of Lieutenant-Colonel Whistler, he was of the opinion that there was no necessity for the continuance of the force at that place.

> From the views taken of the state of affairs on the Mexican frontier by the general officer [Arbuckle] who has succeeded General Gaines in the immediate command in that quarter, and the instructions he has received, the belief is entertained, that by this time the United States troops at Nacogdoches have been withdrawn, and returned to their respective stations within our borders.[56]

Thus ended the occupation of eastern Texas. The year had brought forth many changes in the country across the Sabine. The occupation of the territory could no longer be of advantage to the United States in the policy of either annexation or recognition; therefore it was abandoned. It remains, however, for us to consider the diplomatic situation which resulted from the occupation.

---

[55] Letter of October 6, 1836, from the *Army and Navy Chronicle,* in *Niles' Register,* LI, 162.

[56] *House Ex. Docs.,* 24 Cong., 2 Sess., I, Doc. 2, pp. 129–130, 142–143.

CHAPTER X

THE MISSION OF GOROSTIZA

Having examined the military activities of 1836, it is time to turn to the diplomatic side of the case. The most important actor was Gorostiza, the special envoy of the Mexican government, who was sent to Washington to handle a most difficult situation. In order to understand his position and that of the United States government, it seems necessary to give a brief statement of the attitude of the government at Washington toward the Texan revolution, showing what measures were taken to preserve neutrality, how the officials carried out the instructions, and what was the attitude of the courts.

The enthusiasm and sympathy of the people of the United States led to frequent acts in the autumn of 1835 and during 1836, which were in violation of the neutrality act of 1818.[1] New Orleans was naturally the point of greatest activity, being the port closest to Texas. Forsyth accordingly addressed a letter to Governor Edward D. White of Louisiana, asking him to interfere in any movements on foot and arrest the parties concerned.[2] He also wrote to Henry Carleton, United States district attorney for the eastern district of Louisiana, saying,

It is the fixed determination of the Executive, faithfully to discharge, so far as his power extends, all the obligations of the Government, and that obligation especially requires that we shall abstain, under every temptation, from intermeddling with the domestic disputes of other nations.

---

[1] Winston, in *The Southwestern Historical Quarterly*, XVI, 27–62, 277–283; Rives, *The United States and Mexico*, I, 362–371; Barker, in *The Mississippi Valley Historical Review*, I, 5–7, 10–15.

[2] Forsyth to White, October 27, 1835, *House Ex. Docs.*, 25 Cong., 2 Sess., III, Doc. 74, p. 3.

Carleton was then instructed to prosecute any violators of the neutrality act.[3]

Castillo, the Mexican representative, in October complained of vessels being outfitted in New York for the purpose of introducing arms and munitions of war into Texas. He also stated that the schooner "San Felipe" had sailed from New Orleans for Brazoria, Texas, without papers from the Mexican consul.[4]

Accordingly Forsyth on November 4 sent instructions to the following United States district attorneys: Benjamin F. Linton at St. Martinsville, Louisiana, J. Mills at Boston, William M. Price at New York, Henry D. Gilpin at Philadelphia, Nathaniel Williams at Baltimore, and John Forsyth, Jr., at Mobile, to the effect that, should the contest begin and hostile attempts be made within their districts, the offenders should be prosecuted.[5]

On November 19 a formal complaint was made by Monasterio, the Mexican Minister of Foreign Relations, which in part said:

> The first subject to which the undersigned thinks proper to call the attention of the Secretary of State of the United States, is the notorious co-operation of a great number of the inhabitants of Louisiana, in aiding and advancing the cause of the insurgent colonists of Texas . . .[They] have . . . obtained, and continue to obtain, daily from New Orleans, succors of every kind, in provisions, arms, ammunition, money, and even in soldiers, who are openly enlisted in that city, who sail from it armed for war against a friendly nation; and by their mere presence render more difficult the pacific solution of a question purely domestic. Societies have moreover been formed in New Orleans, which publicly direct or interfere with affairs foreign to their country, either through the instrumentality of the press, or by meetings called ostensibly for the determined object of rendering general throughout the United States the views of a few individuals [speculators] with regard to Texas.[6]

Before this letter was written Forsyth had instructed Butler to inform Monasterio that Jackson looked with regret upon the

---

[3] Forsyth to Carleton, October 27, 1835, *House Ex. Docs.*, 24 Cong., 1 Sess., VI, Doc. 256, p. 4.

[4] Castillo to Forsyth, October 29, 1835, *House Ex. Docs.*, 24 Cong., 1 Sess., VI, Doc. 256, p. 8.

[5] Forsyth to District Attorneys, November 4, 1835, *ibid.*, 36.

[6] Monasterio to Forsyth, November 19, 1835, *ibid.*, 10–11.

state of affairs in Texas. As the United States desired to remain
at peace, measures had been taken to enforce neutrality; it also
wished to execute in good faith the treaty of limits. In case of
a protracted war, neither Mexico nor Texas would be permitted
to encroach upon the territorial limits of the United States, or
make American soil a battleground.[7]

On December 7 Jackson sent his message to Congress, which
stated that the United States was to remain neutral.[8] One portion of the message, especially, attracted the attention of Castillo, the Mexican representative before Gorostiza's appointment.
The statement was: "It has been thought necessary to apprize
the Government of Mexico, that we should require the integrity
of our territory to be scrupulously respected by both parties."
Castillo asked if Jackson recognized limits which were not those
expressly determined by the treaty.[9] Forsyth answered that
remarks made by the President in a message to Congress were
not deemed a proper subject upon which to enter into an explanation with the representative of a foreign power.[10]

In January, 1836, a note was addressed to Monasterio which
expressed the position of the United States at this time. It stated
that measures had been taken to enforce the neutrality act. Then
followed this statement:

For the conduct of individuals which the Government of the United
States cannot control, it is not in any respect responsible; and the Mexican Government well understands how far the funds, and the exertions
and the combined efforts, of individuals may be made to contribute to
the aid of parties in a foreign contest, without, in the slightest degree,
implicating the Government of this country.[11]

---

[7] Forsyth to Butler, November 9, 1835, *House Ex. Docs.*, 24 Cong., 1
Sess., VI, Doc. 256, p. 3.

[8] Richardson, *Messages and Papers of the Presidents*, III, 151.

[9] Castillo to Forsyth, December 11, 1835, *House Ex. Docs.*, 24 Cong.,
1 Sess., VI, Doc. 256, p. 12.

[10] Forsyth to Castillo, December 16, 1835, *ibid.*, 29.

[11] Forsyth to Monasterio, January 29, 1836, *ibid*, 38–39.

Shortly after this, Forsyth informed Castillo that, as the Mexican Minister of Foreign Relations had directly addressed him on the subject of observance of neutrality, further discussion of the subject would be carried on at the City of Mexico rather than at Washington.[12] To put the matter in plain terms, the position of the United States was extremely awkward, and the importunities of Castillo would increase the difficulty of the situation. To carry on the question at long range would, for the time being, free the hands of the government.

But Mexico was not to be denied. It was determined to send Manuel Eduardo Gorostiza, in the capacity of envoy extraordinary and minister plenipotentiary, to the United States. Gorostiza was a tried diplomat, having previously represented Mexico at the Court of St. James. He was appointed on January 19, 1836,[13] and arrived at New York early in March, accompanied by his secretary, M. J. Gamboa, and M. M. Espinosa, attaché. He was detained by illness,[14] and did not take up his duties at Washington until March 24, when he was formally presented to the President.[15]

On April 4 Gorostiza made a complaint to the effect that he had read in certain Tennessee and Kentucky papers that Felix Huston of Natchez was in Tennessee engaged in enlisting, at his own expense, a corps of five hundred men whom he intended to lead to Texas in May. He said that similar things were traceable to the crusade of the so-called commissioners of Texas, among others, the project of raising a company at the expense of the ladies of Nashville.[16]

---

[12] Forsyth to Castillo, February 13, 1836, *House Ex. Docs.*, 24 Cong., 1 Sess., VI, Doc. 256, p. 30.

[13] Monasterio to Forsyth, January 19, 1836, *House Ex. Docs.*, 25 Cong., 2 Sess., XII, Doc. 351, pp. 725–726.

[14] Castillo to Forsyth, March 8, 1836, *ibid.*, 732.

[15] Gorostiza to Forsyth, and Forsyth to Gorostiza, March 24, 1836, *ibid.*, 732–734.

[16] Gorostiza to Forsyth, April 4, 1836, *House Ex. Docs.*, 24 Cong., 1 Sess., VI, Doc. 256, pp. 13–15.

Forsyth immediately sent a letter to James P. Grundy, the United States district attorney at Nashville, to make proper inquiries, and if there were any violators of the law, to institute proceedings at once. Similar instructions had been sent to Grundy's predecessor, William T. Brown. Letters of like import were sent to Lewis Sanders at Frankfort, Kentucky, and to R. M. Gaines at Natchez, Mississippi.[17]

Up to this point the attitude of the government has been examined, but there is another side to the matter, namely, the carrying out of instructions by the various authorities.

As early as October 21, 1835, Henry Carleton, the United States district attorney for the eastern district of Louisiana, had written to the State Department that there was no doubt that certain persons intended to proceed to Texas to help in the revolution. But when the matter was carefully investigated, he stated that it was difficult to apply the act of 1818, "for it does not appear that any regular *enlisting or entering as soldiers* has taken place within the meaning of the statutes, or that any definite or tangible *military expedition or enterprise* has been set on foot or begun."[18]

In New York an interesting case arose which throws more light on the attitude of the American authorities than any other. The Mexican consul, Gonzales, who had been informed of Forsyth's instructions regarding neutrality, informed District Attorney Price that a meeting was called at the Shakespeare Hotel on November 7 for the purpose of aiding the cause of Texas, and that a notice had been published in the newspapers that a committee had been appointed to solicit and receive subscriptions. Gonzales considered that this was the first step toward direct interference.[19]

---

[17] Forsyth to Grundy, April 9, 1836; Forsyth to Brown, February 24, 1836; Forsyth to Sanders, April 9, 1836; Forsyth to Gaines, April 9, 1836; *House Ex. Docs.*, 24 Cong., 1 Sess., VI, Doc. 256, pp. 37–38.

[18] Carleton to Forsyth, October 21, 1835, *House Ex. Docs.*, 25 Cong., 2 Sess., III, Doc. 74, p. 3.

[19] Gonzales to Price, November 10, 1835, *ibid.*, 7.

The grand jurors for the district of New York in the second circuit, to whose consideration the matter was presented, propounded the following inquiry to the court:

Is it, or not, a violation of the 6th section of the act of Congress passed on the 20th day of April, 1818 . . . that meetings should be held in this district, and committees appointed to provide means and make collections for the purpose of enabling the inhabitants of Texas to engage in a civil war with the sovereignty of Mexico, now at peace with the United States?

The reply of the court was as follows:

In answering the foregoing inquiry, the court will confine itself to the facts stated, and the section of the law referred to. The inquiry is, whether meetings held in this district, (or State), and committees appointed to provide means and make collections *for the purpose of enabling the inhabitants of Texas to engage in a civil war with the sovereignty of Mexico*, is a violation of the section of the law referred to?

That section of the act is as follows: ''And be it further enacted, That if any person shall, *within* the territory or jurisdiction of the United States, begin to set on foot, or provide or prepare the means for, any military expedition or enterprise, to be carried on from *thence* against the territory or dominions of any foreign prince or State, or of any colony, district, or people with whom the United States are at peace, every person so offending shall be deemed guilty of a high misdemeanor, and shall be fined not exceeding three thousand dollars and imprisoned not more than three years.''

This section applies only to military expeditions and enterprises to be carried on from the United States against any foreign Power with which we are at peace. No person shall begin or set on foot, or provide or prepare the means for, any military expedition or enterprise, to be carried on *from* thence; that is, from the United States, or the territory within their jurisdiction. Donations in money, or anything else, to the inhabitants of Texas, to enable them to engage in a civil war with the sovereignty of Mexico, is in no sense beginning, or setting on foot, or providing the means for, a military expedition *from the United States* or their territory. The answer, therefore, to the question put by the grand jury, is, That the facts stated do not amount to any offence, under the 6th section of the act referred to.[20]

---

[20] Enclosed with Price to Forsyth, November 13, 1835, *House Ex. Docs.*, 25 Cong., 2 Sess., III, Doc. 74, pp. 5–8.

On November 13 Gonzales protested against another meeting at Tammany Hall. He also said that a recruiting office had been opened at 62 Front Street for those desiring to take up arms in the Texan cause.[21] Price wrote to Forsyth that he would look into the matter,[22] but nothing appears to have been done.

The governor of Louisiana followed Forsyth's instructions by publishing a proclamation regarding the observance of neutrality in the New Orleans papers. But the attitude of the state authorities was shown by a letter from Martin Blache, secretary of state of Louisiana, who stated that such offences being cognizable by United States tribunals, the national authorities could probably exert a more efficient action in repressing them.[23]

John Forsyth, Jr., wrote that there was no question but that the neutrality act had been grossly violated both in letter and spirit by citizens of Mobile and of Alabama. While he was absent in October, several public meetings were held for the purpose of raising men and money, and a company of thirty had been actually equipped and despatched from Mobile. He said:

> I am at a loss to determine whether your instructions should be applied to the cases that have passed; whether they should be retrospectively obeyed; or whether this last proposition is not negatived by the conclud- ing paragraph of your letter, which reads thus: ''You are therefore earnestly enjoined, *should this contest begin*, to be attentive to all move- ments of a hostile character against either party, &c; and to prosecute, without discrimination, all violation of those laws of the United States which have been enacted for the preservation of peace.''

He asked for further instructions and promised that any new cases which might arise would be prosecuted.[24] In spite of this fact a large number of men continued to be raised in Mobile for the Texan service.[25]

---

[21] Gonzales to Price, November 13, 1835, *House Ex. Docs.*, 25 Cong., 2 Sess., III, Doc. 74, pp. 8–9.

[22] Price to Forsyth, November 13, 1835, *ibid.*, 5.

[23] Blache to Forsyth, November 16, 1835, *ibid.*, 9–10.

[24] Forsyth, Jr., to Forsyth, November 18, 1835, *ibid.*, 10–11.

[25] Barker, in Texas State Historical Association, *The Quarterly*, IX, 236.

One of the war vessels of the Texan navy was the "Brutus," purchased for the service early in 1836.[26] She outfitted in New Orleans in December, and several of the insurance companies of New Orleans asked that she be prevented from sailing, because outfitting for war against Mexico.[27] After examining twenty witnesses without obtaining information, and proper affidavits not being filed, Carleton refused to institute proceedings, stating that he was not legally required to institute proceedings upon common report. He stated that, though it was commonly reported that armaments had been fitted out at New Orleans, and soldiers enlisted, no person could be found in the entire population who would make an affidavit of the facts or indicate a single witness to establish them.[28] A few prosecutions were made in New Orleans, but the cases were not prosecuted with vigor, and they were usually dismissed for lack of evidence.

A similar coolness to prosecute, and in many cases even to investigate, was evinced in Mississippi, Tennessee, and Kentucky.[29] Troops were raised there in large numbers, also in Ohio, a state of affairs which continued until well into 1836.[30]

---

[26] Dienst, in Texas State Historical Association, *The Quarterly*, XII, 196.

[27] *House Ex. Docs.*, 25 Cong., 2 Sess., III, Doc. 74, p. 12.

[28] *Ibid.*, 12–23.

[29] *Ibid.*, 23–24.

[30] Barker, in Texas State Historical Association, *The Quarterly*, IX, 236, 240. A letter from S. P. Carson to President Burnet from Nashville contains the following passage: "I inclose you a correspondence with Gen'l Dunlap who has been exerting himself in our cause and who will soon be in Texas. Seventy men are now ready to leave under Captain Grundy who is the *prosecuting Atty.* for the United States for this District, and had *formal orders* to arrest and prosecute every man who may take up arms in the cause of Texas or in any way *Violate* the Neutrality of the U. S. He says he will prosecute any man under his command who will take up arms *here* and he will accompany them to the boundary line of the U. S. to see that they shall *not violate her Neutrality* and when there, if the boys think proper to step over the line as *peaceable Emigrants* his authority in this Govt will cease and he thinks it highly probable that he will take a peep at Texas himself. Thus you will see how the neutrality of this Govt is *preserved* by her civil officers. You will perceive by the accompanying correspondence the monied arrangement I have made with Genl Dunlap to forward on the Volunteers under his command." Carson to Burnet, June 1, 1836, *Tex. Dipl. Corr.*, I, 93.

During the month of April, as we have already seen, Forsyth and Gorostiza were busy completing the treaty of limits, which resulted in the exchange of ratifications on April 20. During the course of this negotiation, Gorostiza became aware that troops had been ordered to the border. In the conference of April 20, the subject was discussed and Forsyth was asked to make a written state ment setting forth the intentions of the United States, a request with which he complied. The memorandum was in three parts: the first stated that, because of the contest in Texas, the movements of some of the citizens of the United States near Red River, and apprehended hostilities of Indians from Mexico against the United States, and of Indians from the United States against Mexico, Gaines had been ordered to the border; the second stated that the troops would protect the boundary commissioners and surveyors; the third, that should the troops, in the performance of their duty, be advanced beyond the point which Mexico might suppose was within the territory of the United States, the occupation of the position was not to be taken as an indication of any hostile feeling, or of a desire to establish a possession or claim not approved by the treaty of limits; such occupation would be provisional and precautionary and would be abandoned when the disturbances in that region should cease.[31]

Gorostiza, in a note on the twenty-third, denied the third position. He stated that the Gaines movement could be looked upon by the Mexican government only in the light of an intervention in her domestic affairs.[32] The Mexican minister at once communicated with his government on the subject. He said that the sending of Gaines to the border was an audacious measure (*paso atrevido*), the cause of which was to favor the Texans.

---

[31] *House Ex. Docs.*, 24 Cong., 1 Sess., VI, Doc. 256, p. 45.
[32] Gorostiza to Forsyth, April 23, 1836, *ibid.*, 18–21.

For my own part, [he wrote] I never will consent that General Gaines should occupy a foot of the territory which is now Mexican; and should the case occur before I receive instructions from you, I will protest personally, and will retire, leaving the ordinary legation here, until the Government may have decided as to the course which that legation is to pursue.

I may be mistaken, but my opinion is, that if we allow the American troops to enter our territory as neutrals, we shall soon or late lose Texas, and that, too, without saving our honor; whereas, if we do not suffer this, we may perhaps preserve Texas, and we shall, at all events, secure the reputation of our country.[33]

Forsyth replied to Gorostiza's protest, stating that the Mexican minister had not understood clearly the observations of Forsyth at the conference of April 20. He said that Gorostiza had taken it for granted that Gaines would be ordered to occupy territory known to be beyond the limits of the United States. He pointed out that the statement was that troops might be advanced beyond the point which *Mexico might suppose* to be within the territory of the United States. He said that the notice was not intended to express intention to occupy a position within the acknowledged Mexican boundary, but to apprize Mexico that if Gaines occupied territory supposed by each government to be within its limits, its purpose was to do its duty to both countries, and that the United States had no intention of interfering in the disturbances of its neighbors.[34]

The answer of Gorostiza was most adroit. He wrote that he was in accord with Forsyth, "so far as regards the assurance that General Gaines' troops will not take a position on any ground known to be beyond the limits of the United States; and as a natural consequence from this principle, that such position can in no case be on ground previously possessed by Mexico, and,

---

[33] Gorostiza to Department of Foreign Relations, April 25, 1836, *House Ex. Docs.*, 25 Cong., 2 Sess., VII, Doc. 190, p. 74.

[34] Forsyth to Gorostiza, April 26, 1836, *House Ex. Docs.*, 24 Cong., 1 Sess., VI, Doc. 256, p. 32.

of course, within its known limits.'' He asked if he were correct on this point.[35]

Forsyth replied that Gaines would not go into the disputed territory unless absolutely necessary. He said that occupation was not the assertion of a right of property. Whether the post occupied should prove to be in Mexico or the United States, it would be abandoned whenever the necessity ceased, ''by the restoration of tranquility to that distracted neighborhood.''[36]

Gorostiza replied that as the government of the United States had not seen fit to take into consideration his observations, nothing remained to be done but to communicate with his government; as it would be proper that the commander of the Mexican army should receive the necessary instructions in case Gaines advanced beyond the known limits.[37] In this, of course, there was a veiled threat.

On the ninth he wrote that he had seen in *The Globe* the instructions of Cass of April 25, authorizing Gaines to advance to Nacogdoches, which was claimed to be within the limits of the United States. He said that he was at a loss to know on what this rested, as he had examined all the correspondence before he left Mexico, and the only thing that he had seen which could be so interpreted was a vague note from Butler of December 21, 1834, the meaning of which had not been explained. He therefore protested against the authorization to Gaines as a violation of Mexican territory.[38]

This brought forth a lengthy and rather undiplomatic reply from Forsyth. He said that Gaines was not ordered to Nacogdoches, but not to go beyond that point. In this, he considered, there was an important distinction, as the terms used limited the authority given and were chosen with the express intention of avoiding misconstruction of the motive of the advance; to

---

[35] Gorostiza to Forsyth, April 28, 1836, *House Ex. Docs.*, 24 Cong., 1 Sess., VI, Doc. 256, pp. 22–23.

[36] Forsyth to Gorostiza, May 3, 1836, *ibid.*, 33.

[37] Gorostiza to Forsyth, May 4, 1836, *ibid.*, 24.

[38] Gorostiza to Forsyth, May 9, 1836, *ibid.*, 26.

protect the frontier against Indians, in the fulfillment of the treaty, troops might justly be sent into the heart of Mexico. He observed that Gorostiza's protest sprang from an idea that the advance of Gaines was founded on a claim to territory.

The wording of the rest is so important that a long quotation seems necessary. Its significance is more forcible when it is remembered that news of San Jacinto had not then reached Washington.

Contrary to his wish, the President finds himself compelled to require the undersigned to remind Mr. Gorostiza that Mexico is not in possession of the territory bordering on the United States, wherever the true line may be. Whether the Government of Mexico will obtain and can maintain possession of it, are questions now at issue by the most sanguinary arbitrament; until they are decided, the undersigned understands Mr. Gorostiza to maintain that the possession of Texas is the possession of Mexico, and that any advance upon the territory claimed as part of Texas by its self-constituted authorities, is considered essentially, and in its effects, a positive violation of the known territory of Mexico. The Mexican Government must be aware, that portions of the territory ever admitted to belong, as well as that claimed to belong, to the United States, is represented in the Texian Government. The known territory of the United States is then now violated by Mexico, since the Government of Mexico is, upon the principle involved, responsible for this usurpation of a right over the jurisdiction of the United States, and this attempt to limit the extent of their territorial possession. This fact of itself would justify an advance of General Gaines to any point necessary to the vindication of the rights of the United States, or to retort an injury upon Mexico, (or Texas, whichever is responsible) for the original wrong. But the President has not designed to vindicate a right or retort a wrong in the orders that have been given. He looks forward patiently to the period, which cannot be far distant, when the territorial rights of the United States will, according to long existing stipulations, be authoritatively designated and marked by competent and trustworthy agents, so as to leave no room for further cavil and dispute; and in the meantime he desires to occupy no position by military force which the circumstances by which the general commanding the troops of the United States is surrounded, do not justify.

Forsyth observed that the claims of the United States were based upon the treaty of limits, and would be settled by the commissioners. He said that Castillo was informed of those claims in the previous November and it was supposed that this was the cause of the special mission of Gorostiza; the United States would maintain only what reason and the facts would justify.[39]

Gorostiza answered at length:

The undersigned [he wrote] in fact does not perceive (perhaps from want of comprehension on his part) the value of the difference noted by the American Government, between not authorizing General Gaines to go to Nacogdoches, and ordering him not to advance beyond Nacogdoches. The undersigned, on the contrary, conceives that it would not be judged necessary to warn that General that he is not to pass beyond a certain determined point, unless he had already supposed to have the power of advancing to that point. Nor can the undersigned admit the doctrine, that the troops of a friendly Power are authorized to enter of their own accord upon the territory of a neighboring Power, however benevolent be the end proposed, and even if the result be evidently advantageous for the latter. Such a principle would in fact destroy the very foundation of the independence of nations: for that which is done to-day entirely with the view of assisting the friend, may to-morrow be undertaken for purposes less pure; the pretext would be equally plausible in each case. And if, for this reason, in such cases, the previous assent has always been required, at least of every Government whose territory is to be protected by foreign troops, what doubt can there be in the present instance, when the representative of Mexico has at once declared, in the name of his Government, that he is thankful for the favor, but does not accept it.

Forsyth had inadvertently spoken of the government of Texas. Gorostiza saw this diplomatic opening and said:

On this point, the undersigned conceives it his duty to declare that his Government neither knows of any such Government in Texas, nor is aware that the American Government knows of any such. All that the Mexican knows of Texas is, that in the Mexican province there are some foreign colonists who had promised to live under the laws of the country, and that those persons, aided by other foreigners, have raised there the standard of rebellion. Whether Mexico can or cannot repress this rebellion, experience will very soon show, especially if those who are neither Mexicans nor Texians cease from interfering illegally or unjustly in a contest entirely domestic.[40]

---

[39] Forsyth to Gorostiza, May 10, 1836, *House Ex. Docs.*, 24 Cong., 1 Sess., VI, Doc. 256, pp. 33–35. The writer has been unable to find the letter to Castillo referred to.

[40] Gorostiza to Forsyth, May 14, 1836, *House Ex. Docs.*, 24 Cong., 2 Sess., I, Doc. 2, pp. 28–30.

It is evident from the above that the situation was becoming exceedingly strained. It is not beyond the range of possibility, that if Santa Anna had continued in his victorious career in Texas, war might have been declared. But the battle of San Jacinto completely changed the aspect of affairs. With the President of Mexico a prisoner and the uncertainty of the resulting political situation in Mexico, the strength of Gorostiza's position was at once destroyed and that of Forsyth correspondingly strengthened. That the Mexican minister fully realized the situation is evinced by the tone of his letters, which became more courtly and suave, although none the less persistent. Covert threats and imperiousness gave way to persuasion.

On May 24 he protested against Walker's resolution to recognize the independence of Texas.[41] To this Forsyth replied:

It is the duty of the President to presume that what is right and just will be done by all the departments of the Government, and any such discussion of matters exclusively before any distinct branch of it, until a decision is made, for which the Government is responsible, would be on his part, both premature and disrespectful.[42]

For several weeks Gorostiza was quiescent, but courage revived when he received information that Mexico had determined to prosecute the war against Texas, and that it would consider any agreements into which Santa Anna may have entered as null and void. This information was conveyed to the Secretary of State on July 9.[43] About this time it became known that Gaines had again received orders to advance as far as Nacogdoches. The Mexican minister at once asked an explanation, to which Forsyth replied, according to Gorostiza, that he would ask the War Department, as nothing was known about it in the State Department. In reporting it to his government Gorostiza wrote: ''He [Forsyth] did so, and I have this day had the satisfaction to

[41] Gorostiza to Forsyth, May 24, 1836, *House Ex. Docs.*, 24 Cong., 2 Sess., Doc. 2, pp. 32–33.

[42] Forsyth to Gorostiza, May 27, 1836, *ibid.*, 33–34.

[43] Gorostiza to Forsyth, July 9, 1836, *ibid.*, 35–37.

hear from his lips that the said statement was entirely unfounded
and that it was in consequence a mere fabrication of the news-
mongers and speculators."[44] The order to Gaines was issued on
the day before Gorostiza wrote to his government, and it is
probable that Forsyth was in ignorance of the fact at the time,
although he must have known the intention. He stayed within
the proprieties of diplomacy, however, in stating the fact. As
the conversation was not reduced to writing, we can depend only
upon Gorostiza's report, which does not state the exact hour
of the conference.

The next move of Gorostiza was to enter a protest concerning
assistance being given to the Texans. He said that various daily
papers reported that over two hundred Kentuckians went by
Grand Gulf, Mississippi, in the "Tuskina," with drums beating
and fifes playing, and that three hundred more would follow.
He also said that seven vessels had been outfitted at Natchez and
embarked with hundreds of volunteers for Texas, stopping to
complete their preparations in New Orleans; that the schooner
"Independence," carrying the Texan commissioners, Collins-
worth and Grayson, had landed at New Orleans and been saluted
as a man-of-war.

> How, in fine [he continued], could the so-called agencies of Texas have
> daily and publicly recruited men in all the cities of the Union . . . , and
> have armed and embarked them by companies? Could these things have
> been done without the knowledge of the federal authorities, especially
> of the officers of the respective custom houses? And if they know them
> and tolerate them, do they not contravene the orders of their own
> Government, rendering its promises of no avail, and its engagements
> illusory?[45]

---

44 Gorostiza to the Minister of Relations. July 12, 1836, *House Ex.
Docs.*, 25 Cong., 2 Sess., VII, Doc. 190, p. 89. The above statement is
taken from the Gorostiza pamphlet, published by that individual to show
the injustice which had been done. As will be shown later, the United
States government did not deny its truth.

45 Gorostiza to Forsyth, July 21, 1836, *House Ex. Docs.*, 24 Cong.,
2 Sess., I, Doc. 2, pp. 38–40.

The government replied that the matter would be immediately investigated and any violators of neutrality punished.[46] Orders were accordingly sent to Gaines to see that neutrality was enforced,[47] a rather amusing method in view of the fact that Gaines, himself, was then the most flagrant violator, as Jackson seemed to admit in his letter to the governor of Tennessee of August 5.

News now reached Gorostiza that Gaines had announced his intention of occupying Nacogdoches ''under the pretext that he has been informed of the murder of two white men by some Caddo Indians, sixty or seventy miles beyond the known limits of the United States.'' The Mexican minister commented ironically:

> As if General Gaines had been commissioned to chastise all those excesses committed (if they had been committed) by Indians against the whites in territories which are not North American [that is, not within the United States]. The undersigned will, however, abstain for the present from any observations on this pretext; nor does he wish to enter now into an examination of certain rumors of a correspondence which is said to have passed between that general and the commander of the Texian forces, and which is not of a very neutral character, if the statements of certain newspapers respecting it be true; nor will he call the attention of Mr. Dickens [acting secretary of state] at this time to the very singular coincidence that only when the Mexican troops are advancing in Texas, those accounts of the excesses of Indians are invented or exaggerated, in order that they may, without doubt, reach the ears of General Gaines.

He asked that his communication be laid before the President, as the continuance of his mission depended upon the answer.[48]

A note from the State Department defended the governmental action in ordering Gaines to go as far as Nacogdoches, and again declared there was no ulterior motive in the proceedings on the border. The hope was expressed that it would be unnecessary for him to go into Mexican territory.[49]

---

[46] Dickins to Gorostiza, July 26, 1836, *House Ex. Docs.*, 24 Cong., 2 Sess., I, Doc. 2, p. 40.

[47] Dickins to Gaines, July 27, 1836, *ibid.*, 40–41.

[48] Gorostiza to Dickins, July 28, 1836, *ibid.*, 43–44.

[49] Dickins to Gorostiza, August 1, 1836, *ibid.*, 44–45.

The following day Gorostiza inquired if the American government had received official information confirming the newspaper accounts that Gaines had occupied Nacogdoches,[50] the reply being that the last despatch received at the War Department was to the effect that he was encamped at Camp Sabine.[51]

On August 4 Gorostiza presented a most strenuous protest against the order authorizing Gaines to occupy Nacogdoches. He pointed out that, on the same theory of interference, it would likewise give the first Mexican general who might reach the Sabine the right of taking a position at Natchitoches, or farther still, in order to drive away the tribes of Indians who might have some intention of entering Mexico. Gorostiza adroitly gave the government an opportunity of throwing the burden upon Gaines. He said that he "has been acting, perhaps without knowing it, under the influence of the friends of Texas, and of the Texians themselves, and that his good faith was constantly beguiled."[52]

The opportunity was ignored; instead, the sending of troops to Texas was brought up. Dickins stated that L. Saunders, the United States district attorney for Kentucky, had found that those who had gone were merely emigrants seeking cheap lands; there had been great excitement because some Kentuckians had been killed in Texas and the papers had published articles to cheer the Texans in their struggle for independence, an explanation which must have amused Gorostiza.[53]

The Mexican minister at this time was in somewhat of a quandary. He knew that orders had been issued to Gaines but he was unable to ascertain whether the overt act had been committed. He ascertained, however, that the order to Gaines had been issued by the War Department the day before Forsyth had

---

50 Gorostiza to Dickins, August 2, 1836, *House Ex. Docs.*, 24 Cong., 2 Sess., I, Doc. 2, p. 46.

51 Dickins to Gorostiza, August 4, 1836, *ibid.*, 46.

52 Gorostiza to Dickins, August 4, 1836, *ibid.*, 48–49.

53 Dickins to Gorostiza, August 16, 1836, *ibid.*, 51.

told him that he was ignorant of the subject. This, of course, completely dispelled any confidence the Mexican representative might have had in the government. In communicating with his own Department of Relations, he said: "I think that no commentaries are needed, to show the true character and value of such conduct."[54]

Gorostiza next called the attention of the State Department to the fact that Texas had declared a blockade of Matamoros. He held that, as Texas was not an independent power, to declare a blockade was an act of piracy.[55] To this the reply was made that the United States had already taken measures to protect its own commerce, and would observe the same strict neutrality as it had in the revolt of the Spanish American colonies.[56] Jackson's letter of August 5 to the governors was also sent to Gorostiza.[57]

The Mexican minister heartily agreed with Jackson's view that Gaines had acted in an unwarranted manner, and then continued:

> But is it also to be understood that the President withdraws or will withdraw from General Gaines the authorization which he had given him on the 25th of April, and had confirmed on the 11th of July, to advance with his troops as far as Nacogdoches? If Mr. Forsyth can answer the undersigned in the affirmative, he will be fully satisfied, and will, in fact, acknowledge that there is no need of Mr. Forsyth's again occupying himself with those notes.[58]

Shortly after this Gorostiza complained that General Dunlap had raised three thousand troops in Tennessee for the Texan service,[59] to which reply was made that the attention of the dis-

---

[54] Two letters, Gorostiza to Minister of Relations, August 18, 1836, *House Ex. Docs.*, 25 Cong., 2 Sess., VII, Doc. 190, pp. 96–97.

[55] Gorostiza to Dickins, August 21, 1836, *House Ex. Docs.*, 24 Cong., 2 Sess., I, Doc. 2, pp. 54–55.

[56] Forsyth to Gorostiza, August 31, 1836, *ibid.*, 55.

[57] Forsyth to Gorostiza, August 31, 1836, *ibid.*, 57–59.

[58] Gorostiza to Forsyth, September 3, 1836, *ibid.*, 61–62.

[59] Gorostiza to Forsyth, September 9, 1836, *ibid.*, 63.

trict attorney of Tennessee had already been called to the matter.[60]

On September 10 Gorostiza wrote that he was convinced that Gaines had occupied Nacogdoches, and urged a reply to his previous communication.[61] Two days later he protested against the action of the collector of the custom-house at New York in allowing the "Brutus," which flew the Texan flag, to enter that port, recognizing the flag, and when the Mexican consul complained, replying that her commander carried a commission from the president of the republic of Texas.[62] Forsyth answered that the action of the collector was not looked upon as a breach of neutrality, as the United States was following out the same course which had been preserved between Spain and her revolted provinces.[63]

On September 23, a personal conference occurred between the secretary of state and the Mexican minister, at which the former attempted to allay the fear of the latter because of the occupation of Mexican soil, but without apparently changing the views of Gorostiza. Two days later he was shown an abstract of two letters from Jackson to Gaines, which cautioned the American general against holding communication with Mexican or Texan leaders, to observe a strict neutrality, and to withdraw from Nacogdoches, if he were convinced that the Mexicans had not incited the Indians to war and that they would cease hostilities; but if these conditions did not prove to be true, he was to summon two thousand volunteers from Arkansas and Missouri, and to advance the whole force to Nacogdoches or to any other point favorable for the protection of the frontier. One of the letters further said: "General Gaines must act according to his own discretion, upon the information he may obtain, always

60 Forsyth to Gorostiza, September 16, 1836, *House Ex. Docs.*, 24 Cong., 2 Sess., I, Doc. 2, pp. 63–64.

61 Gorostiza to Forsyth, September 10, 1836, *ibid.*, 66–67.

62 Gorostiza to Forsyth, September 12, 1836, with inclosures, *ibid.*, 71–74.

63 Forsyth to Gorostiza, September 20, 1836, *ibid.*, 78–79.

bearing in mind the neutral position of the United States with regard to the contending parties in Texas, and the obligations of the treaty in reference to the Mexican authorities.''[64]

On October 1 Gorostiza protested against American troops fraternizing with those of Texas, and demanded a reply to his previous requests that the troops be withdrawn.[65] The State Department, after a delay of nearly two weeks, flatly refused to comply.[66] There was no recourse; the resources of diplomacy were exhausted, and on October 15 Gorostiza demanded his passports.[67]

Five days later they were issued to him with a polite note.[68] He shortly after left the country and arrived at the City of Mexico in the middle of December.[69] Before his departure he published, at Philadelphia, a pamphlet in Spanish in which he reviewed the boundary question and gave portions of the correspondence between him and the Department of State.[70] These were distributed to various members of the diplomatic corps at Washington. The publication of the correspondence was looked upon as a breach of diplomatic propriety, and the matter was called to the attention of the Mexican government, which, however, upheld its minister.[71]

---

[64] *House Ex. Docs.*, 24 Cong., 2 Sess., I, Doc. 2, pp. 81–83. Jackson's letters bore date of September 4, 1836.

[65] Gorostiza to Dickins, October 1, 1836, *ibid.*, 88.

[66] Dickins to Gorostiza, October 13, 1836, *ibid.*, 89–92.

[67] Gorostiza to Dickins, October 15, 1836, *ibid.*, 96–101.

[68] Dickins to Gorostiza, October 20, 1836, *ibid.*, 101.

[69] *Niles' Register*, LI, 320.

[70] Gorostiza, *Correspondencia que ha mediado entre la Legacion Extraordinaria de Mexico y el Departamento de Estado de los Estados-Unidos, sobre paso del Sabina por las tropas que mandaba el General Gaines.* A translation appears in *House Ex. Docs.*, 25 Cong., 2 Sess., VII, Doc. 190, pp. 61–120.

[71] Report of Forsyth, December 2, 1837, *Sen. Docs.*, 25 Cong., 2 Sess., I, Doc. 1, pp. 29–36.

CHAPTER XI

THE TREATY OF LIMITS BETWEEN THE UNITED STATES AND THE REPUBLIC OF TEXAS

With the opening of diplomatic relations between the United States and the republic of Texas, the boundary question entered upon a new phase. On the eighteenth day of November, 1836, W. H. Wharton was given his instructions as minister plenipotentiary of the new republic to the United States. His mission had two great objects, to obtain the recognition of the independence of Texas, and annexation. It was believed that the latter might be brought about by a treaty, in which full provision should be made for the protection of Texan interests, one of which was the question of boundaries, at that time undefined by Texan congressional action.[1]

In regard to the boundaries, the instructions in part read:

We claim and consider that we have possession to the Rio Bravo del Norte. Taking this as a basis, the boundary of Texas would be as follows. Beginning at the mouth of said River on the Gulf of Mexico, thence up the middle thereof, following its main channel, including the Islands to its most northerly Source, thence in a direct line to the United States boundary under the treaty of De Onis at the head of Arkansas river, thence down said river and following the United States line as fixed by said De Onis treaty to the Gulf of Mexico at the mouth of Sabine . . . The said treaty of De Onis calls for the West bank of Sabine, and the South bank of Red and Arkansas rivers as the line. It is believed that the chartered limits of Louisiana calls for the middle of Sabine, if so there will probably be no difficulty in making our line to correspond with that of Louisiana—so as to give to us the right of landing, Ferries etc without molestation on the West Side.

The same alteration should be made if practical as to the Red River and Arkansas river lines, by fixing them in the middle of those rivers,

---

[1] Marshall, in Texas State Historical Association, *The Quarterly.* XIV, 281–285.

but should this be objected to, it is presumed the right of landing, and the free use and controul of the banks on our side to low water mark will be secured to us.[2]

Private instructions were also given to Wharton concerning the occupation of Texan soil by American troops; to quote:

President Burnet wrote officially to Genl. Gaines, that it would be agreeable to the Government of Texas, should he establish his head-quarters at, or occupy the post of Nacogdoches for the purpose of restraining the Indians.

You [Wharton] will endeavor to ascertain the real views of the United States government in occupying that post, and whether it is seriously contemplated to insist on the River Neenes as the constructive line under De Onis' treaty, instead of the Sabine, as laid down in Millish's [Melish's] map of 1818, which is positively and definitely fixed by said treaty as the boundary line. This government cannot admit of any construction that will fix the line at the Neches, or make any variations of this kind from the said treaty of De Onis, and should there be any attempt on the part of the United States government to move the line to the Neches, and thus claim the country between that River and Sabine, you will solemnly protest against it as an infraction of said Treaty of De Onis, and an invasion of the rights and territory of Texas.[3]

A month later the Texan government, by an act of congress, defined the boundaries, the governmental act agreeing with those as laid down in Austin's instructions to Wharton. It was also provided that the president negotiate with the United States for ascertaining and defining the boundary as previously agreed in the treaties with Spain.[4] Shortly after, General Memucan Hunt was sent to the United States as minister extraordinary to assist Wharton. In his instructions no mention was made of the boundary, but the negotiation of a treaty of commerce was urged.[5]

---

[2] Austin to Wharton, November 18, 1836, *Tex. Dipl. Corr.*, I, 127–134.

[3] Private instructions to Wharton, *ibid.*, I, 135–140.

[4] *Laws of the Republic of Texas*, I, 133–134.

[5] Henderson to Hunt, December 31, 1836; Henderson to Forsyth, December 31, 1836, *Tex. Dipl. Corr.*, I, 161–166.

On January 11 Wharton presented the views of his government on the boundary question to Forsyth, the secretary of state of the United States. He said that he had recently been informed that the Caddo were meditating an invasion of Texas; in consequence he requested that United States troops should continue to occupy Nacogdoches or some other point on the frontier, but he further declared that the continued occupation of Nacogdoches or of any other point west of the Sabine would settle nothing in relation to the boundary, the Texan government expecting to have the boundary settled according to the treaty of 1819.[6] Recognition and annexation, however, were uppermost in the minds of Wharton and Jackson, and the minor question of boundary received no immediate attention.[7]

Jackson's course at this time was extremely cautious. Morfit's report on Texan conditions was not overly favorable, neither was it such as to withhold the President. To other causes Jackson's course must be attributed. The wave of enthusiasm which had swept over the country in the spring of 1836 had somewhat subsided, and the northern opposition to slavery was beginning to crystalize against the acquisition of Texas. Gorostiza's spirited protests and ultimate withdrawal presaged war. Fortunately a way was opened opportunely by which Jackson might hope to see the coveted country brought to the verge of acquisition and without a war.

Upon his release from a Texan prison, Santa Anna was sent to Washington, where he held out the idea that, when he was sent back to his own country, he could secure the recognition of Texan independence or the annexation of Texas to the United States for a compensation. If the former were attained, Texas could thereafter follow her own course and annexation might eventually be accomplished without a war. Jackson's course was probably influenced by Santa Anna's first suggestion. He de-

---

[6] Wharton to Forsyth, January 11, 1837, *Tex. Dipl. Corr.*, I, 175.

[7] Wharton to Houston, February 2, 1837, *ibid.*, I, 179–181.

termined upon recognition, one of his last official acts being the appointment of a chargé to Texas.

The claims set up by Texas, and subsequent legislation concerning public lands, brought about a collision with Arkansas. The first of the Texan land laws was passed on December 22, 1836; it provided that a general land office and ten sub-offices were to be established and opened on June 1 of the following year. One of these was to be located at the house of George Wright on Red River. The district about it was to be known as the Red River District and was to be bounded by a line beginning at the Sulphur Fork of Red River and running up that river to the crossing of Trammel Trace, thence on that trace to the Sabine River, up that river to its source, thence due north to Red River, and from there to the point of beginning. This law did not meet with the approval of Houston, but was passed over his veto.[8]

President Houston took no steps to carry it out, and in his message at the opening of the second session, advised that some plan be formulated which would ascertain all the located lands of the country, in order that the vacant lands might be taken up. He stated that the northeastern boundary especially needed attention, but that the treaty of 1819 so well defined the boundary that no trouble was anticipated. He urged that provision be made for the appointment of a commissioner to run the boundary.[9]

On June 12, 1837, the Texan congress passed a supplementary land act which provided that the law was to go into operation on October 1. It further declared that all *empresario* grants had ceased on the day of the declaration of independence and that all vacant lands were the property of the republic.[10]

It must be remembered that the United States at this time was proceeding on the assumption that the Neches instead of the Sabine was the boundary. If such were the case, the territory

---

[8] *Tex. Dipl. Corr.*, I, 193; *Laws of the Republic of Texas*, I, 216–224.

[9] Crane, *Life and Select Literary Remains of Sam Houston of Texas*, 282–287.

[10] *Laws of the Republic of Texas*, I, 263–264.

north of the thirty-third parallel and extending from the eastern boundary of Texas above the Sabine, to the western boundary of Arkansas as determined by an act of the United States Congress in 1824, a territory seventy-five miles east and west, and fifty miles north and south, would have belonged to Arkansas. The Red River land district was within this disputed territory.[11]

Governor Conway of Arkansas informed Forsyth that Texas had laid off a land district which embraced Miller County and about half of Lafayette County in Arkansas. Forsyth replied that Texas would not be allowed to encroach upon the territory of the United States.[12] He immediately protested against the action of the Texan government.

> This information [he said] has been received with great surprise, the more especially as provision was made by Congress at its last session for running the boundary line between the two countries. During the unsettled state of this line, the Government of the United States has carefully refrained from extending the limits of its occupation in that quarter, and I have now the honor to request that you will forthwith apprise the Government of Texas that while the question is pending, no encroachments can be permitted upon the territory occupied by the United States.[13]

Catlett, the Texan chargé at Washington, immediately informed his government of this, and advised that the matter be settled as soon as possible, suggesting that a commission be appointed to act with one from the United States.[14] His advice was anticipated, however, by the Texan congress, which, on June 12, 1837, passed the act for the settlement of the eastern boundary. The president was authorized to appoint a commission to run and mark the boundary from the point where the Sabine River

---

11 Reynolds, in Arkansas Historical Association, *Publications,* II, map opposite 236.

12 *Ibid.,* II, 234.

13 Forsyth to Catlett, June 17, 1837, *Tex. Dipl. Corr.,* I, 230.

14 Catlett to Henderson, June 17, 1837, *ibid.,* I, 229–230.

crossed the thirty-second parallel to the Red River, as provided
in the treaty of 1819. The commissioner was to receive fifty
dollars per day from the time that he reached the point of departure on the Sabine until the line was completed. The compensation of the commissioner was to cover all expenses and the
total cost was not to exceed three thousand dollars.[15]

A change had recently taken place in the Texan Department
of State, R. A. Irion having taken the place of Henderson. Wharton had returned to Texas and Hunt was now the only representative at Washington. Irion informed Hunt of the action
of congress and instructed him to urge the appointment of a
United States commissioner. In negotiating a treaty he was
told to be governed by the stipulations of those of 1819 and 1828.
"It is not, at the present time," he wrote, "intended to run this
line farther than Red River. Owing to the provision that the
General Land Office shall open on the 1st of October next, agreeably to existing laws, it becomes very important that this line
should be defined previously to that time if practicable, for it
should be the base of the surveys in that quarter. In a very
short time after notification this Government can have a commissioner on the spot."[16]

On July 14 Irion wrote to Hunt concerning the protest of
Forsyth. He said that it was true that the citizens of Red River
County, which was located in the disputed territory and was
known in Arkansas as Miller County, had sent representatives
to the Texan congress and that a land district had been established in that county, but the president had not as yet made appointments necessary to put the land law in operation; as Houston was then absent at Nacogdoches, Irion did not feel like making
an authoritative statement, but promised to lay the matter before
the president upon his return. On his own authority he remarked
that it was not the disposition of his government to disturb in

---

[15] *Laws of the Republic of Texas,* I, 271–272.
[16] Irion to Hunt, June 26, 1837, *Tex. Dipl. Corr.,* I, 232–234.

any way the present friendly relations between the two countries.[17]

Hunt next informed Forsyth that a commissioner had been appointed for the purpose of running the boundary and requested that a similar agent be appointed by the United States. Hunt was here forestalling the actual appointment to hasten the action of the United States. A commissioner had not yet been appointed, but he evidently relied upon the fact that the Texan government could get a representative on the ground at short notice, if necessary.[18]

The protest of Forsyth had its effect upon Houston, for on August 10 he issued a proclamation calling a special session of congress to discuss the boundary question.[19] In his message to congress Houston reviewed the events of the past year concerning the boundary, and said that there was no doubt that the disputed territory would be shown to belong to Texas as soon as the limits were defined. He said that a commissioner had not yet been appointed, as no intelligence had been received concerning the course which would be pursued by the United States. He stated that the Texan government would omit nothing that could lead to an amicable adjustment, and that it was the duty of congress to consider what could be done to modify the land law.[20] On September 30 the Texan congress suspended the law until further action might be taken.[21]

On October 3 the committee on foreign relations, to which had been referred the president's message, reported that they recommended that a commissioner and surveyor be immediately appointed to run the line, and that the appointments be com-

---

[17] Irion to Hunt, July 14, 1837, *Tex. Dipl. Corr.*, I, 241–242.

[18] Hunt to Forsyth, August 4, 1837, *ibid.*, I, 252.

[19] *House Journal*, Tex. Cong., called Sess., beginning September 25, 1837, and regular Sess., beginning November 6, 1837, pp. 15–17.

[20] Crane, *Life and Select Literary Remains of Sam Houston of Texas*, 280–281.

[21] *Laws of the Republic of Texas*, II, 3.

municated at once to the minister at Washington that he might urge the United States government to make similar appointments. The Texan commissioner was to run the boundary according to the treaty of 1828 and to end his work at the intersection of the Red River and the hundredth meridian.[22] The report of the committee was adopted, but the nominations were not made at once.[23]

On December 1 a committee of two was named by the Texan senate to urge upon Houston the necessity of appointing a commissioner. In compliance Shelby Corzine was nominated on the fifth, and the senate unanimously confirmed the choice the same day.[24]

Congress again turned its attention to the land law, and on December 16 passed an act which was intended to consolidate all land legislation into a single statute. It changed the unit for land surveys from the district to the county.[25] Section 39 said:

> *Be it further enacted,* That the several land offices contemplated and established by this act, shall commence and go into operation on the first Thursday in February next.—*Provided,* however, that the operations of the land office in the county of Red River, shall not extend to any portion of the territory near the supposed boundary line between this and the United States government of the north, and *provided,* also, that should any person obtain a certificate for land from said board of land commissioners for the county of Red River, who at the date of the passage of this act shall reside east of the boundary line hereafter to be run between Texas and the United States, said certificate shall be void.[26]

Further discussion of the boundary was provoked by the action of the Texan congress, which, on December 18, organized Red River County in the disputed district. The boundaries as defined were as follows:

---

22 *Tex. Dipl. Corr.*, I, 296–297.

23 Irion to Hunt, December 31, 1837, *ibid.*, I, 277–281.

24 *Secret Journals of the [Texan] Senate*, 92–93. Referred to hereafter as *Secret Journals.*

25 *Laws of the Republic of Texas*, II, 64.

26 *Ibid.*, II, 75.

Beginning at the mouth of the Bois d'Arc, running up that stream [Red River] to Carter Cliffs, crossing thence south to a point west of the head of Bid [Big] Cypress, east to its head, and down that to Sodo Lake, thence east to the line of the United States, with that line to Red river, up that to the beginning.[27]

This included nearly all of the present counties of Bowie, Red River, Franklin, Titus, Morris, and Cass.

La Branche, the United States chargé d'affaires at Houston, promptly protested against this. He wrote:

Having been informed that land offices are about to be opened within the territory under the jurisdiction of the United States on Red River, and that commissioners for that purpose have been duly appointed under authority of the government of Texas, notwithstanding the remonstrances of the Honble John Forsyth, Secretary of State of the United States, it becomes my duty, in the name of the government I have the honor to represent, to protest, as I now do solemnly protest against such encroachment on said territory.[28]

Two days later he addressed another letter to Irion in which he inquired if it were true that an act had been passed to define the boundaries of Red River County,[29] to which inquiry he received an affirmative answer.[30]

La Branche now presented a spirited protest against the action of the Texan government. He requested that his communication be laid before President Houston, whom he hoped would take measures which would prevent unfortunate results.[31] The reply of Irion, inspired by Houston, was a masterly refutation of the assumption of the United States. He stated that Texas had continually urged the United States government to appoint a commissioner to run the line, but that nothing had been done. Houston's course in refusing to put the land law into operation and calling a special session of congress to con-

---

[27] *Laws of the Republic of Texas*, II, 89.
[28] La Branche to Irion, January 13, 1838, *Tex. Dipl. Corr.*, I, 281.
[29] La Branche to Irion, January 15, 1838, *ibid.*, I, 282.
[30] Irion to La Branche, January 16, 1838, *ibid.*, I, 282.
[31] La Branche to Irion, January 16, 1838, *ibid.*, I, 283–284.

sider the boundary question was reviewed. It was also pointed
out that congress had made provision for a commission and that
a commissioner had been appointed. It was pointed out that
the conditions of the land law and the act for defining Red River
County were different; in the former the act was to go into
operation at a given time and the appointment of officers to
carry it into effect devolved upon the president; in the latter
case congress passed the laws and elected the officers, thus placing it beyond the power of the executive to interfere.

The history of the disputed territory was then reviewed. It
was shown that, as early as 1824, the state government of
Coahuila and Texas had considered that it had jurisdiction over
that region; that in 1826 land grants had there been made by
both Mexico and Coahuila and Texas, and that as late as 1835
Colonel Benjamin Milam had been appointed commissioner to
issue titles to settlers in that district. These transactions were
known to the United States government, but no protest had been
made to Mexico. He observed that Mexico at one time had a
military force at the "Spanish Bluffs" on Red River. In
February, 1836, the citizens of that district sent members to
the convention which declared independence and adopted the
constitution. In view of these things, it was evident that the
subject was beyond the control of Texas and that her claim was
just.[32]

On February 26, 1838, La Branche replied at great length
and with an ardor much greater than the exigencies of the case
demanded. He criticized the attitude of Houston and the course
pursued by congress, and made light of the arguments showing
that the territory in dispute was Texan soil. He claimed that
several members of the Texan congress had protested against
Senator Ellis of Red River County taking his seat, on the grounds
that he came from Arkansas, thus showing that even in the minds
of members of that body there were grave doubts concerning the

---

[32] Irion to La Branche, February 13, 1838, *Tex. Dipl. Corr.*, I, 291–296.

ownership of that territory. He pompously declared that he would lay Irion's letter before Forsyth.[33] The letter did not deserve a reply and none was given.

It is time to return to events at Washington. On August 4, 1837, Hunt formally asked that Texas be annexed to the United States.[34] This was declined on August 25. The reasons assigned were, that it was a question whether such action would be constitutional, and that, as a state of war existed between Texas and Mexico, the United States, by annexing Texas, would annex a war with Mexico. Forsyth argued that the United States was restricted by treaty obligations and should not forfeit her high character by such an act.[35] On September 12 Hunt again addressed Forsyth on the subject, but to no avail.[36] He did not give up hope, however, at the executive rebuff, still having faith that congress would take favorable action.

While the larger question was up for consideration, it was but natural that the boundary should remain in the background. On September 18 Hunt reported to his government that he had not yet received a communication from Forsyth regarding the appointment of a boundary commissioner.[37] A month later he wrote that the United States senate had not yet confirmed the nomination of a commissioner, that Governor Reynolds of Mississippi was the nominee, and that his name had been before the senate for several months.[38]

The question was not pressed, however, by Hunt, as he had reason to believe that the administration had commenced to view the subject of annexation in a more favorable light, as he believed that the popularity of the idea was growing in congress.[39] In

---

[33] La Branche to Irion, February 26, 1838, *Tex. Dipl. Corr.*, I, 298–310.

[34] Hunt to Forsyth, August 4, 1837, *Congressional Debates*, XIV, Pt. 2, App., 117–121.

[35] Forsyth to Hunt, August 25, 1837, *ibid.*, 121–122.

[36] Hunt to Forsyth, September 12, 1837, *ibid.*, 122–124.

[37] Hunt to Irion, September 18, 1837, *Tex. Dipl. Corr.*, I, 258–259.

[38] Hunt to Irion, October 21, 183i, *ibid.*, I, 266–267.

[39] Hunt to Irion, November 15, 1837, *ibid.*, I, 267–268.

November Hunt went to North Carolina on private business, leaving the legation in charge of P. W. Grayson. On December 5 Grayson wrote to Irion, stating that he believed that there was no solid foundation on which to build a hope that annexation would be carried.[40]

On December 31, Irion wrote to Hunt deploring the fact that the northeastern states were opposed to annexation. To quote from his letter:

> The policy of those States has generally been characterized by a disinclination to extend the territory of the U. States to the South West, and judging from recent demonstrations that feeling will probably continue, *if we have to exist separately,* until, pursuing the destiny indicated to us by that significant and beautiful emblem of our nationality, the evening star, inviting alluringly westward the unavoidable accession of *star* after *star* to our Banner, this now small Republic will embrace the shores of the Pacific as well as those of the Gulf of Mexico; presenting to them the spectacle of an immense cotton and sugar growing nation in intimate connection with *England,* and other commercial and manufacturing countries of Europe, whose relations shall have been permanently adjusted on equitable principles of reciprocal interest; when, they perchance, in reminiscence, recur[ring] to their policy of the present times, may have to deplore the loss of that ascendency in manufacturing and the carrying trade that they now so triumphantly enjoy, and which could be rendered perpetual by a different course of policy.

In this appears to be expressed for the first time in diplomatic correspondence the idea of a close alliance with England as a motive force to be used to urge the United States into annexing Texas. After reviewing the work of organization of government that had gone on in Texas, Irion further observed:

> The land laws have been amended and the General Land Office is to open on the first thursday in February next, for the location of land. Connected with the latter subject is the unsettled boundary line between the U. States and Texas.
>
> Congress was called together . . . in consequence of the remonstrance of Mr. Forsyth . . . . This matter is one of serious import to Texas at the present time, for it appears that the citizens of that border are

---

[40] Grayson to Irion, December 7, 1837, *Tex. Dipl. Corr.,* I, 273.

determined to organize under the authorities of this Republic, which, from the tone of Mr. Forsyth's communication, I am apprehensive, may occasion unpleasant collisions in that quarter, and perhaps lead to a disagreeable controversity [*sic*] between the two Governments, which would, under existing circumstances, be a most unfortunate event for us, and should, if possible, be prevented.

Irion then described the action of Congress in providing for a commissioner and mentioned the fact that Corzine had been appointed. He continued:

> The country through which it [the line] will pass is rapidly settling, to whose inhabitants the uncertainty of the boundary is a source of much vexation, and seriously impedes improvement, as well as the administration of justice.
>
> It is hoped that the U. State's Government will not further postpone the appointment of a commissioner; and I am directed by the President to instruct you to solicit again said appointment. The fixation of this line is the more necessary, inasmuch as the prospect of immediate annexation is so very remote as hardly to be considered in the range of possibilities.[41]

A month later Hunt had become convinced that congress would not take action to annex Texas. He wrote, ''Ardently as I have desired the accomplishment of the measure and unwilling to abandon hope as long as there remained the slightest prospect of success, I can no longer repel the conviction that the measure is utterly impracticable under existing circumstances.'' Feeling that he had not succeeded, he asked for his recall. He further observed that in a recent conversation Forsyth had insisted that the Neches was the true eastern limit of Texas and that he had replied that Texas would not renounce its claim to the territory as far as the Sabine, repeating the desire of his government to run the line as far as the Red River and no farther at that time.

---

[41] Irion to Hunt, December 31, 1837, *Tex. Dipl. Corr.*, I, 277–281. For the Texan-English alliance, see Reeves, *American Diplomacy under Tyler and Polk*, 115; Adams, *British Interests and Activities in Texas*, 112–114; Smith, *The Annexation of Texas*, 94–96. Reeves, Adams, and Smith appear to have overlooked this early expression of the idea, which they suppose was not advanced until Houston's second administration.

Forsyth then asked him how far west Texas contemplated running the northern boundary, to which Hunt replied, "As far as the Pacific Ocean." Forsyth then "insisted upon making the operation a single one and running the line the whole distance." Hunt answered that this was contrary to the wishes of his government. Forsyth then inquired if Hunt had full power to make a treaty for the establishment of the boundary, to which the Texan minister was forced to answer that he had not. In consequence he immediately addressed his government, asking for full powers. He added a postscript to the effect that he had heard that Van Buren was about to make a change in his cabinet and that there were hopes that the new appointments would be made with a view to annexation. In consequence he changed his mind about desiring to be recalled.[42]

Hunt's hopes were raised higher by an interview with Calhoun, who confided to him that the "government was considering the policy of despatching a private mission to Mexico to treat for her acquiescence in any negotiations between Texas and this government relating to annexation." A month later, however, Hunt ceased to be optimistic. The correspondence of La Branche had reached the Secretary of State most inopportunely for Texas. Forsyth informed the Texan minister that it was his disagreeable duty to direct the United States marshal to arrest any Texan surveyors found operating in the territory claimed by Arkansas. In spite of arguments advanced and the conciliatory attitude of Hunt, Forsyth was obdurate, saying that the governor of Arkansas would be instructed to support the marshal. Hunt reported to his government that the United States had continually delayed the fixation of the line, and that Forsyth had but recently informed him that the time limit of the treaty of 1828 with Mexico had expired, and must be renewed with Texas before commissioners for that purpose could act.[43]

---

[42] Hunt to Irion, January 31, 1838, *Tex. Dipl. Corr.*, I, 284–289.
[43] Hunt to Irion, March 3, 1838, *ibid.*, I, 310–313.

In order to reassure Forsyth, and if possible prevent his intentions from being carried out, Hunt, soon after the above interview, sent him a copy of the Texan land law, section 39 of which
provided that the operations of the land office in Red River
County should not extend to any portion of the territory near the
supposed boundary.[44] Forsyth replied on the following day that
he had examined section 39 and considered, that if it were intended to prevent collisions, it was not as definite as could have
been wished. Its efficiency, he thought, would depend upon the
manner of its execution; if carried out with a proper respect to
the rights of the United States, the authorities in Arkansas might
not find it necessary to act under the instructions which he had
given.[45]

Governor Conway experienced great difficulty in carrying
out the instructions of the State Department. In March the general assembly of Arkansas passed an act to enforce the authority
of the state; the act proved inefficacious, for in November his
message told of his failure in enforcing the law. The officers
of Miller County resigned or failed to serve, and the governor
was unable to induce citizens to go there and accept office. The
United States district attorney also failed to take action. In consequence the governor recommended that Miller County be abolished and annexed to another county.[46]

On March 21, Irion sent full powers to Hunt to enter into
the negotiations of a convention to confirm the treaty of limits.
if the United States insisted.

This Government [he said] does not wish to run the line at present
farther than the 100dth degree of West longitude to a point on Red River
in latitude nearly 33° 30′, leaving a distance of eight or nine degrees to
be run at a future time when it can be done with less hazard and expense.
    The region north of Red River through which the line will pass is

---

[44] Hunt to Forsyth, March 8, 1838, *Tex. Dipl. Corr.*, I, 315.

[45] Forsyth to Hunt, March 9, 1838, *ibid.*, I, 318.

[46] Reynolds, in Arkansas Historical Association, *Publications*, II, 234–
235.

inhabited by hostile Indians, which circumstance would render it necessary to send a considerable guard to accompany the Commissioners and
Surveyors. It is hoped that the Government of the U. States will not
insist on running the line beyond the point above indicated on Red River.

On the same day he again addressed Hunt; he pointed out
that it would be necessary to procure, if possible, the appointment of a commissioner on the part of the United States. He
again took up the question of running the boundary beyond the
hundredth meridian, saying, ''Should the U. States' Government insist on running the line the whole distance, I am at a
loss to advise you what to do. Congress having made no provision for running it farther than the 100dth. degree of West
Longitude on the Red River.''[47]

On April 13 Hunt received his full powers. He communicated
the fact at once to Forsyth, who expressed a willingness to open
negotiations and to recede from his previous demand to establish the line all the way to the Pacific. He ascribed as the reason
for Forsyth's previous attitude on this subject, that the United
States was anxious to get San Francisco Bay and his insistence
was to force Hunt to relinquish the right of Texas to extend the
boundaries beyond what they were under Mexico.

I will take care [he observed] in the wording of an article on the
subject, that this claim to additional territory, be not overlooked. As a
seperated Power, the splendid harbours on the South Sea or Pacific Ocean,
will be indispensable for us; and apart from the great increase of territory by an extension of the line, the possession of the harbour of St.
Francisco alone, is amply sufficient, for any increased difficulties or ex-
pence, should there be any in regard to a claim of territory to the Pacific,
in a final treaty of Peace with Mexico.

Hunt and Forsyth now visited New York together and on the
trip talked over the negotiations.[48] The agreement was reached
with little difficulty. In the treaty of 1828, the commissioners

---

[47] Two letters, Irion to Hunt, March 21, 1838, *Tex. Dipl. Corr.*, I, 318–
321.

[48] Hunt to Irion, April 13, 1838, *ibid.*, I, 323–325.

were given considerable latitude; a portion of the third article read: "They shall make out plans and keep journals of their proceedings; and the result agreed upon by them shall be considered a part of this treaty, and shall have the same force as if it were inserted therein."[49] Hunt objected to this, desiring that a clause be inserted which would leave it discretionary with either government to object to the agreement within three months or less after they might fix and report the boundary. To this President Van Buren objected on the ground that it would be necessary to enter into a new treaty, if any change were made in the original. Hunt waived the point,[50] and the convention was signed on April 25, 1838.

The convention provided that each government was to appoint a commissioner and a surveyor, who were to meet within a year after the exchange of ratifications. It was agreed that the commissioners were to have the powers before mentioned, and that until the line was run, each government was to continue to exercise jurisdiction in all territory over which its authority had been exercised. The line was to be marked from the mouth of the Sabine, where it entered the Gulf of Mexico, to the Red River, and the remaining portion was to be run at such time as was convenient to both governments. The ratifications were to be exchanged at Washington within six months.[51] It may be noted here that the convention specified the Sabine; the question, however, as to the Sabine or Neches became a subject of discussion by the boundary commissioners.

Hunt had accomplished all that was possible in view of existing circumstances. He was convinced that annexation would not receive the approval of congress. The conclusion of the boundary convention was a positive accomplishment, and he could return to Texas feeling that he had attained a definite

---

49 *Treaties, Conventions*, (Malloy, ed.), I, 1083–1084.
50 Hunt to Irion, April 28, 1838, *Tex. Dipl. Corr.*, I, 325–326.
51 *Treaties, Conventions*, (Malloy, ed.) II, 1779–1780.

result. On June 5 he tendered his resignation and immediately set out for home.[52]

On May 24 the convention was submitted to the Texan senate[53] and was soon after ratified.[54] In the recess of congress Peter W. Grayson was appointed to fill the position made vacant by the resignation of Hunt;[55] his untimely death intervened,[56] and Anson Jones was appointed.[57] In the first letter addressed to the new minister, Irion urged that he exert himself at the earliest opportunity to procure the appointment of a United States commissioner.[58] Again, a month later, he deemed it necessary to urge the matter upon Jones.[59] The minister, however, did not arrive at Washington until September 23, where he found both Van Buren and Forsyth absent from the city. Vail, the acting secretary, informed him that nothing could be done regarding the boundary commission, as the President had not yet signed the ratification.[60]

On October 2 Van Buren returned to the capital and on the ninth Jones was presented.[61] On the following day he addressed a note to Vail, pointing out that the time for ratification would expire in fifteen days and that he was then prepared to make the exchange on the part of Texas.[62]

In the United States senate the convention had experienced no difficulty and the ratification was advised by that body on May 10; Van Buren signed it on October 4, and on the twelfth

52 Hunt to Irion, June 5, 1838, *Tex. Dipl. Corr.*, I, 330.

53 *Secret Journals*, 110.

54 Irion to Grayson, June 12, 1838, *Tex. Dipl. Corr.*, I, 330–331. It is impossible for me to state on what day the convention was ratified, as the *Secret Journals* are deficient in this data.

55 Irion to Grayson, June 12, 1838, *Tex. Dipl. Corr.*, I, 330–331.

56 Catlett to Irion, July 29, 1838, *ibid.*, I, 341–342.

57 *Secret Journals*, 113.

58 Irion to Jones, August 7, 1838, *Tex. Dipl. Corr.*, I 342–343.

59 Irion to Jones, September 7, 1838, *ibid.*, I, 344.

60 Jones to Irion, September 26, 1838, *ibid.*, I, 344–346.

61 Jones to Irion, October 13, 1838, *ibid.*, I, 346–347.

62 Jones to Vail, October 10, 1838, *ibid.*, I, 347–348.

the ratifications were exchanged.[63]   On the same day Jones formally withdrew the offer of annexation.[64]

A month later Jones sent the ratifications of the treaties of indemnity for the brig ''Pocket,'' which had recently been exchanged, and that of limits, to his government.   The greatest care was taken to insure their safety; he wrote:

I have had [them] safely packed in a box . . . and forwarded . . . through our Consul, Mr. Henry H. Williams of Baltimore and directed to the care of Mrssrs McKinney and Williams of Galveston.   The Box was sent by Mr. Williams per the schooner Axis from that post for Galveston on the 7th Inst in the charge of Captn. John Allen her commander, who promised to take it in his Cabin, and deliver it as directed.[65]

---

[63] *Treaties, Conventions,* (Malloy, ed.) II, 1779.

[64] *House Ex. Docs.,* 25 Cong., 3 Sess., I, Doc. 2, p. 33.

[65] Jones to Irion, November 16, 1838, *Tex. Dipl. Corr.,* I, 350.

CHAPTER XII

THE SURVEY OF THE TEXAS-LOUISIANA BOUNDARY

After the exchange of ratifications, the next work to be done was the appointment of the commissioners. Texas had already appointed Shelby Corzine, but he eventually declined to accept.[1] During the recess of congress, C. S. Taylor was appointed; on November 13, 1838, Houston asked the senate to confirm the nomination, but no action was taken.[2] As Houston's term was about to expire, the filling of the position devolved upon Lamar.

The new president experienced considerable difficulty in selecting men who would accept or were acceptable to the senate. He first nominated Branch T. Archer as commissioner, C. R. Johns surveyor, and Hamilton Bee clerk.[3] Because of private business Archer declined; Johns' name was also withdrawn. Doctor Isaac N. Jones was then appointed commissioner, and George W. Smyth surveyor. Jones found it impossible to serve and David Sample was selected to fill the vacant position.[4] This nomination was rejected by the senate by a vote of six to seven.[5] Lamar then presented the name of P. B. Dexter, but this was also rejected, the senate at the same time confirming the nominations of Smyth and Bee.[6]

On November 27, the name of Memucan Hunt was presented and the senate confirmed it by a vote of ten to two.[7] General

---

[1] Irion to Jones, November 29, 1838, *Tex. Dipl. Corr.*, I, 350–354.

[2] *Secret Journals*, 113.

[3] Webb to LaBranche, May 27, 1839, *Tex. Dipl. Corr.*, II, 52.

[4] Amory to Dunlap, July 24, 1839, *ibid.*, II, 53–54.

[5] *Secret Journals*, 140.

[6] *Ibid.*, 141–143.

[7] *Ibid.*, 143–144.

Hunt was a prominent figure in Texas.   On June 1, 1836, he and General Thomas J. Green, and Colonel J. Pinckney Henderson had arrived at Velasco on the steamer ''Ocean'' from New Orleans with two hundred and thirty volunteers.[8]   As has been seen, in December he was commissioned to act as minister extraordinary at Washington in conjunction with W. H. Wharton, and on February 28, 1837, after the retirement of Wharton, was made resident minister, a position which he held until June 12, 1838, when his resignation was accepted.[9]   In December he became Secretary of the Navy in Lamar's cabinet, a position from which he soon retired.   As he was the minister who closed the negotiation of the boundary treaty, the appointment was peculiarly fitting.[10]

In January, 1839, the congress of the United States passed an act to carry into effect the boundary convention.   It provided that the salary of the commissioner was to be twenty-five hundred dollars, that of surveyor two thousand, and of clerk twelve hundred.   The sum of one thousand dollars was voted for contingent expenses.   John H. Overton was appointed commissioner, John K. Conway surveyor, and John J. Clendenning clerk.   The latter, however, resigned shortly after,[11] and John Henry Young was appointed.[12]   In order that the commission might have the assistance of an officer of the United States corps of topographical engineers, Major James D. Graham was ordered to join the commission[13] and Lieutenant T. J. Lee to act as his assistant.[14] McUne Barrow of the parish of Rapides, Louisiana, was appointed assistant to Conway.

---

[8] Bancroft, *North Mexican States and Texas*, II, 273.

[9] *Tex. Dipl. Corr.*, I, 23.

[10] *Treaties, Conventions*, (Malloy, ed.), II, 1780.

[11] Vail to Overton, July 8, 1839, *Sen. Docs.*, 27 Cong., 2 Sess., III, Doc. 199, pp. 3–5.

[12] Forsyth to Young, October 28, 1839, *ibid.*, 8.

[13] Vail to Overton, July 8, 1839, *ibid.*, 3–5.

[14] Overton to Forsyth, January 20, 1840, *ibid.*, 14.

The joint commission met at New Orleans on August 7, 1839, Dexter then occupying the position of commissioner for Texas. Conway was unable to be present and the preliminary arrangements had to be made without him. Provision was made for the purchase of stores and for transportation to the mouth of the Sabine. It was determined that a compass, one four-pole chain, one two-pole chain, a theodolite, chronometer, quadrant, and sextant were necessary. Owing to the hostility of border Indians, it was believed that an escort of fifty men would have to be furnished by each government. The absence of Conway and the prevalence of yellow fever in New Orleans determined the commission to adjourn, to reassemble at the mouth of the Sabine on October 15.[15]

Owing to the unhealthfulness of the season, the commission did not meet at the appointed time and place, but assembled on November 12 at Green's Bluff on the Sabine River, about thirty-five miles from its mouth. Overton and Conway, Sample, Smith and Bee were present, Sample acting in the place of Dexter. As the astronomical instruments had not arrived, the officers of the commission moved up the river about fifteen miles to Mills-paugh's Bluff, where they encamped.

On November 23 McUne Barrow, Conway's assistant, arrived in camp. On the following day he was killed by the accidental discharge of his rifle. His remains were interred under a solitary pine tree on the west bank of the river.[16]

On December 11 Captain S. J. Pillans of the Texan army, who had been directed to assist in topographical work, and Young, who had been appointed clerk by the United States government, arrived. On January 20, 1840, Memucan Hunt joined the commission to take the place of Sample, whose appointment had not been confirmed by the Texan senate. Major

---

[15] Overton to Forsyth, August 10, 1839, *Sen. Docs.*, 27 Cong., 2 Sess., III, Doc. 199, p. 12

[16] Journal of the Joint Commission, *ibid.*, 57. This will hereafter be referred to simply as Journal of the Joint Commission.

Graham and Lieutenant Lee, in charge of the instruments, arrived at the mouth of the Sabine on the first of February, and were joined there by the commission on the twelfth.[17]

In the previous November, Lamar had approved an act of the Texan congress which provided for the appointment of a commissioner, surveyor, and clerk to carry out the boundary convention. The salary of the commissioner was fixed at $2000, that of surveyor at $1500, and of the clerk at $1000. In addition to the sum of $3000 provided by the act of June 12, 1837, $5000 was set aside. The remainder of the previous act was repealed. The salaries of the commission were to run during the period actually consumed in the work, a reasonable time being allowed for going and coming.[18] On January 18, 1840, a joint resolution was approved which provided for $5000 more, but this fund was not to be applied until the work was completed.[19]

When the joint commission was finally assembled, it was not properly supplied, the Texans being without instruments, a state of affairs which led to future difficulties.[20] The map by which the commission was to be guided was also lacking; the convention had provided that the line should be ''as laid down in Melish's map of the United States, published at Philadelphia, improved to the first of January, one thousand eight hundred eighteen.''[21] This map could not be found in the State Department. Forsyth had previously written to Francis Hopkinson, a map dealer of Philadelphia, to obtain one, but without success,[22] and when the actual work of surveying the boundary was begun in May, the commission had no copy of the map.[23]

---

[17] *Sen. Docs.*, 27 Cong., 2 Sess., III, Doc. 199, pp. 57–58.

[18] *Laws of the Republic of Texas*, 4 Cong., 2 Sess., 230–231.

[19] *Ibid.*, 229.

[20] Graham to Overton, February 16, 1840, *Sen. Docs.*, 27 Cong., 2 Sess., III, Doc. 199, pp. 16–19.

[21] *Treaties, Conventions*, (Malloy, ed.) I, 1083; *ibid.*, II, 1779.

[22] Forsyth to Hopkinson, October 23, 1839, *Sen. Docs.*, 27 Cong., 2 Sess., III, Doc. 199, p. 7. Two letters, Hopkinson to Forsyth, October 26 and 29, 1839, *ibid.*, 13.

[23] Forsyth to Hopkinson, June 29, 1840, *ibid.*, 10.

From the first the work of the joint commission was disturbed by differences and controversies. The first of these occurred over the use of instruments. The Texans being unprovided with them, Hunt stated that he supposed they would have to depend upon those brought by Graham. That officer understood this to mean that the Texans would be willing to take the results of his work. This, however, Hunt declined to do, insisting that as long as his surveyor could not have independent use of the instruments, thereby arriving at his own computations, he considered it indispensable to wait until instruments could be procured by his government.[24]

The second difficulty was of a more serious kind, and grew out of an interpretation of the meaning of the treaty. The convention stated that the boundary extended from the mouth of the Sabine where that river enters the Gulf of Mexico.[25] The first question to be decided was, what stream was meant by the Sabine, and the second, what was the mouth? The difficulty grew out of the peculiar nature of the opening into the sea; the water from the Neches and Sabine entered the Gulf through what was commonly known as Sabine Pass, a stream seven miles long and varying in breadth from a half mile to a mile.[26] Above this was an expanse of water known as Sabine Lake; this was sixteen miles long and in its broadest part seven miles wide. At its northwestern extremity was the mouth of the Neches entering through a single stream from the northwest. In the center of the northern shore, entering through three mouths, was the Sabine flowing from the north.[27]

It had served the purpose of the Jackson administration to assume, in its dealings with Mexico, that the Neches rather than

---

[24] Graham to Overton, February 16, 1840, *Sen. Docs.*, 27 Cong., 2 Sess., III, Doc. 199, pp. 16–19.

[25] *Treaties, Conventions*, (Malloy, ed.) II, 1779–1780.

[26] Map of Sabine Pass, drawn by Lee, accompanying *Journal of the Joint Commission*.

[27] Map of the River Sabine, drawn by Lee, accompanying *Journal of the Joint Commission*.

the Sabine was the boundary meant by the treaty of 1819.[28] When Texan independence was recognized, it put a new phase on the boundary question. Whether or not Texas was annexed, it would not be good policy. to press a claim for a large piece of territory. The intentions of the government on this point may best be shown by quoting from a letter from Forsyth to Overton which said:

> Soon after the conclusion of the treaty for defining the limits between the United States and Mexico, this Government was led to believe that the river Neches, which, as well as the Sabine, flows into the Sabine lake, was the most considerable of those two streams; that it was navigable, while the Sabine was too shallow for that purpose, and that the general direction of the Neches corresponded better than that of the Sabine to the course which, according to the treaty, the boundary line was to take. Recent examinations, however, made under the direction of the Department of War, in the accuracy of which there is reason to confide, tend to show that the information referred to was, at least to some extent, incorrect. In the present state of information, that question is still pending, and requires particular examination, by the commission of which you are a member, with a view to its final adjustment. You will, therefore, make the necessary inquiries, note all the facts bearing upon it, and regulate yourself by the result of them.[29]

While waiting for the assemblage of the commission. Overton visited New Orleans and while there examined the question. "The result of that examination thus far," he wrote. "leaves me but little hope of being enabled to sustain the pretensions of the United States to Neches as the boundary. The question, however, shall be submitted to the decision of the commission.''[30]

This matter was left in abeyance at first while the question as to the mouth of the Sabine was decided. The question was opened in an exchange of notes on February 22, 1840; Hunt asked Overton to present a formal *projét* of the manner in which

---

[28] Van Buren to Poinsett, August 25, 1829, *Congressional Debates*, XIV, Pt. 2, App., 127–130.

[29] Forsyth to Overton, October 23, 1839, *Sen. Docs.*, 27 Cong., 2 Sess., III, Doc. 199, pp. 7–8.

[30] Overton to Forsyth, January 20, 1840, *ibid.*, 14.

he proposed to commence.[31] To this Overton replied that he proposed "to begin on the Gulf of Mexico, at the mouth of the Sabine
River in the sea, continuing thence north along the western bank
of that river and of the lake, to the point of intersection of the
western bank with the thirty-second degree of north latitude,
thence due north to the Red River."[32]

To this Hunt replied that before presenting his views on the
construction of the treaty, he wished to know if the government
and citizens of Texas were to be granted the right of erecting
wharves and works of all descriptions on the west side of Sabine
Pass, Sabine Lake and Sabine River.[33] Overton answered that
in the conversation which he had had with Hunt, in which this
matter had come up, he had referred only to commercial privileges of the inhabitants, and not to those of the government. He
expressed his doubts as to the jurisdiction of the commission in
such matters.[34]

Hunt replied that up to this time he had acted in the spirit
of compromise and had solicited his government to allow him to
settle points of dispute without communicating with it, but such
would be the case no longer unless the Texan government and
citizens were allowed the privilege of erecting wharves and works
of all kinds on the shore of the main channel of Sabine Pass,
Sabine Lake, and Sabine River.[35] Overton answered that the
Mexican treaty of 1828, which was the basis of the convention
with Texas, stated what the rights of both parties were, and that
"no act of the commission . . . can add to, take away, or
in any wise affect, the vested rights of either country." He
stated that he simply desired to carry out the convention in strict
fairness and justice.[36]

---

[31] Hunt to Overton, February 22, 1840, *Sen. Docs.*, 27 Cong., 2 Sess.,
III, Doc. 199, p. 20.

[32] Overton to Hunt, February 22, 1840, *ibid.*, 20–21.

[33] Hunt to Overton, February 24, 1840, *ibid.*, 21.

[34] Overton to Hunt, February 28, 1840, *ibid.*, 21–22.

[35] Hunt to Overton, February 29, 1840, *ibid.*, 22.

[36] Overton to Hunt, February 29, 1840, *ibid.*, 22–23.

Hunt replied at length, stating that Overton, in a previous conversation, had agreed to the right of Texan citizens to erect wharves for commercial purposes, and he could not see why the erection of factories, navy-yards, and fortifications by the Texan government would not likewise be admissable. He pointed out that the treaty said "that use of the waters and navigation of Sabine River to the sea shall be common to the respective inhabitants of both nations," without mentioning the rights of either government, a point which he believed should be definitely settled.

Hunt next entered into the question of the mouth of the Sabine. He argued that Sabine Pass and Sabine Bay, or Lake, were not Sabine River. As Overton insisted on proceeding by the strict letter of the treaty, and as the commission was not in possession of Melish's map which would settle the question, he offered as a solution of the difficulty that the commission begin its work at the mouth of Sabine Pass, continue along the middle of this inlet and Sabine Lake to the mouth of the Sabine River, thence along its western bank. If this were unsatisfactory, Hunt suggested that they might leave the disputed part to their respective governments and proceed at once from the mouth of Sabine River where it emptied into the lake.[37]

He followed this with an additional proposal on the following day, to the effect that each commission begin at the mouth of Sabine Pass and proceed as far as the point where Sabine River emptied into the lake, each according to its own construction of the treaty, and thence proceed together. The work could then be submitted to the governments for decision.[38]

To all the points raised by Hunt, Overton replied on March 5. He said that an expression of opinion that the treaty gave certain commercial privileges to Texas had been construed into a pretension to grant or cede rights to Texas. As regarded the

[37] Two letters, Hunt to Overton, March 2, 1840, *Sen. Docs.*, 27 Cong., 2 Sess., III, Doc. 199, pp. 23–27.

[38] Hunt to Overton, March 3, 1840, *ibid.*, 27–28.

mouth of the Sabine, he considered that the treaty was plain when it spoke of the line to begin "on the Gulf of Mexico at the mouth of the Sabine in the sea." He considered that Sabine Lake was only a widened part of the river.[39]

Hunt replied that Sabine Lake should not be considered a part of the river, any more than Long Island Sound was a part of Hudson River, Delaware Bay a part of Delaware River, or Albemarle Sound a part of Roanoke River; other instances were also mentioned. He then pointed out that, owing to the expense which would be incurred by delay, the unfortunate condition of those residing in the disputed territory in which anarchy prevailed, and the danger from Indians, it was desirable that they proceed at once. He therefore offered another proposition which said:

> Commence at what you represent and claim as the west bank of the entrance of Sabine river in the sea, designating it by the erection of a mound or stone pillar, and the taking of the latitude and longitude of its location, continuing along the west bank of what is represented and claimed by you as the west bank of Sabine river . . . , making, as we may progress on the west bank, similar evidences of which I claim as the termination of Sabine lake or bay, on its south side, at its connection with Sabine pass or inlet; and another of like description at the point I claim as the termination of Sabine river in the lake or bay.[40]

Overton replied that there were numerous examples of where rivers widened as did the Sabine; he cited as examples Tappan Sea in the Hudson, Lake Pepin in the Mississippi, Lake St. Peter in the St. Lawrence, three lakes in the Calcasieu, and various others. He said that he greatly regretted the unfortunate results of delays, but observed, "This delay, I will here beg leave to say, has not been caused by the United States." He further remarked that unless the work might begin at once, he would ask for an adjournment of the commission, and proposed that they meet on the following day to decide what was best to be done.[41]

---

[39] Overton to Hunt, March 5, 1840, *Sen. Docs.*, 27 Cong., 2 Sess., III, Doc. 199, pp. 28–32.

[40] Two letters, Hunt to Overton, March 7, 1840, *ibid.*, 32–38.

[41] Overton to Hunt, March 9, 1840, *ibid.*, 38–41.

This proposal was not acceded to; notes were exchanged which were filled with unpleasant insinuations, personalities, and evident ill-will.[42] As neither would yield, it was decided to forego operations until the matter could be presented to the respective governments, and the commission adjourned, Major Graham being sent to Washington to consult with the State Department.[43]

The position of the Department of State was fully given in a letter from Forsyth, which stated that Overton should not have allowed himself to be drawn into irrelevant discussions. He confirmed Overton's opinion that the joint commission had no power to settle such matters as the use of boundary waters. In regard to the boundary he said:

> The claim set up by the Texan commissioner to the centre of that part of Sabine river called Sabine pass, and to Sabine lake, is preposterous, and must not be entertained a moment. The river prescribed by the treaty as forming the boundary is the Sabine, having its mouth on the sea in the gulf of Mexico, and the line is to run along its west bank from the point at which it empties into the sea.

In case that Hunt might seek to delay the actual operations by a renewal of the discussion or set up new pretensions, Overton was instructed to withdraw from the commission with all the persons acting under him and report the fact to the State Department.[44]

On May 15 Overton informed Hunt of the decision of Forsyth[45] The Texan commissioner replied that his government had expressed the hope that the United States would yield one-

---

[42] Hunt to Overton, March 11, 1840; Overton to Hunt, March 15, 1840 *Sen. Docs.*, 27 Cong., 2 Sess., III, Doc. 199, pp. 41–46.

[43] Overton to Hunt, March 15, 1840; Hunt to Overton, March 16, 1840; Overton to Forsyth, March 16, 1840, *ibid.*, 45–48.

[44] Forsyth to Overton, April 8, 1840, *ibid.*, 9–10.

[45] Overton to Hunt, May 15, 1840, *ibid.*, 2. The pagination of document 199 is peculiar; the first part contains 74 pages; this is followed by maps, and after them the paging begins with 1. The above letter and others of May 15 and 16 are after the map.

half the pass and lake; but if this could not be obtained, to propose Hunt's second proposition, namely, each commissioner to follow his own construction until the point was reached where Sabine River entered Sabine Bay. In support of his previous contention, he quoted a letter of Joel R. Poinsett, which spoke of the Sabine and Neches as emptying into Sabine Bay.[46]

Overton replied that he had nothing further to add and that it rested with the Texan commissioner; he stated that, if the answer were unfavorable, he desired to leave on the morrow.[47] Hunt saw that this was final and reluctantly consented to yield, stating that if there were any unnecessary delay on the part of the United States in carrying the work to completion, the proposition would not be considered as binding on the government of Texas.[48]

The Texan commission assembled at Green's Bluff on the west side of the Sabine about ten miles above the lake on May 3 and was joined there by the United States commission on the fifteenth. On the nineteenth the joint commission left the encampment and descended the river in two boats to the residence of Captain Green on the east shore of the lake, a short distance above the beginning of Sabine Pass. On the twenty-first they proceeded to the shore of the gulf and erected a circular mound of earth fifty feet in diameter and about seven feet high; this was surmounted by a pole thirty-six feet high with a keg covered with pitch at its top. A bottle was buried at each of the cardinal points of the compass four feet from the center, in each of which was deposited a paper bearing the following description:

Be it remembered that on the 21st day of May, 1840, the demarcation of the boundary between the United States and the republic of Texas was begun at this point, being in conformity with the provisions of the convention for the demarcation of the said boundary, concluded and signed

---

[46] Hunt to Overton, May 15, 1840, *Sen. Docs.*, 27 Cong., 2 Sess., III, Doc. 199, pp. 2–3.

[47] Overton to Hunt, May 15, 1840, *ibid.*, 3–4.

[48] Hunt to Overton, May 16, 1840, *ibid.*, 4.

by the respective plenipotentiaries of said countries at Washington, the 25th day of April, 1838.

Witness our signatures this 21st of May 1840.

JOHN H. OVERTON, *Commissioner of the U. S.*
JOHN R. CONWAY, *U. S. Surveyor.*

Witness—

J. D. GRAHAM, *Major U. S. Engineers*
MEMUCAN HUNT, *Commissioner on the part of the Republic of Texas.*

By the Commissioner.

GEO. W. SMYTH, *Surveyor of Texas.*
JOHN HENRY YOUNG, *Clerk to U. S. Comm'r.*[49]

The mound was located in latitude 29° 41′ 27.5″ north, and longitude 93° 50′ 14.2″ west of Greenwich. From that point the commission proceeded along the west bank of Sabine Pass and Lake to a point of woods known as Aurora, opposite to which the night was passed on a keel boat. On the following day the survey was continued along the west shore of the lake. When the mouth of the Neches was reached, the commission paused to consider the question of this being the river designated in the treaty. Because of the fact that the river flowed from the northwest, and therefore did not correspond to the general direction of the boundary, and because above the juncture with the Angelina it was an inconsiderable stream; and as the Sabine flowed generally north and south and was the larger stream, being navigable for steamers of 130 tons burden for about two hundred miles; also in view of the editions of Melish's map published earlier and later than the missing map mentioned in the treaty, and because of the testimony of old residents that the Sabine had always borne that name—the commission decided that the Neches could not be the Sabine of the treaty. The point being settled without difficulty, the commission proceeded, entering the Sabine proper and advancing to Huntly, which was forty miles from the point of

---

[49] *Journal of the Joint Commission,* 59–60.

beginning. Here it was announced that Hunt was to retire from the commission and that George W. Smyth was to continue the work.[50] Daniel Wilber and Andrew B. Gray, two Texas engineers, had also recently joined the commission.

On May 22 the entire party embarked near Huntly on the steamboat "Albert Gallatin" to continue the survey. They proceeded daily without difficulty or unusual incidents to vary the monotony of the river voyage, arriving at Gaines' Ferry on the twenty-seventh. Here they joined Lieutenant Lee and Captain Pillans, who had ascended the river in March after the temporary adjournment of the commission, Lieutenant Lee having been placed in charge of the astronomical apparatus during the absence of Major Graham. On April 1 he was joined by George C. Meade, who had been appointed assistant astronomer. Lee, with his assistance, had been engaged since the adjournment in making a series of astronomical and magnetic observations.

A day's delay occurred at Gaines' Ferry, owing to the fact that arrangements had not been made for transportation above this point; the master of the "Albert Gallatin" was finally induced to convey the party to the intersection of the thirty-second parallel, and the commission proceeded. Above Gaines' Ferry navigation was frequently interrupted by overhanging trees and the crookedness of the river. On the thirty-first the steamer was stopped for several hours by a raft in the river, and a similar obstruction was met with on the following day. As they neared Logan's Ferry, they found the river wide and navigation easy.[51]

As Logan's Ferry was found to be close to the thirty-second parallel, the steamboat was discharged and a camp was formed on the Louisiana shore. Lee and Meade were despatched to find a suitable place for an encampment; the point they selected was

---

[50] *Journal of the Joint Commission,* 60–61, and note. Smyth was appointed May 1, 1840, and confirmed by the Texas Senate, November 16, 1840. *Secret Journals,* 184, 186.

[51] *Journal of the Joint Commission,* 61–63.

found to be about a mile north of the thirty-second parallel. and thither the whole party repaired on June 3. The following day an observatory was erected on a commanding position on the thirty-second parallel, about two miles east of the river. Until the sixteenth the men were employed in clearing away obstructions and in taking observations. Owing to the brightness of the moon, considerable difficulty was experienced by the astronomers operating with reflecting instruments. As the unhealthy season was near at hand and the funds of the commission were getting low, being sufficient only to transport the party to Red River where it could take transportation by water, it was determined to adjourn until the first of the following November.[52]

It was not until November 23 that the Texan Congress provided funds for continuing the work, on that date ten thousand dollars being voted. Owing to the tardiness of the appropriation, the commission did not meet until February 14. 1841. Overton remained at his home until notified on December 25, 1840, of the readiness of the Texan commissioner to proceed with the work. The party started at once, reached New Orleans on January 2, and remained there until the fifteenth, procuring supplies and making arrangements. They set out on horseback by way of Opelousas and Alexandria, where they embarked for Shreveport, arriving there on February 1. On the seventh they were joined by Lieutenant-Colonel James Kearney of the United States Topographical Engineers, who had been appointed to take the place of Major Graham. He was accompanied by Lieutenant Blake, who was to act as assistant; Lieutenants Johnson and Allen also joined the commission as assistants. The entire party reached the former place of encampment on February 14.[53]

Owing to the state of the weather, the work of observation was delayed for several days. Sextants which were forwarded from Washington in January had not arrived, and in order to save expense, Overton, following the suggestion of Smyth, decided to

---

[52] *Journal of the Joint Commission,* 63–64.
[53] *Ibid.,* 64–65.

discharge all but twelve of his camp followers. Little was accomplished until the twentieth of March, when Lieutenant Sitgreaves arrived from New Orleans with the sextants.

Rainy weather set in, but the work of observation continued between the storms. By the twenty-eighth Kearney had determined their position with sufficient certainty to justify the removal of the transit to the bank of the river to determine the meridian, when the stream suddenly rose, inundating the banks on both sides and interrupting the work. By the thirty-first the land between the observatory and the river, a distance of nearly two miles, was almost entirely under water. On the first of April Lieutenant Allen had to repair to Fort Jesup because of sickness, and the clerk, J. H. Young, resigned and left.

On the fourth it was determined to survey a line north to a point above the overflow, then to run a line west to the meridian and thence survey northward, leaving the lower line to be marked after the water subsided. On the fourteenth the camp was removed to the position selected for the second observatory. Thus at the end of two months, owing to water and weather, practically nothing had been accomplished.

Several days were spent in verifying their position, and the timber was cleared for about three miles along the meridian. On the twenty-third a granite block ten feet long and nine inches square was imbedded five feet in the ground. On the south side was engraved "meridian boundary, established A.D. 1841"; on the east side "U. S.", and "R. T." on the west side.[54]

The work now progressed rapidly. from one to four miles being surveyed daily. Each mile was marked by a mound of earth five feet high and fifteen feet in diameter. Each mound was surmounted by a wooden post eight feet in length. "U. S." being carved on the east side and "T" on the west. The south side was numbered to indicate the number of miles north from

---

[54] *Journal of the Joint Commission,* 66–67.

the thirty-second parallel. At the foot of each mound a bottle was buried containing an inscription.

The work proceeded daily without interruption until May 14, by which time thirty-six miles had been surveyed and marked. On that day the party remained inactive and the members of the commission and army officers repaired to Greenwood to take part in memorial ceremonies that had been proclaimed because of the death of President Harrison.[55]

On the eighteenth they reached the shore of Ferry Lake. a sheet of water about three miles across. An island near the center was named Neutral Island and the forty-sixth mound was located near the center. The lake was crossed on a large ferry scow, three days being consumed in getting the men and camp paraphernalia across. Owing to the peculiar formation of the northern shore, which was much cut up by inlets and swamps, considerable difficulty was experienced in marking the line on the north side of the lake, but whenever practicable mounds were erected. When "Jim's Bayou," one of the arms of the lake, was reached, it was necessary to wade into the water and cut through forests of cypress. Rafts were constructed but proved to be of little use; the heat was excessive; the men showed great reluctance about going into the water and the officers found it necessary to take the lead. For two days this kind of work continued, and after cutting through a deep swamp and overflow, the highland was reached.[56]

On June 5 the thirty-third parallel was reached. Here a post marked "33° latitude" was erected, and on either side a tree was planted. This marked the division line of Arkansas and Louisiana. Here Overton was taken sick from exposure in crossing the swamps. The work, however, continued. On the ninth Mr. Gray was thrown from his horse, but was not seriously injured. Two days later a shortage of bread occurred and the

---

[55] *Journal of the Joint Commission,* 68–70.

[56] *Ibid.,* 70–72.

men refused to work, delaying the advance for a day. Overton's illness became distressing, Conway, Bee, and Blake were attacked by fever, and most of the employees were sick. The work, however, was pushed on in spite of obstacles.[57]

On June 14 the encampment was moved to the south bank of Sulphur Fork. The men who could work assisted the wagons through an overflowed swamp and across a tributary, over which the oxen and mules swam with the wagons empty. The two following days were spent in constructing rafts to transport the camp equipage across the stream, which was over two hundred feet wide, and on the sixteenth the crossing was accomplished. From this point the work went rapidly and on June 24 the Red River was reached, the line being found to be 106 miles 2083 feet in length from the thirty-second parallel.[58]

With the completion of this survey, the history of the western boundary of the Louisiana Purchase as an international line abruptly ends. The reopening of the question of the annexation of Texas, the acquisition of that territory with its self-defined boundaries, and the war with Mexico, by which a vast domain was added to the United States, caused new boundary questions to arise. The demarcation of the western boundary of the Louisiana Purchase was no longer a national matter.

---

[57] *Journal of the Joint Commission,* 72–73.
[58] *Ibid.,* 73–74.

BIBLIOGRAPHY

PRIMARY SOURCES

UNITED STATES GOVERNMENT PUBLICATIONS

Acts passed at the first Session of the twenty-fourth Congress of the United States. Washington, n.d.

American State Papers, Foreign Relations. 6 vols. Washington, 1832–34.

Annals of Congress, 7 Cong., 1 Sess.; 8 Cong., 1 Sess.; 8 Cong., 2 Sess.; 9 Cong., 1 Sess.; 9 Cong., 2 Sess.; 10 Cong., 1 Sess.; 16 Cong., 1 Sess.

Compilation of the Messages and Papers of the Presidents, 1789–1897. 10 vols. Washington, 1899. James D. Richardson, ed.

Congressional Debates, VII, XII, XIII, XIV.

Department of the Interior—Census Office.

    Census of 1900, Population. 2 vols. Washington, 1901.

    Census of 1900, Statistical Atlas. Washington, 1903.

House Ex. Docs., 24 Cong., 1 Sess., VI, Docs. 249, 256; 24 Cong., 2 Sess., I, Doc. 2; 25 Cong., 1 Sess., Doc. 42; 25 Cong., 2 Sess., III, Docs. 74, 78, VII, Doc. 190, XII, Doc. 351; 25 Cong., 3 Sess., I, Doc. 2; 61 Cong., 2 Sess., Doc. 357.

Revised Statutes passed at the first Session of the forty-third Congress. Washington, 1878.

Senate Docs., 24 Cong., 2 Sess., I, Doc. 20, II, Docs. 84, 189; 25 Cong., 2 Sess., Docs. 1, 199; 25 Cong., 3 Sess., I, Doc. 1.

Treaties, Conventions, International Acts, Protocols, and Agreements between the United States and other Powers, 1776–1902. 2 vols. Washington, 1910. William M. Malloy, compiler.

OTHER PRIMARY MATERIALS

ADAMS, JOHN QUINCY.

    Memoirs of. 12 vols. Philadelphia, 1874–1877. Charles Francis Adams, ed.

ALTAMIRA, EL MARQUES DE.

    Testimo de un Parecer dado en los Auttos fechos en Vertud de Real Cedula en qe S.M. manda se la Informe sobre surttos Abusos Commettidos en la Provincia de Texas en el Tiempo que se expressa; y Tambien de un Parrapho de ottro Parácer dado en los proprios Auttos, uno y ottro del Sor Audittor Grâl de la Guerra, in Yoakum, *History of Texas*, I, 381–402.

AMANGUAL, FRANCISCO.

    Diario de la derrota de Novedades ocurridas en la partida del mando del Sor. Capn Dn Franco Amangual. Año de 1808. MS notes in Bolton Collection, University of California.

AMERICAN HISTORICAL ASSOCIATION.
Annual Reports, 1907–8. Texan Diplomatic Correspondence. 3 vols Washington, 1908–11. George Pierce Garrison, ed.

AMERICAN PHILOSOPHICAL SOCIETY.
Documents relating to the Purchase and Exploration of Louisiana. Boston, 1904.

ARREDONDO, JOAQUÍN DE.
Report of the Battle of the Medina, August 18, 1913. Translated by Mattie Austin Hatcher, in Texas State Historical Association, *Quarterly*, XI, 220–232.

AUSTIN, STEPHEN F.
Mapa original de Texas por el Ciudadano Estevan F. Austin presentado al Exmo. Sor. Presidente, por su autor 1829. Original in Archive of the Secretaría de Fomento, Department of Cartography. Photograph in Bolton Collection, University of California.

BARBÉ-MARBOIS, FRANÇOIS MARQUIS DE
The History of Louisiana, particularly of the Cession of that Colony to the United States of America. Philadelphia, 1830.

BENTON, THOMAS HART.
Thirty Years' View. 2 vols. New York, 1854.

BOLTON, HERBERT EUGENE.
Athanase de Mézières and the Louisiana-Texas Frontier, 1768–1780. 2 vols. Cleveland, 1914.

BOURRIENNE, LOUIS ANTOINE FAUVELET DE.
Memoirs of Napoleon Bonaparte. 4 vols. London, 1836.
Concerning Philip Nolan, in Texas State Historical Association, *Quarterly*, VII, 308–317. Andrew Cunningham McLaughlin, ed.
Documentary Progress of Texas Revolutionary Sentiment as seen in Columbia, in Southern History Association, *Publications*, VII, 25–31, 85–95, 200–206, 238–246. Eugene Campbell Barker, ed.

DUNBAR, WILLIAM.
Journal of a Voyage commencing at St. Catherines Landing, on the East Bank of the Mississippi, proceeding downwards to the Mouth of the Red River and from thence ascending that River, the Black River and the Washita River as high as the Hot Springs in the Proximity of the last mentioned River, in American Philosophical Society, *Documents relating to the Purchase and Exploration of Louisiana.*

ELLICOTT, ANDREW.
The Journal of . . . for determining the Boundary between the United States and the Possessions of his Catholic Majesty in America. Philadelphia, 1802.

FILISOLA, VICENTE.
Memorias para la Historia de la Guerra de Tejas. 2 vols. Mexico. 1848.

FRENCH, B. F.

Historical Collections of Louisiana. 4 vols. New York, 1846–53.

GALLATIN, ALBERT.

The Writings of. 3 vols. Philadelphia, 1879. Henry Adams, ed.

GARDEN, GUILLAUME DE, COMTE.

Histoire Générale des Traités de Paix et autres Transactions principales entre toutes les Puissances de l'Europe depuis la Paix de ·Westphalie. 14 vols. Paris, 1848–1859.

GOROSTIZA, MANUEL EDUARDO DE.

Correspondencia que he mediado entre la Legacion Extraordinaria de Mexico y el Departamento de Estados de los Estados-Unidos, sobre el Paso del Sabina por las Tropas que mandaba el General Gaines. Mexico, 1837.

GREGG, JOSIAH.

Commerce of the Prairies. 2 vols. New York, 1845.

HARRIS, DILUE.

The Reminiscences of, in Texas State Historical Association, *Quarterly.* IV, 85–127, 155–189.

HITCHCOCK, ETHAN ALLEN.

Fifty Years in Camp and Field. New York, 1909. W. A. Croffut, ed.

JAMES, EDWIN.

Account of an Expedition from Pittsburgh to the Rocky Mountains, performed in the Years 1819 and '20 . . . under the Command of Major Stephen H. Long. 2 vols. Philadelphia, 1822–23.

JEFFERSON, THOMAS.

The Limits and Bounds of Louisiana, in American Philosophical Society, *Documents relating to the Purchase and Exploration of Louisiana.*
The Writings of. 10 vols. New York, 1892–99. Paul Lester Ford, ed.
The Writings of. 20 vols. New York, 1903. Memorial edition.
Writings. 9 vols. Washington, 1853–54. H. A. Washington, ed.

LEWIS, MERIWETHER.

Original Journals of the Lewis and Clark Expedition, 1804–1806. 8 vols. New York, 1904–05. Reuben Gold Thwaites, ed.
The History of the Expedition under the Command of Lewis and Clark. 4 vols. New York, 1893. Elliott Coues, ed.

Lucien Bonaparte et ses Mémoires, 1775–1840. 3 vols. Paris, 1882. Th. Iung, ed.

MADISON, JAMES.

The Writings of. 9 vols. New York, 1900–10. Gaillard Hunt, ed.

Manifiesto del Congreso General. Mexico, 1836.

MARTENS, GEORG FRIEDRICH VON.

Recueil des principaux Traités d'Alliance, de Paix, de Trêve . . . conclus par les Puissances de l'Europe. 8 vols. Göttingen, 1817–35.

MONITEUR.

Gazette nationale: ou, Le Moniteur universal.

MONROE, JAMES.
The Writings of. 7 vols. New York, 1898–1903. Stanislaus Murray Hamilton, ed.

MOORE, JOHN BASSETT.
A Digest of International Law. 8 vols. Washington, 1906.

MORSE, JEDEDIAH.
A Report to the Secretary of War of the United States, on Indian Affairs, comprising a Narrative of a Tour performed in the Summer of 1820. New Haven, 1822.

NAPOLEON I.
Correspondance . . . publiée par Ordre de l'Empereur Napoleon III. 32 vols. Paris, 1858–70.

Niles' Weekly Register.

ONIS, LOUIS DE.
Memoir upon the Negotiations between Spain and the United States of America which led to the Treaty of 1819. Baltimore, 1821. Tobias Watkins, trans. Spanish ed., Madrid, 1820; Mexican ed., Mexico, 1826.

PADILLA, JUAN ANTONIO.
Memoria sobre los Indios infieles de los Provincia de Tejas, 1819. MS, Béxar Archives. Copy in Bolton Collection, University of California.

Papers bearing on James Wilkinson's Relations with Spain, 1787–1789, in *The American Historical Review,* IX, 748–766. William R. Shepherd, ed.

Papers relating to Bourbon County, Georgia, 1785–1786, in *The American Historical Review,* XV, 66–111, 297–353. William R. Shepherd, ed.

PICHARDO, JOSÉ.
El Nuevo Mexico y Tierras adyacentes Mapa Levantado para de la Demarcacion de los Limites de los Dominios Españoles y de los Estados Unidos por el P.D. José Pichardo quien lo dedica al Exmo. Sôr. D. Francisco Xavier Venegas Virrey de esta N.E. &c Ano de 1811. Cartography Department of the Secretaría de Fomento. Photograph in the Bolton Collection, University of California.

PIKE, ZEBULON MONTGOMERY.
Papers of Zebulon M. Pike, 1806–1807, in *The American Historical Review,* XIII, 798–827. Herbert Eugene Bolton, ed.

The Expeditions of . . . to the Headwaters of the Mississippi River, through Louisiana Territory, and in New Spain, during the years 1805–6–7. 3 vols. New York, 1895. Elliott Coues, ed.

POINSETT, JOEL ROBERTS.
Contestacion del Ministro Americano, a la Escitativa de la Legislatura des Estado de Mexico. Mexico, 1829.

Esposicion de la Conducta Politica de los Estados-Unidos para con las nuevas Republicas de America. Mexico, 1827.

Manifiesto de los Principios Politicos del Escmo. Sr. D. J. R. Poinssett. Mexico, 1828.

Notes on Mexico made in the Autumn of 1822. London, 1825.

REPUBLIC OF TEXAS.
> *House Journal, called Session, beginning September 25, 1837, and regular Session, beginning November 6, 1837.* Houston, 1838.
>
> *Journal of the Permanent Council* (October 11–27, 1835), in Texas State Historical Association, *Quarterly*, VII, 250–278; IX, 287–288. Eugene Campbell Barker, ed.
>
> *Laws of the . . .* 2 vols. Houston, 1838.
>
> *Laws . . . passed at the second Session of the fourth Congress.* Houston, 1840.
>
> *Ordinances and Decrees of the Consultation, Provisional Government of Texas and the Convention, which assembled at Washington March 1, 1836.* Houston, 1838.
>
> *Secret Journals of the Senate . . . , 1836–1845,* Ernest W. Winkler, ed., in Texas Library and Historical Commission, [accompanying the] *First Biennial Report, 1909–1910.*

ROBERTSON, JAMES ALEXANDER.
> *Louisiana under the Rule of Spain, France, and the United States, 1785–1807.* 2 vols. Cleveland, 1911.

ROYCE, CHARLES C.
> *Indian Land Cessions of the United States,* in Smithsonian Institution, Bureau of American Ethnology, *Eighteenth Annual Report.* 2 vols. Washington, 1900.

STIFF, EDWARD.
> *The Texan Emigrant.* Cincinnati, 1840.

TEXAS LIBRARY AND HISTORICAL COMMISSION.
> *First Biennial Report, 1909–1910.* Austin, 1911.

Texas Revolution Documents, in Southern History Association, *Publications,* VIII, 104–118, 343–362. Eugene Campbell Barker, ed.

TYLER, LYON GARDINER.
> *Letters and Times of the Tylers.* 3 vols. Richmond, 1885–1896.

VERGENNES, CHARLES GRAVIÈR, COMTE DE.
> *Mémoire historique et politique sur la Louisiane.* Paris, 1802.

WARD, HENRY GEORGE.
> *Mexico in 1827.* 2 vols. London, 1828.

WILKINSON, JAMES.
> *Memoirs of my own Times.* 3 vols. Philadelphia, 1816.

WOOD, W. D.
> *Sketch of the early Settlement of Leon County, its Organization, and some of the Early Settlers,* in Texas State Historical Association, *Quarterly*, IV, 203–217.

SECONDARY AUTHORITIES

ADAMS, EPHRAIM DOUGLAS.
British Interests and Activities in Texas, 1838–1846. Baltimore, 1910.
ADAMS, HENRY.
History of the United States of America. 9 vols. New York, 1889.
BANCROFT, HUBERT HOWE.
History of Arizona and New Mexico. San Francisco, 1889.
History of California. 7 vols. San Francisco, 1886–90.
History of Mexico. 6 vols. San Francisco, 1883–88.
History of the North Mexican States and Texas. 2 vols. San Francisco, 1884–9
BARKER, EUGENE CAMPBELL.
Difficulties of a Mexican Revenue Officer in Texas, in Texas State Historical Association, *Quarterly,* IV, 190–202.
Land Speculation as a Cause of the Texas Revolution, in Texas State Historical Association, *Quarterly,* X, 76–95.
Organization of the Texas Revolution, in Southern History Association, *Publications,* V, 451–476.
President Jackson and the Texas Revolution, in *The American Historical Review,* XII, 788–809.
Stephen F. Austin and the Independence of Texas, in Texas State Historical Association, *Quarterly,* XIII, 257–284.
The San Jacinto Campaign, in Texas State Historical Association, *Quarterly,* IV, 236–345.
The Texan Revolutionary Army, in Texas State Historical Association, *Quarterly,* IX, 227–261.
The United States and Mexico, 1835–1837, in *The Mississippi Valley Historical Review,* I, 3–30.
BOLTON, HERBERT EUGENE.
Guide to Materials for the History of the United States in the Principal Archives of Mexico. Washington, 1913.
Notes on Clark's "The Beginnings of Texas," in Texas State Historical Association, *Quarterly,* XII, 148–158.
Some Materials for Southwestern History in the Archivo General de Mexico, in Texas State Historical Association, *Quarterly,* VI, 103–112.
Spanish Activities on the lower Trinity River, 1746–1771, in *The Southwestern Historical Quarterly,* XVI, 339–377.
The Jumano Indians in Texas, 1650–1771, in Texas State Historical Association, *Quarterly,* XV, 66–84.
The Spanish Abandonment and Re-occupation of East Texas 1773–1779, in Texas State Historical Association, *Quarterly,* IX, 67–137.
The Spanish Occupation of Texas, 1519–1690, in *The Southwestern Historical Quarterly,* XVI, 1–26.

The Founding of Mission Rosario: A Chapter in the History of the Gulf Coast, in Texas State Historical Association, *Quarterly*, X, 113–139.

The Native Tribes about the East Texas Missions, in Texas State Historical Association, *Quarterly*, XI, 249–276.

BROWN, JOHN HENRY.

History of Texas from 1685–1892. 2 vols. St. Louis, 1893.

Life and Times of Henry Smith, the first American Governor of Texas. Dallas, 1887.

BUCKLEY, ELEANOR CLAIRE.

The Aguayo Expedition into Texas and Louisiana, 1719–1722, in Texas State Historical Association, *Quarterly*, XV, 1–65.

Cambridge Modern History, The. 13 vols. New York, 1902–12.

CHADWICK, FRENCH ENSOR.

The Relations of the United States and Spain. Diplomacy. New York, 1909.

CHAMPIGNY, JEAN, CHEVALIER DE.

Etat-present de la Louisiane avec tous les Particularites de cette Province d'Amerique, pour servir de suite a l'Histoire des Etablissemens des Européens dans les deux Indies. Amsterdam, 1781.

CHITTENDEN, HIRAM MARTIN.

The American Fur Trade of the Far West. 3 vols. New York, 1902.

CLARK, ROBERT CARLTON.

The Beginnings of Texas, in Texas State Historical Association, *Quarterly*, V, 171–205.

Comprehensive History of Texas, A. 2 vols. Dallas, 1898. Dudley G. Wooten, ed.

COX, ISAAC JOSLIN.

General Wilkinson and his later Intrigues with the Spaniards, in *The American Historical Review*, XIX, 794–812.

The Early Exploration of Louisiana. Cincinnati, 1905.

The Louisiana-Texas Frontier, in Texas State Historical Association, *Quarterly*, X, 1–75.

The Louisiana-Texas Frontier, in *The Southwestern Historical Quarterly*, XVII, 1–42.

The Southwest Boundary of Texas, in Texas State Historical Association, *Quarterly*, VI, 81–102.

CRANE, WILLIAM CAREY.

Life and Select Literary Remains of Sam Houston of Texas. Philadelphia, 1885.

DE SHIELDS, JAMES T.

Cynthia Ann Parker. The Story of her Capture at the Massacre of . . . Parker's Fort . . . and of her Recapture at the Battle of Pease River by Captain L. S. Ross of the Texian Rangers. St. Louis, 1886.

DIENST, ALEXANDER.
The Navy of the Republic of Texas, in Texas State Historical Association, *Quarterly,* XII, 165–203, 249–275, XIII, 1–43, 85–127.

DUNN, WILLIAM EDWARD.
Apache Relations in Texas, 1718–1750, in Texas State Historical Association, *Quarterly,* XIV, 198–274.

FICKLEN, JOHN R.
Was Texas included in the Louisiana Purchase? in Southern History Association, *Publications,* V, 351–387.

FOURNIER, AUGUST.
Napoleon I, a Biography. 2 vols. New York, 1911.

FULLER, HERBERT BRUCE.
The Purchase of Florida. Cleveland, 1906.

GARRISON, GEORGE PIERCE.
Texas, a Contest of Civilizations. Boston, 1903.

GAYARRÉ, CHARLES ETIENNE ARTHUR.
History of Louisiana. 4 vols. New York, 1903.

GREENHOW, ROBERT.
The History of Oregon and California. Boston, 1844.

HEINRICH, PIERRE.
La Louisiane sous la Compagnie des Indies, 1717–1731. Paris, 1908.

HOSMER, JAMES KENDALL.
The History of the Louisiana Purchase. New York, 1902.

HODGE, FREDERICK WEBB, ed.
Handbook of American Indians north of Mexico, in Smithsonian Institution, Bureau of American Ethnology, *Bulletin 30.* 2 vols. Washington, 1907–10.

HOUCK, LOUIS.
A History of Missouri. 3 vols. Chicago, 1908.

HOWREN, ALLEINE.
Causes and Origin of the Decree of April 6, 1830, in *The Southwestern Historical Quarterly,* XVI, 378–422.

KENNEDY, WILLIAM.
Texas: the Rise, Progress and Prospects of the Republic of Texas. 2 vols. London, 1841.

LE PAGE DU PRATZ.
Histoire de la Louisiane. 3 vols. Paris, 1758.

LYMAN, THEODORE.
The Diplomacy of the United States. Boston, 1826.

McCALEB, WALTER FLAVIUS.
The Aaron Burr Conspiracy. New York, 1903.
The First Period of the Gutierrez-Magee Expedition, in Texas State Historical Association, *Quarterly,* IV, 218–229.

McMaster, John Bach.
  History of the People of the United States from the Revolution to the Civil War. 8 vols. New York, 1888–1913.
Manning, William R.
  Texas and the Boundary Issue, 1822–1829, in *The Southwestern Historical Quarterly,* XVII, 217–261.
Marshall, Thomas Maitland.
  The Southwestern Boundary of Texas, 1821–1840, in Texas State Historical Association, *Quarterly,* XIV, 277–293.
Martin, François-Xavier.
  The History of Louisiana from the Earliest Period. New Orleans, 1882.
Monette, John Wesley.
  History of the Discovery and Settlement of the Valley of the Mississippi. 2 vols. New York, 1848.
Parton, James.
  Life of Andrew Jackson. 3 vols. Boston, 1866.
Paxson, Frederick Logan.
  The Independence of the South American Republics. Philadelphia, 1903.
  The Last American Frontier. New York, 1900.
Phillips, Paul Chrisler.
  The West in the Diplomacy of the American Revolution, in University of Illinois, *Studies in the Social Sciences,* III, Nos. 2 and 3.
Polk, James Knox.
  The Diary of . . . 4 vols. Chicago, 1910. Milo Milton Quaife, ed.
Potter, R. M.
  Escape of Karnes and Teal from Matamoras, in Texas State Historical Association, *Quarterly,* IV, 71–84.
Reeves, Jesse S.
  American Diplomacy under Tyler and Polk. Baltimore, 1907.
  The Napoleonic Exiles in America, in Johns Hopkins University, *Studies in Historical and Political Science,* Series XXIII, 531–656.
Reynolds, John Hugh.
  The Western Boundary of Arkansas, in The Arkansas Historical Association, *Publications,* II, 211–236.
Rives, George Lockhart.
  The United States and Mexico, 1821–1848. 2 vols. New York, 1913.
Robertson, William Spence.
  Francisco de Miranda and the Revolutionizing of Spanish America, in American Historical Association, *Annual Report, 1907,* I, 189–528.
Rose, John Holland.
  The Life of Napoleon I. 2 vols. London, 1902.
Schouler, James.
  History of the United States of America under the Constitution. 6 vols. New York, 1880–91.

SHEPHERD, WILLIAM R.
  Wilkinson and the Beginnings of the Spanish Conspiracy, in *The American Historical Review*, IX, 490–506.
SLOANE, WILLIAM MILLIGAN.
  The Life of Napoleon Bonaparte. 4 vols. New York, 1910.
SMITH, JUSTIN H.
  The Annexation of Texas. New York, 1911.
SPENCER, JOAB.
  Missouri's Aboriginal Inhabitants, in *Missouri Historical Review*, III, 275–292.
The Texas Almanac, 1868. Galveston, 1868.
TURNER, FREDERICK JACKSON.
  The Diplomatic Contest for the Mississippi Valley, in *The Atlantic Monthly*, XCIII, 676–691, 807–817.
  The Policy of France toward the Mississippi Valley in the Period of Washington and Adams, in *The American Historical Review*, X, 249–279.
THWAITES, REUBEN GOLD.
  A brief History of Rocky Mountain Exploration. New York, 1904.
VAN TYNE, CLAUDE H.
  Review of Channing's "A History of the United States," III, in *The American Historical Review*, XVIII, 603–605.
VILLIERS DU TERRAGE, MARC DE, *baron.*
  Les dernières Années de la Louisiane française. Paris, 1903.
WHEELER, OLIN D.
  The Trail of Lewis and Clark. 2 vols. New York, 1904.
WILLIAMS, ALFRED M.
  Sam Houston and the War of Independence in Texas. Boston, 1895.
WINKLER, ERNEST WILLIAM.
  The Cherokee Indians in Texas, in Texas State Historical Association, *Quarterly*, VII, 95–165.
WINSOR, JUSTIN.
  The Westward Movement. Boston, 1897.
WINSTON, JAMES E.
  Kentucky and the Independence of Texas, in *The Southwestern Historical Quarterly*, XVI, 27–62.
  Virginia and the Independence of Texas, in *The Southwestern Historical Quarterly*, XVI, 277–283.
WOOTEN, DUDLEY G.
  See *Comprehensive History of Texas.*
YOAKUM, HENDERSON.
  History of Texas from its first Settlement in 1685 to its Annexation to the United States in 1846. 2 vols. New York, 1856.

INDEX

Adaes Indians, 125.

Adams, John, negotiation of treaty at end of the Revolutionary War, 1.

Adams, John Quincy, appointed secretary of state, 53; negotiation of the treaty of 1819, 54, 55, 58, 59, 60–63; yields claim to Texas, and advances claim to Oregon, 55; negotiations with Vives, 68–69; opposes sending representative to Mexico, 71; debate in Congress, 161–162.

Ais. *See* Eyeish.

Alabama Indians, 131, 181.

Alamán, Lúcas, Mexican secretary of foreign relations, 74, 84–85; negotiation of treaty of 1828, 76, 77, 78, 86; report on Texas, 91–93; dealings with Butler, 98–100.

Almonte, Colonel Juan N., 107, 115.

Amangual expedition, 25.

Apache Indians, 127, 128, 129.

Aranama Indians, 128.

Arbuckle, Brigadier General, 145, 185.

Archer, Branch T., 138, 225.

Arkansas, difficulties with Texas, 91, 93–94, 98–99, 209–210, 220.

Arkensa Indians, 133.

Arkokisa Indians, 126.

Armstrong, minister to France, advises forceful occupation of Texas, 38; dealings with Talleyrand, 41; negotiation in 1806, 43; quarrels with Bowdoin, 44.

Attacapa Indians, 126.

Aury, Luis de, 46–47.

Austin, Stephen F., 137, 183.

Bancroft Library, *preface*, v.

Barbé-Marbois, negotiates treaty of 1803, 7–8.

Baratarian pirates, 47.

Barrow, McUne, 226, 227.

Batres, Mexican boundary commissioner, 84.

Bayard, Samuel O., 97.

Bayou Pierre, occupied by Spaniards, 12, 26, 28; evacuated by Spaniards, 30.

Bean, E. P., activities in eastern Texas, 93, 94.

Bee, Hamilton, 225, 240.

Belknap, Major, 185.

Benton, Thomas H., 59; candidate for minister to Mexico, 73.

Berlandier, Luis, 84.

Berthier, French minister to Spain, negotiation with Spain in 1800, 1–2.

Bidai Indians, 126, 131.

Biloxi Indians, 131, 133, 181.

Blasco, José Mariano, Mexican secretary of the treasury, 111.

Index

Cushing, Colonel T. H., ordered to Natchitoches, 27–28; demands withdrawal of Spanish troops from Bayou Pierre, 28; checks ardor of Claiborne, 29.

Dallas, George M., candidate for minister to Mexico, 72, 73.

Dean, Captain, 171–172.

Delaware Indians, 131, 132, 149, 172.

De Lisle map, 5, 36.

De Onis, Spanish minister to the United States, negotiation of treaty of 1819, 50–63.

Dexter, P. B., 225, 227.

Donelson, Jr., John, 97.

Dunbar, William, 9, 10, 12.

Dunbar-Hunter expedition, 15.

Dunn, James, 174.

Du Pratz, 5, 36.

Edwards grant, 134, 135.

Edwards, Larkin, 172.

Edwards, Ninian, appointed minister to Mexico, 72; attack on Crawford, 72; resignation as minister to Mexico, 72.

Ellis, Powhatan, United States minister to Mexico, 116–117; opinion regarding treatment of Butler, 121.

Emet Indians, 127.

England, suggestions of alliance with, against Spain, 38, 39, 40; mediation of, with Spain, declined, 54; *see* also Great Britain.

Erving, George W., minister to Spain, 50, 52–53, 57.

Ervipiame Indians, 127.

Esteva, José Ignacio, Mexican plenipotentiary, 79, 84.

Estrada, de, 110–111.

Everett, S. H., 178.

Evía, Joseph de, map, 20.

Expeditions: Amangual, 25; Dunbar-Hunter, 15; New Mexico, from, in 1804, 25; Freeman, 15, 22, 25, 28; Gaona, 149, 152; Lewis and Clark, 8, 9–10, 14–15, 24; Long, James, into Texas, 67, 67 *note;* Lucero, 25; Melgares, 16, 25; Pike, 15–16, 25; Robin, 21; St. Denis, 36; Sibley, 12, 15, 26, 125, 127; Viana, 25, 28.

Eyeish Indians, 125.

Fagoaga, Francisco, Mexican secretary of state and foreign relations, 100.

Fields, Richard, 132, 134.

Filisola, General Vicente, 135, 176.

Flores, Manuel, 149, 155–156, 172, 174, 175–176.

Floridas, French proposals to Spain in 1800, 2; Jefferson's suggestion of cession to United States, 9; proposal of cession by Spain in 1818, 54; Jackson's invasion of, 56, 57, 58; land grants, 65-66, 68–69; cession, 70.

Folch, Vicente, plan for Spanish defense of Florida, 23–24.

Forbes, John, 139.

Forsyth, John, utterances hostile to Spain, 56; minister to Spain, 63–67; secretary of state, 107; instructions to Butler, 113–114; recalls Butler, 116; conference with Gorostiza, 157, 204; attitude concerning Gaines' occupation of Nacogdoches, 194, 195-198; protests against Texas land law, 212; completes negotiation of treaty of limits with Texas, 221–222; settles boundary commission disputes, 234.

Index.

Index.

209; land law of December 22, 1836, 209; land law of June 12, 1837, 209, 210–211; land law of December 16, 1837, 213; annexation, 216–217, 218, 219; alliance with England, hinted at, 217. *See also* Alamán, Milam, Terán, Van Buren.

Texas-Louisiana boundary commission, Texas commissioners selected, 225–226; U. S. commission selected, 226; assembling of the joint commission, 227; equipment, 227, 228; Texas Congress passes act providing for, 228; controversies, 229–235; additional funds voted by Texas, 238; adjournment, 238; reassembles, 238.

Texas-Louisiana boundary survey, 235.

Texas Indians, 126.

Texas rangers, 137.

Thompson, Waddy, 161.

Thorn grant, 134.

Tohaha Indians, 127.

Toho Indians, 127.

Toledo, Mexican revolutionist, 46.

Tonkawa Indians, 127, 136.

Tornel, José María, Mexican minister to the United States, 85, 94; retires, 95; insulted by Butler, 119–120.

Torrens, José A., Mexican chargé d'affaires at Washington, 73.

Toussaint l'Ouverture, 2.

Towaash Indians, 180.

Towakana Indians, *see* Tawokani Indians.

Treaties: at the end of the Revolutionary War, 1; of March 21, 1801, between France and Spain, 2;

Treaties (*continued*) —
of San Ildefonso, 2;
of 1795, 6, 17;
of the Neutral Ground, 30.
proposed in 1806, 43.
of 1819, negotiation, 50–63; approved by the Senate, 63; Spain refuses ratification, 64–69; second ratification by United States Senate, 70; ratified by Spain, 70;
of 1828, with Mexico, negotiation of, 76; ratified by the Mexican Senate, 85; arrives in Mexico after the time limit has expired, 85; exchange of ratifications delayed, 86; date of ratification postponed, 95; ratified, 97; additional articles added in 1831, 95, 96–97, 106; delay in putting into effect, 106–108; completion of treaty urged by Butler, 110; final steps, 111–112; ratifications exchanged, 116–117; later additions, 142, 194;
of 1832, with Mexico, 163;
of commerce with Mexico, 79, 82–83, 96–97;
of Velasco, 175;
between government of Texas and the Cherokee, 139;
of limits with Texas, negotiation, 218–291; final agreement, 221–222; ratified by Texan Senate, 223; ratified by United States Senate, 223–224; Texas commissioners selected, 225, 226; United States commissioners selected, 226.

LIST OF MAPS

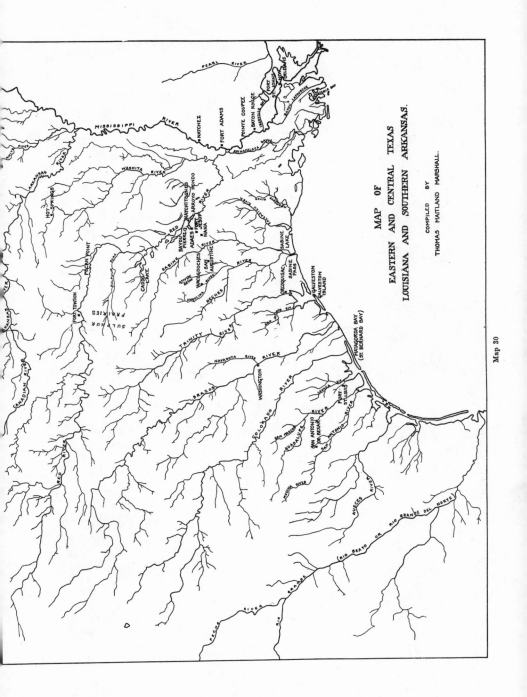

MAP OF
EASTERN AND CENTRAL TEXAS
LOUISIANA AND SOUTHERN ARKANSAS.

COMPILED BY

THOMAS MAITLAND MARSHALL.

Map 30